PRESENTING YOURSELF
SUCCESSFULLY TO
COLLEGES

Also by Howard Greene and Matthew Greene:

Greenes' Guides to Educational Planning: The Hidden Ivies

Greenes' Guides to Educational Planning: Inside the Top Colleges

*Greenes' Guides to Educational Planning:
Making It into a Top College*

*Greenes' Guides to Educational Planning:
Making It into a Top Graduate School*

Greenes' Guides to Educational Planning: The Public Ivies

PRESENTING YOURSELF SUCCESSFULLY TO
COLLEGES

[HOW TO MARKET YOUR STRENGTHS AND MAKE YOUR APPLICATION STAND OUT]

Howard R. Greene, M.A., M.Ed.,
and Matthew W. Greene, Ph.D.

Quill
A HarperResource Book
An Imprint of HarperCollinsPublishers

HarperCollins books may be purchased for educational, business, or sales promotional use. For information please write: Special Markets Department, HarperCollins Publishers, Inc., 10 East 53rd Street, New York, NY 10022.

FIRST EDITION

Designed by Stratford Publishing Services, Brattleboro, Vermont

Library of Congress Cataloging-in-Publication Data have been applied for.

ISBN   0060934603

05 06 RRD 10 9 8 7 6 5

Contents

Preface

We have enjoyed the challenges and rewards of guiding students in their pursuit of a college education since 1968. Over the years, we have witnessed the ebb and flow of the admissions process, from the days of robust rivalry for acceptance into selective colleges to the extraordinary competition that exists today. As the number of college candidates has climbed dramatically at the very selective colleges and universities, some of the rules of the admissions game have changed. Selection criteria have shifted from overall academic performance, counselor recommendations, personal interviews, and test scores to academic performance in the highest available level of courses, test scores, and the presentation package. The personal interview plays a role in the evaluation process in only a handful of institutions.

Since high school and college enrollments began to mushroom in the 1990s, it has become difficult for guidance counselors to know their large roster of advisees intimately and write informative, insightful evaluations of them for admissions committees. Candidates must make the case for themselves to be selected from a large pool of appealing candidates.

We have advised thousands of talented young men and women on the importance of the personal presentation to college admissions officers choosing among the many qualified candidates. One of the most rewarding elements of our counseling work is helping high school seniors discover what makes them special, what they have accomplished that has import for a successful college experience, and how they will add value to the college community. Only then can earnest candidates write the kind of personal statements and creative essays that will convey to colleges who they are and what they stand for.

We have read tens of thousands of essays of varying quality over the years, and we know of students who hurt their chances for acceptance by submitting a poor presentation package to the college of their dreams. We have also seen students gain admission because they have done an outstanding job of telling admissions officers who they are and why they will make a significant addition to their campus. From our counseling work and communications with college admissions directors, we know there is a need for a guide to presenting oneself.

Note that we use the terms *presentation* and *package,* marketing words that often give a negative connotation. We do not wish to have students "package" themselves, or have others do so for them. What we mean by presenting a strong application package to colleges is informing the admissions committees about all of your accomplishments and strengths in accurate, honest, informative, enthusiastic, complete, and meaningful applications.

There is an abundance of guides on how to write a winning essay for the college of your choice. Many omit mention of other important elements in the admissions process. Much more is involved than simply writing a creative or well-crafted essay to convince a seasoned, and often cynical, admissions team to accept you. There are other key pieces to the puzzle that eventually provide a full picture of a candidate.

In this book, we address the other pieces of a complete and effective college application, including the factual responses (e.g., to questions such as Why do you wish to attend our college or university? Why do you see yourself and our university as a good match? What did you do last summer and how did it affect your thinking and goals for the future?); a personal résumé that incorporates meaningful activities and experiences in athletics, the performing arts, or community service in a coherent fashion; a portfolio of artwork, writing, or research; cover letters to coaches, specialty teachers, and admissions officers; and recommendations.

Other guides often fail to put their model essays in any context. No two candidates should write in the same style and on the same subject. Conveying who you are to a college means that you have to write from your own background and experiences. You need to understand why one student would write in a particular manner or on a particular subject, while another would choose to take an entirely different direction.

We have taken all of this into account in writing this guide for you. Our examples of essays, statements, exhibits, résumés, and letters are drawn from the files of the many students whom we have counseled in recent years. Every sample essay represents a real person who was successful in his or her quest to enroll in an excellent college.

In our recent book *Making It into a Top College: Ten Steps to Gaining Admission to Selective Colleges and Universities,* we devote an entire step to how students can present or market themselves to colleges. We have been encouraged by students, parents, and educators to expand this discussion, to provide more examples of what will help students write about themselves more easily and enhance their odds of acceptance. Although this guide is intended to assist high school juniors and seniors in preparing and submitting their applications to colleges, it should also prove helpful to guidance counselors, parents—frequently the chief supporters and advisors for their children—and classroom English teachers who provide workshops and assignments on college essay writing.

We hope readers will find this guide and the models we present useful in understanding the important role of presentation in the college admissions process and the nature of the presentation process itself.

Introduction

Henry David Thoreau, on hearing a century ago that the newest technological feat of the telegraph system would speed up communications between Maine and Texas, wondered what Maine and Texas had to say to each other. The same question applies today with the previously unimagined advances in technology that enable us to communicate instantaneously with virtually anyone anywhere in the world. As a candidate for acceptance to a selective college, you can communicate with admissions committees simply by filling out an application and pushing a button that will relay your personal information to them via the Internet or fax. We now have a miraculous set of inventions that have speeded up interaction between you and the admissions officers. But like Thoreau, we must ask the question: Is what you have to communicate to these people of interest to them, and how will it affect their opinion of you?

The need for a guide on how to present yourself as an applicant to the college admissions committees is underscored by the changes in the admissions decision process. The transition from high school to college has been one of the most significant rites of passage for generations of individuals. The ritual of a nerve-wracking personal interview with an admissions officer has been replaced by the written essays and self-descriptions required by almost all colleges and universities. For a variety of practical and public policy reasons, most colleges no longer grant personal interviews, let alone require them, as an essential element in selecting their entering class. A survey of admissions officers by the National Association of College Admissions

Counselors reveals that only 10 to 11 percent of member colleges give any weight to personal interviews in the decision process.[1]

The reality is that as the number of applicants to all of the competitive colleges has soared, it has become impossible for limited admissions staff to interview all candidates. The civil rights movement and federal laws regarding any and all forms of discrimination have also contributed to the demise of required interviews. College administrators do not wish to provide a situation for potential discrimination based on any personal factors. Further, it would be unfair to thousands of candidates to require them to travel to campus for an interview at considerable personal expense.

Academic performance in a challenging curriculum continues to be the number one factor considered in evaluating candidates. Another significant factor that has increased in importance in recent years is standardized test scores. This means that a strong personal presentation in writing that offers compelling reasons for admitting you, whether you are an excellent student or have average test scores or a spotty academic record, takes on even greater importance in persuading admissions committees to select you over other qualified candidates.

The goal of all selective colleges and universities today is to build a community of diverse individuals who range across the spectrum of our society in terms of their talents, intellectual interests, and socioeconomic, ethnic, racial, religious, and geographic backgrounds. This is how a college builds a dynamic community in which each student grows intellectually and emotionally from rubbing shoulders with peers who may differ in many ways from him or her. Most parents of present-day college applicants recall that the prevailing philosophy in their school days was to be a well-rounded individual, a person who had a balance of interests and activities that appealed to colleges. This is not the case today, when the goal is to build a well-rounded class composed of many unique individuals. The more commitment and talent in one or several specialties a student demonstrates, the more

---

[1]Annual survey of college admissions directors, 2000.

likely he or she is to stand out in the competition for admission. This principle holds true for the uniqueness a candidate displays by virtue of his or her background exposures and experiences. The only way admissions committees can make these distinctions in evaluating thousands of candidates is to rely on the personal application and supplemental documentation—which you are responsible for providing.

At all selective colleges, making admissions decisions is now a committee process, far different from the days when an admissions director could make a decision at his or her own discretion. Today all the members of the admissions committee review all candidates' dossiers and make determinations on whom they will accept. The application, with its request for detailed personal information, plays a critical role in helping committee members choose candidates from a large pool of qualified individuals. This fundamental change means that a socially confident high school senior cannot count on a winning personality and charm to convince a seasoned admissions officer to offer him or her a place in the incoming class. The good news for applicants is that they do not have to suffer the anxieties and, for many, the actual fear of facing a stranger in a brief meeting with the thought that this person could determine their educational fate. With the moment of relief this knowledge brings, however, comes the realization that the ability to write with intelligence, clarity, and feeling, in presenting yourself to a committee of strangers on paper, can play a significant role in the decision to admit or reject you. Our experience in counseling thousands of bright and well-educated young men and women makes it clear that the written essays and overall personal presentations are the most challenging tasks in the entire process of applying, even for those students who rank in the top portion of their class and perform well on standardized tests.

Parents express great concern about the stress their children exhibit while preparing their applications and the tension that can easily develop between parent and child over this stage of applying to college. This is often the step in the admissions process that keeps them from applying to the colleges they have dreamed of entering and for which they have worked assiduously through their high school years. We think of one young man, for instance, who had an outstanding academic high school record yet was completely stymied on how to present himself to the admissions committee at the University of North Carolina, the school he had set his sights on early in his college search. He possessed a particular passion, but it took a brainstorming session with us for him to recognize what he should reveal about himself, and that all he needed was to create the right opening to develop his full statement. Here is what he wrote: "During the winter of my sophomore year of high school I developed a fifth limb. Like most other people, I have two arms and two legs, but now I also have a sword. I am a competitive fencer." In his personal statement, described by the North Carolina admissions office as "an important factor in our decision to admit this bright student," he went on to tell how he discovered a sport for someone without the size or skills to stand out in basketball, football, lacrosse, or ice hockey. He did a masterful job of educating the reader on the particular physical and mental skills necessary to excel in fencing, and how he developed them through hard work and persistence. His thoughts and good writing showed originality, strength of character, and a personality that won him not only acceptance to the university but also a place on the university's varsity fencing team.

In this book, we provide sample personal essays, statements of interests, letters of support, interest/activity résumés, and portfolios of students' work in a variety of talents and skills. The essays are on a wide range of topics and in styles of writing that are appropriate for students to use. Samples we've chosen from the files of thousands of clients of Howard Greene and Associates reveal the presentations of artists, musicians, school leaders, athletes, scientists, international students, students with learning disabilities, and other types of applicants. These students shared their thoughts and their writing with us and now with you. We provide recommendations for good writing together with examples of effective and less effective writing styles. One of our goals is to help you appreciate the basic principles of good prose, citing resources and authorities that will guide you to develop your own manner of expression.

We discuss essays as they developed from an initial idea to a rough draft to a final copy that impressed admissions committees. The reader will come to understand that writing about oneself *is* hard work, but there are defined techniques for developing an idea and bringing it to successful fruition. We call attention to the different kinds of writing that young men and women often display and the attitudes that lie behind these differences. Girls, for example, often have to be encouraged to speak about their accomplishments with confidence and energy, while boys sometimes have to be encouraged to be reflective and intimate in their description of themselves. You will learn the difference between relating your particular strengths and accomplishments and boasting or overselling yourself to the admissions committees.

We envision *Presenting Yourself Successfully to Colleges* as a support for you, the applicant, regardless of your particular strengths, interests, and experiences at a critical moment in the admissions procedures. We will help you wrestle with the process of putting together a winning application package. Rather than intimidating the uninitiated with models of highly sophisticated or clever writing that only a small number of high school students are capable of producing, we concentrate on examples of quality presentations that were the result of much preliminary thought and discussion, as well as the hard work of writing and rewriting. They represent the efforts of many different types of students, and we hope you will recognize parts of yourself in some of them. Our tone is always upbeat and, we hope, infectious: if the students you read about here can master the art of writing first-rate personal essays, so can you!

You have noted by now that our focus is not exclusively essay writing. Much more makes up your presentation to admissions committees, for example, activity résumés and talent portfolios. We want you to envision your application as an organic whole composed of many parts that reveal who you are in the deepest sense. As you begin this challenging exercise, remember the meaning of the verb *essay:* it means to try to do, to examine, or to weigh. You are being invited by a committee of judges to examine what has shaped your ideas and ideals, your present strengths and those you wish to develop, your expectations for the college experience, and your hopes for your future. *You* are the subject of your application materials, no matter what topic you choose to write on. Demonstrating your effort to understand yourself is at the heart of the personal statement.

We can all easily distance ourselves in our writing from the issues and motives that deeply move us, treating the subject of ourselves rationally and superficially. This is not what you should do in conveying your personal world to the admissions committees. They really do want to know as much as possible about you. Through trial and error, effort and self-examination, you will be amazed by what you will write about and how well you will write it. The panel of jurists will be delighted, and sometimes amazed, by the insights and reflections you have revealed to them. This is what will move them to offer you a place in their community. We hope that many of the writing samples in this guide will strike a chord in you, giving you the confidence to convey through your writing what you really want colleges to know about you.

We do not minimize the hesitations and doubts facing applicants to college. Even outstanding students and gifted writers, who may not think they need help in their writing, will want to see how others have learned to reveal their accomplishments and personalities without boasting or appearing self-centered. We include in these pages excerpts from a few essays and statements considered unsatisfactory by both admissions officers and us, and some dos and don'ts of the essay writing and presentation process.

Almost all the students we have counseled have had trouble getting started with their writing. Choosing appropriate topics is the first hurdle they face, so we offer pertinent advice in Chapter 2 of this guide. Next comes the greater challenge for many writers: formulating your ideas well enough to put them in writing. This is often the point at which applicants throw up their hands and declare, "I can't write anything! I have nothing to say!" Graham Greene, one of the greatest storytellers of the twentieth century, once explained to an aspiring writer what he did if he was struggling to get his thoughts to the point where he could express them: Greene would review the topic that was giving him great difficulty just before going to sleep for the night. He would almost always wake up aware that what he called "the ghost writer in the cellar" had cleared up his problem while he was asleep.

You have so many important ideas that lie just below the surface of your awareness, waiting to be tapped. Thought, reflection, brain-storming with teachers, counselors, friends, or parents, a long walk, or a good night's sleep can suddenly bring to your conscious mind exactly what you want to say and how you will write your message.

By following the guidelines and models of good writing we present in this book, you will find your own voice and turn a personal experience into a story that reveals much about you and catches the attention of an admissions committee.

CHAPTER ONE

Presenting Yourself to the Colleges of Your Choice

The Importance of Stating Your Case to the Admissions Committees

"Applicants are not judged simply by the number of Advanced Placement or other advanced credits amassed at the end of senior year," the dean of admissions and financial aid at Harvard University declared at a recent annual meeting of the College Board. He advises students "to assess what your talents are or might be, and what it is you truly love and value." In a letter to Harvard's 6,000 volunteer alumni interviewers, he wrote, "Interviews [by these alumni] are actually more important than ever. The principal reason: the personal qualities of our students have never mattered more . . . the intangibles are determinative. Will this person be a great educator of other students? What will she or he be like as a prospective roommate, or working fifty hours a week on the *Crimson,* or in a seminar, or on the lacrosse team, or in late-night discussions?" He went on to comment that these are the skills that distinguish the most appealing individuals in the large pool of candidates with outstanding grades, academic transcripts, and test scores.

To personalize, enliven, and strengthen your application to selective colleges, you need to present some of the intangible qualities that will make you an appealing candidate. In a letter to school counselors and alumni interviewers, Karl Furstenberg, the dean of admissions and financial aid at Dartmouth, summarized the importance of providing more than statistical information to the admissions committee.

The following are the factors that will influence the decision to admit a candidate and that the dean hopes to discover from the materials in the applicant's folder:

> Obviously, the first and highest priority for admission is the academic accomplishment and intellectual quality of the student . . . But it is the presence of the intangible measures of academic accomplishment, promise, and dedication that really distinguish the exceptional applicants from the "solid" ones. The key difference between the two groups is intellectual curiosity. This quality eludes precise measurement, but we always look for it . . . We seek critical thinkers and creative problem solvers, all with the independence of mind and personal confidence to assert their ideas; students, who by virtue of their intellectual leadership, will both delight and challenge their professors and their peers . . . There is an intangible dimension to extracurricular records, and we must be attuned to those human qualities—integrity, leadership, compassion, open-mindedness, sense of humor, independence, energy—that will continue to enrich the Dartmouth community.

Stanford University further emphasizes how essays and other documentation play a key role in the lengthy and exhaustive review of the 16,000 applications they receive every year. Again, the personal writing and supplemental information will influence the committee as they consider more than the quantifiable information of grades, test scores, and courses taken.

> The thorough and elaborate evaluation process in which almost the entire admissions staff is involved each winter and spring cannot be reduced to a quantifiable formula. We attempt to blend the information contained in references with the data from academic credentials. We spend many hours (including nights, weekends, and holidays) reading and rereading files. Each application is carefully reviewed, sometimes by as many as

five admissions officers. Each admission officer reads hundreds of folders from a wide variety of applicants, thereby acquiring a strong sense of the strength of the pool of which each of you may be a part . . . Also of importance to us are applicants' essays and the references they present from teachers and others who know them well. We take into consideration personal qualities—how well an individual applicant has taken advantage of available resources, whether he or she has faced and withstood unusual adversity, and whether the applicant shows promise as a contributing community member.

We can cite the philosophy and goals of the admissions committees of the hundreds of other excellent colleges and universities that we hope you have considered in your search, and all of them will articulate the same message that Harvard, Dartmouth, and Stanford do here. You now have the framework within which to decide how you will make yourself a candidate the committees want to invite into their respective colleges. Without a presentation or marketing plan, you may well be relegated to the rejection pile because you did not make yourself known beyond the academic data.

What "Marketing Yourself" Means

As we wrote in *Making It into a Top College: Ten Steps to Gaining Admission to Selective Colleges and Universities,* one of the most important elements in the admissions process is presenting yourself fairly and accurately to each college you would want to attend. What does an overburdened admissions committee do when forced to make choices among candidates whose folders would be difficult to distinguish if the names were left out? Self-marketing is a concept that confuses many candidates. In a culture that thrives on marketing products, ideas, and individual personalities, the idea of marketing oneself to academic institutions can be easily misinterpreted. Our objective is to clarify what is appropriate and helpful marketing for an applicant to selective colleges.

The extraordinary rise in the number of qualified students seeking admission to the better colleges and universities today presents a challenge for you to demonstrate your individuality and accomplishments. You should determine that you will not allow yourself to fall into a faceless category of candidates who are judged by a selection committee solely on the basis of statistical and quantifiable information. *You* know that you are far more than the sum of your grades and test scores; your objective is to convey a complete image so that you will not become just another face in the crowd of applicants. Marketing yourself becomes essential. Your objective is to force the committees to select you, because you have made them aware of your individuality and the positive influence you will have in their community. It is all too easy for the committee to fall back on the quantitative factors in choosing another applicant over you when they do not have a full portrait of you. You should not allow this to happen either because you do not take the time to assemble a distinguishable presentation package or because you feel it is wrong to promote your own case, seeing it as boastful and self-centered. If you show, not say, what you have accomplished in your high school years, you are not boasting; rather, you are laying out a palette of colors—meaning your strengths and accomplishments—that create the portrait of an exciting and attractive person.

We believe in the ideal expressed by the great jurist Oliver Wendell Holmes that "the best test of truth is the power of the thought to get itself accepted in the competition of the market." Promoting yourself in the competitive marketplace of college admissions must have as its foundation truthful information. You can be assured that anyone who tries to present an inaccurate portrayal of himself or herself will ultimately be found out, so we have no hesitation in encouraging you to present who you are in all important respects with candor and sincerity.

We are comfortable using the term "presenting yourself" in our counseling work and in this guide, and we want you to feel the same way. Marketing has come into universal usage because the college admissions process has become a free marketplace driven by the classic forces of supply and demand. This commercial tinge might make you uneasy about presenting yourself to the admissions committees, but you should understand that all colleges and universities today use the language of the commercial marketplace in making themselves known to prospective students. Admissions officers spend many hours laying out a strategic marketing plan to convince strong high school students to consider their college rather than their competitors' institutions. They will respect and appreciate your efforts to present yourself as informatively as you can, enabling them to make an intelligent choice from among so many qualified candidates. Keep in mind the goal behind most colleges' admissions efforts: to build a class of individuals who represent a wide array of talents, interests, academic strengths, and socioeconomic, racial, and ethnic backgrounds.

Marketing yourself in college admissions is composed of three essential factors:

- Assessing your strengths;
- Assessing the colleges that closely match your strengths;
- Communicating these strengths clearly, enthusiastically, and interestingly to the targeted colleges by supplementary documentation.

Building your full presentation package takes considerable thought and effort, but the resulting success in acceptance to the colleges of your choice will make it well worth your while. Consider the case of James, who had his sights set on applying to Dartmouth on the Early Decision plan. A strong academic student in an excellent suburban high school, he was aware that he would be vying for a place against a highly competitive group of Early Decision candidates. James understood that his grades, which put him in the top decile of his class, and his SAT scores, all of which were above 700, would not ensure him acceptance to one of the most selective colleges in the country.

Here is some of the documentation James assembled and presented to Dartmouth's admissions office. One item was a press release he had written and sent to the local newspapers regarding a program for senior citizens he started:

September 29, 2001

UPDATE ON CONNECT-SENIORS

CONNECT-SENIORS, a program that provides computers and training for senior citizens, founded by 12th Grade honor student James Jones, announces that the Southern New England Telephone Company (SNET) has joined the CONNECT-SENIORS team as a corporate partner. Jones pursued SNET as the DSL provider when it became clear that senior care housing facilities were without funds to cover projects of this scope. To carry out his program of helping senior citizens who lived in a residential care facility learn how to use computers, Jones advertised for used computer donations and invited his school mates to volunteer weekly training sessions for the residents of the local senior residential facility. In addition, he has arranged with the director of his lower school to have these young students connect with the senior citizens as e-mail "pen pals" in order to give the Seniors both the opportunity and motivation to refine their computer skills on an ongoing basis.

Jones views CONNECT-SENIORS as a model for a national program that will allow senior citizens in care facilities to stay connected to their family and the outside world. He became aware of the need for creating such access for the elderly to the electronic world while working as a caseworker for his U.S. Congressman. The need was driven home further when his own grandmother bemoaned the lack of ready access to his brother who was away at college and difficult to reach, and other members of her large and far-flung family. SNET is currently in discussions with Jones regarding his concept of a national alliance between schools and corporations to bring CONNECT-SENIORS to a larger audience of the elderly.

James also responded to the essay questions required to complete Dartmouth's application, including this one: "What else should we know? Tell us more about yourself, explain an interest, describe a talent, or raise an issue of concern. Anything goes!"

One of you is relaxing in your dorm room, a state of the art environment where everything is at your fingertips. The thermostat, DVD player, remote light switches, a portable telephone, your laptop that lets you e-mail your professors and your friends, and even order in the late night pizza that is an essential part of studying for exams; all of the creature comforts are available at the touch of your computer command. You live in a dormitory modeled on the concept of the residential college system at Oxford. There is a Master and a Dean overseeing course scheduling, lectures, and there are Master's teas, informal barbecues, and planned academic and athletic events on a regular basis. Your dorm mates share many similar interests while there are many new friends to be made over the semester. You are a sophisticated Internet user, surfing the Web for up-to-the-minute research on your personal and academic interests. You can pull down any and everything, almost, that you want to know. You are able to spend a good deal of time electronically communicating with your family members, many of whom live in different time zones, which matters not at all in your ability to carry on a dialogue with them. You attend your classes during the day and gather at night with your friends to discuss, debate or collaborate on the topics presented to you by your professors and to carry on the research necessary to complete a paper that is due in the near future. In the truest sense, it is your passion for learning and sharing with your peers and your family that keeps you energized.

One of you is eighty-five and lives in a life care facility for the elderly. Television provides the only means for educating yourself and keeping up with the outside world. None of the electronic conveniences are at hand for you to control your environment. You can never find your oldest grandson in his dorm room during the hours when you are permitted to use the telephone in your facility, so you are losing touch with him. Overworked staff who have to "triage" all requests from residents are unable to handle anything but the most pressing issues. You have no access to the wealth of information so readily available to most people on the Internet. You feel like you became cut off from those you care about when the technology overwhelmed and intimidated you. You retired from your work and were unable to keep yourself current once there was no daily impetus to learn the latest technology. Your health seems to be deteriorating as your intellectual pursuits diminish.

It does not have to be this way!

Several factors converged when my grandmother mentioned how much she missed her grandson, my older brother, when he returns to college after each break. At the same time, I was bothered by the status of the elderly constituents I had worked with this past summer. I learned from my visits to several senior residential centers on behalf of my Congressman, for whom I was working, that the residents were so intimidated by the advanced technology that they had simply stopped trying to find solutions to their personal problems. I could sense that they had withdrawn from the outside, feeling unable to access a world now stored electronically. I worried that no one would be available to help them learn how to utilize a tool that was, in many ways, made for them to remain mentally active and engaged with their family and friends in the outside world. I thought of my grandmother as a typical example of how these circumstances were isolating them increasingly.

I decided to speak with my brother to see if there was anything we could do to redress this sad situation. The temptation is to think that age defines one's ability to make a difference in society. Initially, my brother and I felt that the problems the elderly had to deal with were beyond the ability of two teenagers to rectify. Of a moment we realized that this sense of hopelessness was how the senior constituents and our own grandmother felt, and that we could not accept this as a final reality. We determined we must act in some way to counteract this attitude.

We could not build elegant residential colleges to bring intellectual activity and friendships to the elderly, of course, but we determined that there are ways to get them connected to an electronic world that would enable them to communicate to anyone they wished and to gain access to information, family, entertainment, and up-to-date news. This is how we came to create the concept of CONNECT-SENIORS. The basic concept is to put computers into the hands of the elderly in residential homes and teach them how to connect, surf, and e-mail by providing ongoing training sessions. Our start has been modest, but successful. We dream of expanding this concept in ever-widening circles that will reach eventually all those who are living in senior housing facilities.

After spending this past summer soliciting used computers from classmates, friends, and their families we realized that this was too large an undertaking for two individuals to carry out. I found the solution in my school where many students have volunteered to join the weekly training sessions for our senior citizens at the residential center in my town. Even the younger children in my school have gotten involved as a part of the solution. Every week, as their introduction to community service as well as to computer skills, they e-mail their Senior pen pals. They ask them all sorts of questions which purposely require their Senior pal to do a little thinking, or research, or just remembering.

Thus far the response from the senior citizens and the students involved has been highly enthusiastic; and the donation of computers is beyond our expectations. Our efforts do not end here, however. There is the potential for a larger program than ours at the local level. We see no reason why such major corporations like Microsoft, AOL, IBM, or regional telephone companies like SNET should not want to partner a CONNECT-SENIORS program on a national basis. We have the model to show them how well it works, so stay tuned in for further news on our progress. Our grandmother is.

In addition to two of his Advanced Placement (AP) course teachers, James asked the principal of his school to write a personal recommendation that described his leadership abilities and the positive impact the CONNECT-SENIORS program had made on the entire school community. Several of the residents of the senior care center took it upon themselves to e-mail the admissions office at Dartmouth to tell them of the change this program made in their lives and the caring manner in which James related to them. Now, who can ignore the appeals of grandmothers?

James also included a detailed résumé of his activities in and out of school, which revealed the breadth of his interests and concerns. An admissions reader could only conclude that he is a young man of great compassion, commitment, and energy.

Note how much more James told about himself through his essay and supplemental documentation than an admissions committee would have learned from a simple line item on the activity checklist that says he performed twenty hours a week of community service. If you reread what the dean of admissions at Dartmouth said his college seeks in a candidate, you can see that James presented himself in this light, and thus he was accepted.

How to Assess Your Strengths and Unique Features

Lists are a wonderful tool for breaking complex concerns into comprehensible parts. What could be more complex than determining your particular strengths, special qualities, and accomplishments? We include here the Admission Strengths Assessment Form we recommend college-bound students complete before they determine which colleges are right for them, and from which they can develop their essays and accompanying materials for presentation to admissions committees. We urge you to reflect on the items covered by this form; chances are high that as you fill it out, you will see a unique individual who has much to present to a college unfold before your eyes. First, work on this form by yourself. You may then want to share it with your family, a trusted friend, a school counselor, or a coach to be certain you have not missed some essential points that others see as making you special. You already know that your parents are your greatest fans and advocates. Although they may not be fully objective regarding your capabilities and accomplishments, they do have a good picture of what makes you stand out, and we encourage you to share your self-assessment form with them. Teachers, coaches, and advisors can help you to be realistic about the level of your talent and potential for success in their field in college.

Ultimately, you should dare to be proud of the achievements, abilities, principles, and personality that will convince admissions officers that you will, indeed, make their community a better place for having you as a member. You are the person who must decide how to help them focus on a fully developed portrait of yourself. You want these committees to see clearly who you really are and just how attractive a candidate you are.

MY ADMISSION STRENGTHS ASSESSMENT

Strengths	Activities	Other Advantages
Academic	**School Activities**	**Strength of Character**
Grades _____	School government _____	Independence _____
Class rank _____	Class officer _____	Reliability _____
Test scores _____	Publications	Courage _____
Honors _____	officer _____	Persistence _____
Special projects ___	Music _____	Patience _____
Extra credits _____	Drama _____	Tolerance _____
Advanced	Clubs _____	Concern for
Placements _____	Other _____	others _____
Outside courses ___		
Related work _____		
Internships _____		

Nonacademic	**Other Activities**	**Skills/Talents**
Sport 1 _____	Community service ____	1. _____
Sport 2 _____	Work _____	2. _____

(continued)

Nonacademic	Other Activities	Skills/Talents
Letters _____	Internship _____	3. _____
Captaincy _____	Religious _____	4. _____
	Political _____	
	Unique travel _____	

Colleges Looking for My Strengths/Talents

College _____ Strengths _____

College _____ Strengths _____

College _____ Strengths _____

College _____ Strengths _____

Marketing Strategy

Communicate my strengths to:

Admissions Committee _____

Faculty members _____

Administrators _____

Arts director _____

Coaches _____

Minority Affairs officer _____

Alumni _____

By means of:

Direct communications by letter, telephone, or e-mail _____

Additional essays _____

Exhibits:

Tapes _____

Portfolio _____

Newspaper clippings _____

Audition _____

Additional recommendations:

Employers _____

Religious leader _____

Community service director _____

Camp or travel program director _____

When and How to Market Yourself

If you follow our tried-and-true Ten Steps approach to the admissions process presented in *Making It into a Top College,* you will understand that creating your presentation package begins when you have developed a strong academic record in high school, taken the appropriate entrance tests, and carefully identified the colleges you wish to attend. You should have a good sense of your strengths and the benefits you will bring to those colleges that appreciate them. Your marketing campaign begins when you file your applications and continues right up to the time when admissions committees begin their final decision sessions. This will be in December for Early Decision candidates and January through March for regular or second-round Early Decision candidates. Actually, you are not finished with your efforts to present yourself before the committees until the final determination is made on your candidacy. This is important for you to understand, and it is why we will explain in subsequent sections of this guide what you can do at each phase of the admissions process to support your case for acceptance.

Many unknowing applicants do not take advantage of colleges' open-file policies. Admissions staffs are interested in examining the folders of qualified candidates right up to the time when final decisions are made. It is possible to be rejected early in the selection process without your knowing this, as the committees make internal decisions on the candidates they identify as definitely unqualified or not interesting enough to consider in comparison to the many highly attractive candidates they will review in depth. No amount of self-marketing is likely to change the committees' minds at this juncture.

You should be applying, to begin with, to those colleges for which your credentials put you seriously in the running.

We can tell you from our experience in admissions work that the greatest challenge for the committees is making choices they are comfortable with in the last phase of the selection process, when they are considering only the most qualified and interesting applicants. How do they choose one strong candidate over another? Many factors now come into play—the strength of the academic curriculum, test scores, personal background, geography, and field of interest. This is when the intangibles loom large—values, character, and specific talents and strengths that say, "This person more than that other one will have a beneficial impact on our campus and will take the most advantage of our great resources." Presenting your special features is a continuing process right up to the last moment. We can assure you that the hard work of planning your presentation strategy in the most appropriate fashion will improve your chances of winning a coveted place in an exciting college.

Assessing the Colleges That Closely Match Your Strengths

In your search for the colleges that will suit the interests and talents you possess in addition to your academic strengths—a process that should start in your junior year of high school—you will discover a good deal about their overall academic programs, specialty departments, major extracurricular activities, and the intellectual and social environment that pervades the campus. You should consider if you can relate to some of these distinctive elements and emphasize them in your presentation to the admissions committees. Your study of the Japanese language and travel to Japan during the summer, for example, could appeal greatly to those colleges that have a major commitment to Asian studies; or your musical talent as a pianist to the School of Music at Vanderbilt; or your rowing ability to a university that is building a competitive crew program; or your community service involvement to virtually any college that cares about service to others. We could go on with hundreds upon hundreds of examples of young men and women who made certain that the admissions com-

---

SUGGESTIONS FROM COLLEGE ADMISSIONS OFFICERS

Be yourself through the admissions process. Don't put on a persona that is not your own.

—Dean of Admissions and Financial Aid, Cornell University

The personal statement is an important part of your application for admission and scholarships. The University uses the statement to learn about you as an individual—your talents, experiences, achievements, and points of view. Think of the personal statement as your opportunity to introduce yourself to the admissions officers who will be evaluating your application.

—Director of Admissions, University of California

Tell about all your personal credentials. Just being number one in the class is not going to make your application successful.

—Director of Admissions, University of North Carolina

Students should do their best to let the admissions office know what is important to know about them, and not be shy about their accomplishments. It is hard to capture yourself on pieces of paper, but it is important to try because that is all the admissions office has to look at.

—Senior Admissions Officer, Swarthmore College

It is important to remember that admissions decisions are not made by gatekeeping computers, but by humans who exercise a considerable amount of human judgment. Tell us, therefore, all that you can about yourself.

—Senior Admissions Officer, Williams College

---

mittees knew what was special about them by the time their application files were reviewed.

We tell all students we counsel how they can help themselves in this process: in any of the forms of presentation from the colleges (remember that they, too, are concerned with informing prospective candidates about what makes them different from their competitors) and in any communication you have with members of the college, note the academic programs about which they boast, the new facilities to which they have committed large amounts of money, the faculty and disciplines they highlight, the athletic, arts, community service, and other special categories they appear to favor. A new performing arts facility, for example, will encourage the admissions committee to admit a higher percentage of artistically talented men and women; the new field house or ice hockey rink will do the same for the athlete; the newly endowed chair in a special discipline will call for the admission of at least several individuals qualified for this department.

You should ask counselors, teachers, arts instructors, coaches, and others who know your strengths to recommend college programs that match your abilities and interests. These professionals receive frequent mailings from their college counterparts regarding new programs and facilities or interest in recruiting more students for particular programs. You can contact individuals on each campus of potential interest and tell them about your background. Always remember that you are helping these people discover you and your potential for enhancing their program. If you are encouraged to apply, contact the admissions office to request an application and any informational materials that relate to your special interest. In this age of electronic technology, there is no excuse for delaying your communication with college representatives in any and all of the fields that relate to your interests and strengths. It is extremely important for you to carry out your college search in this manner, rather than deciding to apply only to a group of colleges your friends favor or that meet your standard solely for the prestige factor.

Communicating Your Strengths by Supplementary Documentation

The key to impressing a committee of admissions officers, who range from wary to slightly cynical when confronted by thousands of similar applications, is to show evidence of your strengths and accomplishments rather than merely tell the committee what a strong candidate you are. Documentation is the key to communicating your individual qualities to these college gatekeepers. To separate you from the pack of eager applicants, they need your personal statements, your essays, your photography, writing, or art portfolio, your résumé of accomplishments and experiences, and your supporting letters of recommendation from those who have been witness to your abilities and character.

When the admissions officers convene to make their selection of the most appealing candidates, they are likely to engage in heated discussion. Each officer is asked to recommend to the committee at large his or her top candidates and defend these choices, since all officers are competing among themselves for the limited places available in the incoming class. This is a classic example of the zero-sum process. If my favorite applicant is accepted by the committee, there will be one less place available for the other officers' favored applicants. Exhibits that document your talents got you to this point in the selection process, and now the admission officer will want to share your presentation with the committee at large. Ideally, there will be a note in your folder from a college coach or professor or drama teacher expressing serious support of you and the contribution you will make to their program.

If more college applicants realized the importance of legitimate documentation, there would be less time wasted in the creation and review of ineffective and oftentimes embarrassing efforts to gain admission to a selective college. Rarely, if ever, has a marginal candidate been accepted on the basis of gimmickry or sensationalism (desperate examples abound of students sending singing telegrams to the admissions committee, sending expensive tapes of themselves making their case for acceptance, e-mailing the director of admission every day for the entire senior year, sending chocolate chip cookies and mom's secret recipe for them), and such efforts push admissions officers beyond the limits of their patience and compassion.

We do not intend for you to adopt the high-powered creative tactics of professional advertising and marketing firms. Admissions officers are serious educators who care about their institution. A show of flamboyance or heavy-handed personal marketing will be seen for what it is: a hoped-for camouflage of the applicant's limited record in high school. An overproduced, flashy, and slick application package, or one that appears to have been assembled by someone other than yourself, can have just as negative an effect on the admissions reader as a sloppy or poorly written application. The show-off, shallow candidate rarely makes it past the first round in the selection process. Trust us on this.

The Value of Recommendations from Those Who Can Speak to Your Strengths

Anyone with a dash of imagination can put together an impressive-looking set of credentials intended to bedazzle even the most seasoned of admissions committees. Students frequently express to us their frustration with the long lists of activities and accomplishments some of their peers include in their application materials. How, they ask, can admissions officers who are pressured by the demands of reviewing thousands of applications discriminate among candidates who have given a great deal of their time and energy to particular clubs, community service, or school leadership positions—to name some prime examples—and those who are along for the easy ride, contributing little to the organizations and activities listed in their applications? The answer we give, although not simple or foolproof, is that the truth will win out, because of careful screening on the part of admissions officers. They will expect to receive supportive and, better still, glowing recommendations from the adults—guidance counselors, teachers, coaches, employers, arts instructors, religious leaders, and others—who oversee student activities. The advisor to the newspaper or debate team will write only in support of the outstanding contributor to their activity; the coach will extol only the abilities and intense commitment of the top athlete who gives the sport his or her all; the director of the dramatic program or orchestra or chorus is going to substantiate the talent and passion of only a few performers in his or her charge; the religious leader at your place of worship who has monitored your serious participation in such areas as teaching younger children, religious services, or outreach programs to those in need of help will want to promote your acceptance.

Although you are asking busy professionals to take the time to compose a thoughtful, instructive letter to the colleges on your behalf, you will invariably discover that they are more than happy to do so if you have been a devoted and hardworking participant in their activity. You should never hesitate to request a recommendation if you are confident that you have, in fact, contributed a good deal to the program.

What should an effective recommendation contain? These are the basic components of a strong supportive statement: a brief but detailed description of the course content the teacher teaches or the program the advisor directs; how long and in what depth he or she knows you; a description of your attitude toward learning and hard work, your ability to work with others in a supportive and collaborative manner, your character traits and sense of fair play, your emotional maturity, your willingness to go the extra measure to accomplish the goals of the class or activity; your natural talent, intellectual, physical, or artistic; and of course your potential for success in their respective field in college. The admissions committees will be grateful, to say the least, for these insights from experienced and responsible adults who have worked closely with you. These recommendations should reinforce what you have written about yourself and your strengths. In some cases, colleges ask for a peer reference in the belief that a classmate or teammate can provide a special perspective on your personality, your values, and the nature of your relationships with your peers.

It is your responsibility to review your relationship and performance in your classes and extracurricular activities to decide who will write the most enthusiastic and informative recommendation on your behalf. Take the time to make a list of all potential recommenders and then narrow your list to the best three or four individuals. Your next task is to approach them to ask if they feel comfortable writing on your behalf when you have finalized your list of colleges. It is more than acceptable to include an additional one or two recommendations if they complement the first two and provide meaningful additional information about you.

EXAMPLES OF CREATIVE MARKETING

How you market your special qualities is limited only by your imagination, organization, and energy. Here are a number of marketing strategies you should review for potential use.

Send to Admissions Office:

- A copy of an award or commendation received in the last two years of high school
- A newspaper clipping about your achievement in a recent debate competition or athletic or math contest
- A special recognition or words of praise written by your teacher about a research paper, project, or performance you completed
- The school newspaper carrying news of your being elected to the National Honor Society, making the headmaster's list, being named a National Merit finalist, or winning a place on the All-County or All-State band, chorus, team, and so on
- A prize story that has appeared in a literary magazine or a drawing, photo, or other artwork

Send to the Appropriate Faculty Member:

- A paper or project of exceptional merit
- A model you have constructed of a building for an architecture or design class
- A software program you have developed
- A description of a business you have started
- Music you have composed or a film you have produced
- A translation prepared by you from a foreign language into English, or vice versa
- News of a conference or seminar on politics or international issues you have attended recently

Summary

In the following chapters, we offer advice and support on how to write an essay worthy of your accomplishments. We also provide you with models for crafting a first-rate résumé and cover letters to administrators, faculty, coaches, and artistic directors. We end this discussion here by reinforcing the importance of presenting yourself in a thoughtful, truthful, and self-confident manner. If you do not believe in yourself, why should a committee of strangers? Don't be shy about speaking up about your capabilities, as long as what you say is substantiated by clear evidence. Do this, and you do yourself and the admissions officers a favor.

CHAPTER TWO

How to Write an Exciting Essay

Getting Started

Most high school seniors with ambitious plans to enroll in a good college approach the search process with energy and enthusiasm. Visits to various campuses, discussions with relatives and friends who attend the colleges they are considering, and a careful review of the colleges' literature are initiated with little hesitation. Once they know where they want to apply, students must complete the individual applications, which include essays. This is the point when many applicants become mired in waves of self-doubt, confusion, and writer's block. This is a natural emotional reaction to the challenge of presenting yourself to a group of strangers judging your qualifications. You can overcome writer's block by following the steps we have described in Chapter 1. If you are willing to work hard, you can create a set of personal essays and statements that will improve your chances of acceptance to selective colleges.

In Chapter 3, we will provide guidelines for writing about yourself, and in Chapter 4 we will offer a number of essays written by students like yourself. Our goal is to explain the major features of a first-rate essay and show you how to get started in writing your own. Samples of essays on different topics that proved successful for various candidates are included to help you understand that writing is a process you can learn, just as these young men and women did.

There is no pat formula for writing the perfect essay. You can easily become confused by the conflicting advice many well-meaning people offer you: essays should be short or long, formal or informal in tone and style, funny or serious, very personalized or more detached, a narrative story or straightforward information, on a safe or a risk-taking topic, and so on. The key to writing your college essays, in our opinion, is the topic you choose or are required to address and the style in which you are naturally accustomed to write. Since you are asked to write about yourself so admissions officers learn who you are rather than what you have done, the style of writing should reflect your personality and thinking, not anyone else's. Your uniqueness will emerge from your writing if you remember this advice. Too many pens stirring the pot will create a stew of many ingredients, only some of which will be your handiwork.

Major Requirements for Good Essay Writing

One of the academic bibles all college students should always have at their elbow as they write is *The Elements of Style*, by William Strunk Jr. and E. B. White. Strunk was a professor of English for many years at Cornell University, and it was he who created this gem, "the little book," as it was referred to by generations of students who took his course in writing. White, who went on from Strunk's class to become one of the finest and most successful essayists in the mid–twentieth century, edited the later editions of this eighty-five-page guide to writing. They offer two fundamental pieces of advice among many good recommendations that will enable you to craft the outstanding essay hiding inside you.

The first:

Choose a suitable design and hold to it. A basic structural design underlies every kind of writing. The writer will in part follow this design, in part deviate from it, according to his skill, his needs, and the unexpected events that accompany the act of composition. Writing, to be effective, must follow closely the thoughts of the writer . . . Planning must be a deliberate part prelude to writing. The first principle of composition, therefore, is to foresee or determine the shape of what is to come and pursue that shape.[2]

[2]William Strunk Jr. and E. B. White, *The Elements of Style,* 3rd ed. (New York: Macmillan, 1979), p. 15.

The second:

Omit needless words. Vigorous writing is concise. A sentence should contain no unnecessary words, a paragraph no unnecessary sentences, for the same reason that a drawing should have no unnecessary lines and a machine no unnecessary parts. This requires not that the writer make all his sentences short, or that he avoid all detail and treat his subjects only in outline, but that every word tell.[3]

If you take this advice to heart, you will save yourself a good deal of insecurity and wasted effort in your writing. We offer additional rules for effective essay writing that have helped thousands of college-bound essayists:

1. Develop a clear main idea or thesis at the very start.
2. Give important and relevant specific examples to support your main idea or thesis.
3. Be coherent in your writing; that is, stick to the main point and do not wander into other unrelated or irrelevant topics.
4. Always use the active voice to give a sense of energy and originality in your thinking.
5. Use good grammar and syntax; otherwise, admissions readers will wonder if you are prepared to meet the standards of their faculty.
6. Use mature language. This means that you should avoid slang, coarse terminology, and commonly used adolescent phrases that will be unrecognizable to anyone over twenty-five.
7. Avoid overblown words and phrases in the attempt to impress the reader with your erudition.
8. Do not overwrite what it is you hope to convey to the reader. Too much repetition of your thought or too many words and pages to make your point will be held against you by the busy reader.

[3]Ibid., p. 23.

9. Do not overstate your point, lest you be accused of inflating your abilities or accomplishments.
10. Avoid at all costs any whiff of gimmickry: for example, a wise-acre remark or a pretentious quotation from an author you are unlikely to have read.
11. Create a mind-catching opening sentence and paragraph that will make the reader eager to read your entire essay.
12. Write, rewrite, and write again with the clear notion that you are not done until you have made three or more passes at your piece.

What Is a Personal Essay?

Strictly speaking, an essay can take any of these forms: a theme, a thesis, a tract, a treatise, a composition, a discussion, an article, a study, a rationale, a dissertation. None of these is appropriate to the purpose at hand, as they all smack of formal schoolwork that centers on other people, events, or creations rather than yourself. We suggest you think of each essay you will write as a "piece," which connotes a more relaxed, intimate, thoughtful reflection on any topic of your choosing that has as its end goal self-revelation for the admissions committees.

Here is E. B. White, who made his living as an essayist, with his observations on this particular form of writing:

> There are as many kinds of essays as there are human attitudes or poses, as many flavors as there are Howard Johnson ice creams. The essayist arises in the morning and, if he has work to do, selects his garb from an unusually extensive wardrobe: he can pull on any sort of shirt, be any sort of person, according to his mood or his subject matter—philosopher, scold, jester, raconteur, confidant, pundit, devil's advocate, enthusiast.
>
> There is one thing the essayist cannot do, though—he cannot indulge himself in deceit or in concealment, for he will be found out in no time. Natural candor is the basic ingredient.[4]

---

[4]E. B. White, *Essays of E. B. White* (New York: Harper & Row, 1977), p. vii.

Here you have further advice on the importance of writing from your own mind and soul with truth and honesty. The subject of the application essay is always you, so you have a head start on what to write about and how you will decide to write. Do you think a narrative story about a trip you took will convey who you are to the admissions committees? Or will a straightforward account of an incident work best? Or will a description of a person who has influenced your life do the job? Or has there been an illness or a tragedy in your life that most defines you? The choice should be yours, and the style and tone in which you write about yourself should be appropriate to the subject. You cannot make a mistake this way.

Edgar Allan Poe, who knew how to make a lasting impact on his readers, said that one of the writer's first considerations in designing an essay is to consider the effect he or she wants to create. Start your essay with this element in mind and then create the story itself. "Keep originality always in view," he urged. All the facts or events of the story must ultimately add up to give the desired effect of the piece. "Consider the point of your writing before anything be attempted with the pen."

To create a personal piece, you should be relaxed and tell the story you instinctively want to tell. There is no wrong choice, since you are the point of the story. Trust your own instincts to write your piece on the topic in the way you feel will best convey the effect and message. You can take risks. Try writing on a topic you consider slightly unusual or personal or controversial. If it makes a significant point, then it is the right topic.

It is fine to be funny or witty. Let your sense of humor be in evidence, and let the readers know that you are fully capable of laughing at yourself. Allow your feelings to show. Work on that opening sentence or two until you are comfortable showing your statement to a close friend or other confidant. Do all this, and you will be well underway with your presentation. Be aware, however, that a personal piece that reveals more than any admissions officer wants to know will not help you be understood and appreciated for who you are.

This is our list of reminders when composing your personal essay:

1. Do not attempt to put everything about yourself into one essay. You need to set your objective, and the topic that will let you meet this objective, at the beginning of your writing and then stay on track. Do not let yourself get derailed by going off in other directions.
2. Do not be pompous, bombastic, arrogant, all-knowing, hostile, or critical of other people as you write about yourself.
3. Do not oversell your strengths and accomplishments or take all the credit for success in your endeavors.
4. Do not write about the difficulty of composing this essay, as many naive candidates do. Demonstrate that you can and have put in the thought and work to create a good piece of writing that will meet the expectations of the admissions committee.
5. Do not expect admissions officers to second-guess who you really are, what your true potential for learning is, or why you did not live up to your promise, because you failed to tell them the full story. The following are frequent examples of this situation:

   - A drop in your grades due to a serious illness
   - Low standardized test scores due to a learning or physical disability
   - Few advanced courses in your record because of the limited offerings in your school
   - Few sports or club activities due to the need to work after school and weekends to help your family
   - Frequent changes of schools because of a parent's job re-location

Don't Get It Right, Get It Written!

Samuel Eliot Morison, a great American historian, offered this practical bit of advice: "A few hints as to literary craftmanship may be useful to budding historians. First and foremost, *get writing!*"

"It took me fifteen years to discover that I had no talent for writing, but I couldn't give it up because by that time I was too famous," wrote Robert Benchley, one of the great social humorists in the middle of the past century. This comment on his feeling about the quality of his own writing is witty and humble. Few individuals think of themselves as great writers, because the work involved in writing is so hard.

Robert Benchley, *Bartlett's Familiar Quotations,* 16th ed. (Boston: Little, Brown, 1992), p. 675.

Please believe that you are not the only individual who has struggled to get started on the actual writing process. All the advice on what is important to include in a personal essay will not guarantee an easy path to putting your ideas in order and writing them down. Most people will spend so much time fretting over what they will say and how they will say it, out of fear of doing a poor job, that they cannot make the transition to writing. They freeze in their thinking, they avoid the task, they give up. Does this sound like you? You will have to conquer this tendency, just as all writers have.

THE PERSONAL WRITING WORKSHEET

Five adjectives that describe me best:

_____

_____

Three of my strengths:

_____

_____

_____

Three of my weaknesses:

_____

_____

_____

Three major experiences that have shaped me:

_____

_____

_____

Which of these experiences reveals something essential about me?

_____

_____

What is that something?

_____

_____

Three individuals who have strongly influenced me:

_____

_____

_____

Which of these individuals would help me to reveal who I am?

_____

_____

How and why?

_____

_____

The most important point I want to make is:

_____

_____

The effect I want to have on the reader is:

_____

_____

I want the tone of my writing to be:

_____ serious

_____ humorous

_____ narrative

_____ descriptive

_____ expository

_____ other

A draft thesis statement:

_____

_____

_____

A draft opening sentence:

_____

_____

_____

A draft concluding sentence:

_____

_____

_____

If you follow the three steps of building your assessment chart that we outlined in Chapter 1 (gauging your strengths, assessing the appropriate colleges, and communicating your strengths), complete the Personal Writing Worksheet, and observe the guidelines we present here, you are ready to begin writing. Now we'll show you a few essays written by students who worked diligently until "they got it written" effectively.

A Reflective Personal Statement

The writer of this thoughtful examination of the role of religion in the lives of individuals and groups took on a sensitive topic that could have met with disfavor from an admissions committee. Amanda believed that an experience during summer travel abroad deeply affected her, causing her to rethink some ingrained attitudes, and that she needed to communicate this to the colleges. Writing about her unusual summer experience in India falls under the essay category of a recent "meaningful experience" and how it affected her thinking. (The essay categories are discussed more fully in Chapter 3.)

Amanda's several drafts did not get off to a good beginning, since she initially declared her rejection of all formal religions. The reader was not encouraged to read further, because the tone was uninviting. With a good deal of rewriting, she was able to present the awe and wonder of her experience and its impact on her value system. The reader senses a story unfolding that will explain what happened to Amanda. This is certainly not the typical, uninspiring summary of "what I did and learned this summer."

FAITH AND FREEDOM AMONG THE TIBETANS

I have struggled over the idea of God and religion for quite some time. I have often found myself examining the role that religion plays in the lives of people who are devoted to a god or some form of a deity. When I read newspaper articles about the conflict between Catholics and Protestants in Northern Ireland or the atrocities in Kosovo, or when I study the pogroms in Russia and genocide during the Crusades, I reinforce my mistrust of institutions that either encourage or unintentionally provide believers with an excuse to use violence against people whose religious views differed from theirs. Then something took place that was to change radically my perception of the role of religious belief in the lives of humankind.

It was not until this past summer, when I lived in the north Indian town of Dharamsala, the seat of the Tibetan government in exile, that I began to reexamine my doubts about religion. I stayed with a devout Tibetan Buddhist refugee family and was swept up in the worship that shapes their daily lives. When the father of my family, Pala, became ill, relatives and friends from all over town came and prayed at his bedside. Every morning as the sun rose, and Amala, the mother, sang deep, melodic prayers, I would light incense on the shrine that hung from the thin newspaper-covered walls.

As I spent more time with my adopted family, I began to understand how belief in the Buddha provided them with a sense of hope and security. In the case of Pala's sickness, it gave the family a reason to believe that he would recover and be able to return to work as a noodle seller on the streets of a nearby town.

During my stay with my family, I was granted permission to attend the Dalai Lama's teachings at the Ing monastery. It was Bagdro, however, a young Tibetan monk who managed to move me more than any religious leader I was honored to meet. He first caught my eye on the bus from Delhi to Dharamsala. I noticed that his wine-colored robes were soaked through with sweat, making intriguing patterns under his shoulder blades and across his chest. We smiled politely to each other, and as I struggled to sleep in the cramped bus in the 120-degree heat, I wondered how he could smile when he must be hotter than I was. By a coincidence that perhaps was meant to occur, a friend who wanted me to hear his story introduced me to him a week later in town, and we smiled in recognition.

I learned that Bagdro is a former political prisoner who was unjustly arrested in Lhasa, Tibet, after he helped organize a peaceful demonstration to protest the violent Chinese occupation of his homeland. He was imprisoned for three years and subjected to starvation and daily brutal beatings. After partially recovering, he managed to escape over the Himalayas into India, where he now dedicates his life to educating the world about what is happening to his people, in the hope of someday freeing his homeland from the control of the Chinese occupiers.

As Bagdro told me his story over steaming cups of sweet milk and tea, I came to a realization that simultaneously troubled and fascinated me. Bagdro has no human rights and to return to his homeland would be suicide. He has no pension plan or social security number, no family, and no material possessions. By Western standards he has nothing. I, on the other hand, have a passport, freedom on every level, and a bank account, not to mention the most important factor in my life, a close and loving family. Yet when I sorted out my feelings towards him of pity, awe, respect, and kinship, I was disconcerted to discover that what underlay all of these emotions was envy.

I found that I craved what he had, something that far outweighed any of my seemingly valuable possessions. I discovered that he had a belief system that has fueled him with the energy to search for and find his inner strength. Seizing this power, Bagdro has used the teachings of Buddhism to survive under severe oppression and loss, to triumph and transcend his circumstances. Not only did his faith enable him to do this, it also gave him the ability to inspire people from other countries and cultures to attempt to lift the hand of oppression and brutality from the Tibetan people. Bagdro's faith, in other words, infuses and sustains his struggle for freedom.

Bagdro's is a benevolent faith, which I never believed existed. Having been exposed to Bagdro, other Buddhists and their ideas, I began to believe that I, too, could cultivate a faith that would help me discover the strength to devote myself to a cause, and even go against the grain of conventional society. I want to "worship" compassion, freedom, justice, generosity, and selflessness. These ideals will become the foundation of my belief system and my comportment in a complex and divided world.

A Pair of Mature Personal Essays

This set of personal statements was written by Karen in response to Yale University's request that the applicant reflect on her attitudes, values, and perception of herself, and tell them something that the committee might not learn from the rest of the application. The choice of subjects is not uncommon among intelligent applicants, but Karen's story of music's significance in her personal development—and the maturity of expression throughout—helped win her a place at Yale.

For eight years I have played the flute. At times I have struggled, doubting my ability ever to master a specific piece, and at times I have played notes that seemed to float effortlessly from the silver instrument at my lips. Regardless of whether I struggled or excelled, my first flute teacher did nothing but praise me. At recitals at a neighborhood church, she would introduce me with great pride, launching into long explanations of the difficulty of the piece I was playing, and, with all due modesty, I probably played better than the other students did at these recitals. After I finished playing, parents and other students would surround me and compliment me effusively, saying things like, "When is your next engagement with James Galway?" Hearing such comments as a sixth-grader was thrilling. I worked at playing the flute day in and day out, trying to learn tricky fingerings and produce a vibrant tone. I loved playing even when I was most frustrated. The exhilaration of mastering a difficult piece of music and sharing it with others was worth all the hard work.

My flute teacher encouraged me to apply to the Interlochen Arts Camp in Michigan. This involved making a recording of solos, scales, and etudes. Playing for a tape made me a little apprehensive, because I had never played the flute outside of my school and my local church. Yet, with the prospect of attending a camp that promised to surround me with flute music and other serious musicians, I overcame my nervousness and sent an application to this famous performing arts camp.

Months later, I received an acceptance in the mail. I was thrilled. The rest of the school year flew by, and then one hot summer day I found myself on a campus filled with 2,000 students toting pointed shoes, and oil canvases, and, most importantly, flutes. But I soon discovered that these kids, budding artists aged 12 to 16, appeared more talented than I had ever imagined, and to my surprise, more talented than I was. When the seating hierarchy in the band was sorted out, I had been placed in the back of the flute section.

I learned over the next month what it meant to struggle. My mind whirled as I heard scales played at laser-like speeds and saw practice cells filled with campers frantically practicing at every hour of the day. Desperate to improve and move up in my section, I also began to practice every second that I could, cutting lunch occasionally and skipping out on time with my friends. When the end of the month came, however, I had shifted only a few chairs forward. Returning home dejected, I told my parents and friends it was a fabulous time, masking my disappointment at the realization that I was not the child prodigy they had all told me I was. In the following year, when people threw extravagant compliments at me, I would smile politely and thank them quietly. Inside, I knew that I was not the musical star they either thought I was or wanted me to be.

With an attitude of humility and determination, I decided to return to Interlochen the following summer and the summer after that. Yet those four-week sessions were different for me. I was no longer so desperately concerned with rising to the top of the flute section. I still worked hard and tried to improve my standing among the other flutists, but this was now only a measure of how much I had improved for myself.

Now as I surveyed this rarefied setting, I realized that I did not need to be the best flutist at the camp to have a rewarding time. There was stimulating music, art, dance, and drama for me to appreciate. There was much for me to learn from the extraordinary people surrounding me—ideas, deep friendships, and other passionate interests. I left my last summer at Interlochen having moved up in the flute section, but more importantly, I left with the realization that my love for music went far beyond the praise of others and my own competitive zeal. Playing the flute is not about being the best in the school, it is about making music that moves me in a way nothing else can. It transports me to a spiritual, transcendent place where all that is important is the message of my music. I find myself expressing emotions I never knew I had and discovering parts of myself I never felt were there: an ability to connect with other people through the lyrical sounds and an ability to interpret and understand someone else's feelings. It is this aspect of music that has made it a central part of my life, and it is in this way music has made my life richer than any amount of praise could provide.

The central themes of Karen's essay, like Amanda's essay, are strongly held beliefs and ideas that were challenged under stressful circumstances, the difficulty of having to develop new ways of viewing one's beliefs, and the gratitude for having been made to change one's ways of thinking. A sense of humility and appreciation for the opportunity to grow in new directions emerges from the stories and serves to make these writers even more appealing candidates to selective colleges.

Here is Karen's second essay, which fits the category of an intimate "significant influence" piece. The reader gains insight into her intellectual curiosity and love of books. In combination, her two presentations speak well of her, far more eloquently than her grade point average and test scores alone.

The store has been empty since last May. A sign still hangs above the door, reading "Cheshire Cat Children's Bookstore," and taped to the front locked door is a collage of pictures of the store throughout its years, together with a note thanking all former customers. This is the first September in Northwest Washington, DC that the window has not been brightened by the Cheshire Cat's hallmark display of live monarch butterflies, their bright orange and black wings emerging from the chrysalises before the transfixed eyes of children.

As a child, I always loved that display. I begged my mother every day at the beginning of September to drop by the shop after school so I could see if any new butterflies had emerged from their cocoons. These visits were never quick. After watching the butterflies fly around inside the window for several minutes, I always ventured into the store, a narrow, cheerful room lined with floor-to-ceiling bookshelves overflowing with the most wonderful looking books I could imagine.

The three Englishwomen who owned the store—all white-haired, thickly accented, and always smiling—knew my mother and me well, since we visited the store at least once a week. Whenever we entered, they hurried to the shelves to pick some new books they thought I might like. Naturally, they had read every book in the store, and they often sat with me as I sorted through the stack of books they had made especially for me. They would gently interrupt my skimming to give me a short plot summary of each one. It would be several hours later before my mother and I would leave the store, a bag of new books in hand.

It was in this magical room that I developed my passion for books. I wanted to read everything there—fiction, biographies, history, poetry. Best of all, the owners encouraged me to do just that, as they picked the best books to set before my wide eyes. As I became older, I did not visit the Cheshire Cat as frequently. By the time I entered high school, there was little left there for me to read. However, in the middle of my sophomore year, as if by a miracle, I learned that there was an opportunity to work at the bookstore. Of course I applied immediately.

Returning to the shop, I found everything exactly as I had remembered: the sweet Englishwomen, the slightly sagging shelves, rows and rows of wonderful and intriguing books. I loved being there again, watching other children wander in with their parents and excitedly select their favorite books. Now I was the one who would stack my favorite books in front of the customers and help them sort through the titles, one at a time so they could savor the delights that awaited them between the covers. When September came, I showed children the butterflies I had loved so much and answered their questions about the process of transforming from a caterpillar into a butterfly.

The Cheshire Cat will always be for me a perfect place, a magical shop, a nostalgic corner of my memory. It was a place where a love of books was nourished like nowhere else. The children who came there always returned numerous times. It was truly the small, personalized neighborhood bookstore, beloved by everyone in the area. Sadly, keeping a special place like Cheshire Cat running was difficult; the desk in the basement was always stacked high with bills and book order forms; and the last remaining owner grew older and retired as the effort to run the shop became too much for her. The children and their parents now turned to the large booksellers in the shopping malls for the ease and convenience factor.

Now when I stand in front of the blackened front window, a sudden wash of emotions and memories sweeps over me, I appreciate how much this place and the people who loved books and wanted to share this love with young readers meant to me. It was here I began my love affair with learning, here that my mind took its first big steps forward intellectually. Looking back on the brightened window filled with live butterflies, I feel blessed to have known this place.

As we move on to more guidelines for essay writing and examples of many different types of successful essays, we leave you with this advice from Isaac Bashevis Singer: "If you write about the things and the people you know best, you discover your roots. Even if they are new roots, fresh roots . . . they are better than no roots at all."

CHAPTER THREE

Principles of Good College Essay Writing

The application essays are one of the most daunting and stressful aspects of the college admissions process for students, for their parents, teachers, and guidance counselors, and for admissions officers. Students must discover, often for the first time in their lives, how to present themselves in writing to a group of strangers in about 500 words. Parents must watch, usually from the sidelines, as their son or daughter struggles with the writing process. Parents mutter to themselves and one another, debating whether and to what extent to encourage, cajole, influence, or ignore their child's efforts. Teachers and counselors attempt to help, without appearing too critical, too distant, or too involved. How much should they edit? What should their expectations be? How much time should they reasonably allow to provide commentary before applications are due? On the other side of the fence sit the admissions officers. They are the final repository of all this writing. They are the audience to whom students are earnestly writing, and they must read hundreds and thousands of essays and applications during each admissions cycle. What should they expect from their applicants? What will they learn from each student's writing? How do they know a student's work is his or her own, and conveys an accurate and useful message about that particular student?

In the center of this maelstrom sits the student, idly tapping the keyboard, staring out the window, commiserating with a friend on the phone, yelling at mom or dad to get off his or her back, and wondering in the dark of night and with clear exasperation just how to describe a significant life experience in two pages at age seventeen. What is a significant life experience, anyway? How do you know one when you see one? Who has had a significant impact on your life? If you talk about your teacher, will your father get upset? If you talk about your grandmother, will your friends think you're ridiculous? Why do they make us do this stuff?!

Essays do not emerge from nowhere. They arise within each individual student. We firmly believe that every applicant can write a good, exciting, interesting college application essay. You do not need to be the top student in Advanced Placement (AP) English to present yourself well in your essay writing. You need only follow some basic guidelines, look within yourself, be true to yourself, and be diligent, and you will succeed in "getting yourself down on paper" in a way that positively supports your applications to selective colleges. Though presenting yourself successfully to colleges is a big task, and writing good essays is the central part of that experience, you can make it through this effort with your integrity, self-respect, and pride intact.

Why Do We Have to Do This Stuff?

Imagine an alternate college admissions universe. Every winter, selective colleges collect applications from hopeful students that contain three major pieces of information: course transcripts with an academic GPA; scores from one or more sets of standardized tests; and class rank, when available. Admissions officers sort through this information trying to build a strong and interesting incoming class. They look for honors, AP courses, a consistently high GPA, high scores on SAT and ACT tests, and a high rank in class to find the best-performing academic students. They may use formulas to help them assess this information and compare students. Then, they sit and scratch their heads. "We have a strong class," they muse, "but who knows if it is an interesting one? If only there was some way to tell what these students were really like as individuals . . ."

Today, part of this admissions universe is a reality. In large part, admissions decisions at selective colleges, both private and public, are made on the basis of your high school curriculum, your standardized test scores, and your rank in class (if your high school provides ranks or decile divisions). Applicants still have a chance to help admissions committees build an exciting class by writing essays and working on their overall presentation to the colleges in order to convey essential information about who they are as students and individuals, their activities in and out of school, their hopes and goals, and the level and nature of their interest in a particular college or university. Despite the evident hassle of writing them, essays offer a unique opportunity to engage the attention of the admissions committee.

Your goal in essay writing should be to come across to readers (i.e., admissions officers) as interesting, intriguing, exciting, bright, heroic, sublime, engaged, enthusiastic, serious, witty, intelligent, educated— any adjective that suggests you would be a valued individual in the class an admissions committee is trying to create at their college. Is it hard to be original among hundreds and thousands of other applicants who are encountering the same quandaries as you? Yes and no. Your goal is to write in a way that will affect the mind and heart of the readers and persuade them to admit you. It is hard to be original when you are writing essays that may strike chords readers have heard many times before. It is not hard to be original if you stick to writing about yourself, to telling true-to-your-life stories, and to being you. Since no one else can be you but *you,* the first rule of thumb is to avoid being vague or abstract. Everything has to come back to how your thoughts and experiences and lessons and mentors and books have affected you, your thinking, and your values.

What Some Colleges Say about Essay Writing and Presentation

As colleges have moved away from the on-campus personal interview as a means of getting to know each student's interests, character, and personality, they have relied more heavily on the open written elements of their applications to discover the intangible qualities of applicants. Here are some comments from selective colleges indicating how essays help them to make their admissions decisions:

Outstanding grades, a strong academic program, and a thoughtfully written personal application are very important to us in the selection process. So are written recommendations, standardized-test scores, and your special talents, strength of character, and intellectual potential. Quite simply, we're interested in the people who will get the most out of a Cornell education.

—Cornell University admissions website, www.cornell.edu

An interview is not a factor in our decision. Your carefully completed application should provide the information we need to make a decision. Think of the required personal essay as an interview in writing . . . Because we do not have the opportunity to meet each one of you personally we would like you to help us to get to know you better. A transcript, test scores, and list of extracurricular activities can tell us only so much about you as a person. In an essay, you can provide additional information beyond the scope of the application that you would like the Admission Committee to consider.

—University of North Carolina at Chapel Hill admissions website,
www.unc.edu/admissions

Do not get overwhelmed by the college application process! At its best, this is a chance to raise your own level of self-awareness and discover the range of options available in higher education. Applying to college is an opportunity for you to find a particular type of place that can best serve your needs. You determine what those needs are and which colleges can deliver on your expectations. When completing an application, make the connection between your personal aspirations and the campus culture you discovered at the college(s) to which you are applying. Before you know it, you will be moving into your dorm room and meeting new friends.

—Eric J. Furda, director of undergraduate admissions,
Columbia University admissions website,
www.columbia.edu.admissions

At U.Va., we take a holistic approach to admission. This means that we consider all of a student's strengths, including academic performance, extracurricular achievements, and personal qualities, in making the admission decision. We like to know what makes you a whole person, someone who is not only a top student but also interesting in some other way, whether for accomplishments in an activity, for unusual personal circumstances, or simply for skillful expression of your ideas. BUT we can't admit the big-man-on-campus or the big-woman-on-campus if he or she is a mediocre student . . . If you don't enjoy writing, work on it. And even students who love to write should work on using lots of specific details, narrowing your topics, and identifying your own opinions. We ask for some written responses as part of our application process because we expect entering U.Va. students to be able to express themselves clearly and concisely. Like your activities, your writing also helps us see you as a whole person.

—University of Virginia informational pamphlet, April 1998

The simple fact is that there is not enough room and the admission committee must make difficult choices. Many times I have received phone calls from an irate high school counselor or parent and retrieved the [rejected] student's file. As I quickly scanned the application, I wondered why we denied this student because she or he looked so good. Then I remember the way the committee discussion had gone in those late night, last-few-slot meetings. The turning point may have been something as simple as the student's intended major, *a turn of phrase in an essay*, a defining comment in a teacher's recommendation, or the desire to have someone from Fargo, North Dakota.

—R. Fred Zucker, dean of admission, financial aid, and student life, University of Dallas, *College Board Review*, fall 1997, p. 19, emphasis added

The essay questions enable an admission dean to look beyond test results, grades and class rank to better understand the applicant and to personalize the process. Although writing ability is important, it is not the only thing that a dean will see. An essay can be well-written but uninformative, meaning that I have no better perception of who you are as a student or as an individual after reading the essay than I did before reading the essay, nor do I see how your strengths are different than those of many other talented applicants. Essays are a way to express yourself, share thoughts, and display creativity. Write from your viewpoint. Stay away from the same topics that others choose to write about. By being an individual, you distinguish yourself from the group and give us the opportunity to see your strengths.

—Amherst College admissions officer

As these comments from a variety of selective college and universities indicate, the essay is given serious consideration as a key personal component in the admissions process. It is not the most important factor, but not the least, either. What the admissions readers are encouraging you to do is to approach the essays carefully and see them as an opportunity to present some part of who you are to the colleges. You can help the admissions reader to see what the most important parts of your application are and what some of your more prominent personal characteristics are. A thoughtful, well-crafted, and personal statement sets you apart from other highly qualified candidates.

Believe the admissions officers when they say they read applications carefully. They are usually looking for reasons to admit you, and you may begin the process with the benefit of the doubt. Poorly written essays and sloppy applications can quickly turn the tables and provide the reader with reasons not to admit you. Boring or nondescript essays may provoke a yawn, a quicker turn of the page, and a dismissal of you as not a very interesting applicant, despite your strong academic credentials.

How do you accomplish the important task of producing a set of essays that present you in the best possible light? In the box are some guidelines on beginning and completing the essay writing process, and on considering the college application essays overall.

TIPS ON ESSAY WRITING AND PRESENTATION FROM A SMALL COLLEGE ADMISSIONS OFFICE

Bates College offers the following advice for applicants on its website. Note that Bates, as a small liberal arts college, still emphasizes the role of the on-campus interview in its admissions process, unlike the great majority of colleges today. Bates gives you these tips to make your application stand out:

1. Tell us how and/or why your most important activities (perhaps an AP physics project, a team captaincy, or a tutorial project in the inner city) have changed you. We want to know what you have learned from your experiences, not just what you have done.

2. View the admissions forms as the place to chronicle your family background, school history, activities, work experiences, and other autobiographical information you want us to know. Be clear and concise and use specific detail.

3. Use the subjective questions (like those asking about a book which has had an impact on you, why you are interested in Bates, or what has been your most important extracurricular activity) and the essay to express your "other" side, that which we may not learn from your courses and grades. The quality of your writing is particularly important here.

4. Take advantage of our invitation to submit evidence of your scholarly and creative endeavors. Present slides of art work, tapes of musical performances, photography, poetry, creative and journalistic writing, independent research and internship reports or whatever else you feel it is important for us to know. Do not tell us only about your successes; tell us about what you truly enjoy doing, what inspires you, and what holds meaning for you.

5. Do not miss the opportunity to have a personal interview. It is a time for you to talk about your interests and goals with a member of the Admissions Committee and to see what Bates can offer you. From our point of view, the interview adds a vital, personal dimension to our decision-making.

(continued)

Bates organizes these points for students considering their application essays:

1. Essay's importance for colleges:
   a. To judge depth of students' understanding of intellectual or social issues, quality and freshness of mind, "lighting up" of issues referred to skeletally elsewhere in application.
   b. To show writing style, technical correctness, and fluency (sentence subordination, paragraph construction/unity, vocabulary, metaphorical versus concrete language, etc.).
2. Subject: Anything of real interest to the student. It should light up another part of the folder.
   a. Autobiographical: Be careful of the obvious "How my trip to France taught me independence." But if reflective, anything—travel, significant personal struggle, family experience—can be an impressive subject.
   b. Social/Political: Ought to be tied to previous student interests. An essay on devotion to environmentalism as an abstract idea carries little weight.
   c. Intellectual interests: Response to works of a particular author, research in certain areas, places where the student has outgrown and reached beyond his/her curriculum.
3. Length: More than two-thirds of a page, and usually less than four pages to ensure being read carefully.
4. Format:
   a. Neat, readable, hand-written or word processed.
   b. Physically prepared by student him/herself (not dad's/mom's secretary, even as typed—it raises doubts about editorial overlays).
5. For weaker writers:
   a. Take real care; start in September-November; rewrite frequently.
   b. Send one to three extra writing samples: in- and out-of-class work, with teachers' comments.

6. How weighted by college:

   Often as a confirmation of a decision if other credentials are clear. The essay can be a powerful "tipper" in close cases, especially with very strong or very poor essays.

   Warning: Faculty admissions readers pay careful attention to essays. As the eventual consumers, they may advocate against admitting applicants with unoriginal or poorly crafted essays.

Bates College admissions website, www.bates.edu/app-tips.

Pieces of the Puzzle: Assembling Your Application

Building your college applications involves assembling a variety of pieces into a coherent whole. You combine your lists of extracurricular, work, and volunteer activities with your essays, your transcript, your standardized test score reports, your personal data forms, and so forth, to create an accurate and understandable portrait of yourself. The requirement to complete several long and short essay questions is an opportunity to put together multiple pieces of your own puzzle in the form of separate but connected samples of writing. Look at each individual college application as a coordinated product. Its elements should work together to present your different sides and interests. You will likely write at least three or four essays of varying length in the process of completing six to ten applications. What you will find is that you can start to put these puzzle pieces together in different ways depending on the needs of each application. You will need to adapt your writing to fit each college's specifications and profile, and you will need to make judgments about the relative merits of your essays and how they work together.

You should avoid repeating yourself in any given application. Although you do want to stress some themes and make clear what is most important to you, you do not want to take two pieces of the puzzle and draw the same picture on them. For example, if you are a musician, you should not write your "meaningful activity" short essay about music and then repeat yourself in the longer personal statement by talking about how much music has meant to your life. Think about other interests, experiences, or ideas you would like to discuss, and use the longer statement to put together a more varied and interesting portrait.

Different Types of Essay Questions—Yet You Are You

There are several different types of essay questions, and you will often need to combine answers to at least two of them on any particular application. One can identify the Why Us, Meaningful Activity, Significant Influence, and Powerful Idea essays as distinct groups in the college applications. Each type of essay asks you for different information and a different approach, but each has an important characteristic in common: they are all about you. In each case, the college is looking to learn about you, not about their institution, hockey, your father, or J. D. Salinger. You might be discussing *The Catcher in the Rye* or your powerful slapshot, but what the college reader is looking for is how you write, how you interpret the text, what you learned about yourself and life through hockey, your sense of humor and values, and so on. Keep in mind that you should remain the focus of your writing. Even if you are revealing yourself implicitly by the telling a story or discussing a serious topic, remember that the admissions officer is asking, "What does this tell us about this student?"

Why Us

You will encounter a common short or middle-length essay topic: Why Penn? Why Georgetown? Why Northwestern? Why Vanderbilt? In some form or another, you will have to answer this question for many college applications and, most important, in conversations with admissions officers, alumni/ae, teachers, friends, parents, counselors, and others. You should at least consider how you would answer this question for each college or university to which you are applying, and at best compose a several-hundred-word essay laying out your reasons for wanting to attend each school. This is the case even if the college does not require this question on its application. Since *you* do not change from school to school, three-quarters of each essay will be the same or very similar. You will answer these questions as best as you can:

- What are my main academic interests?
- What are my possible choices of major?
- What are my possible career choices?
- What are my main extracurricular, social, and community interests?
- In what ways do I hope to continue them in college?
- What type of institution and environment am I looking for in a college or university (big, small, liberal arts, preprofessional, conservatory, urban, rural, suburban, single-sex, diverse, traditional, etc.)?

Remember, this portion of the essay is about you, not about them. In other words, do not tell the university all about who and what they are. They know their strengths and weaknesses well enough. To avoid clichés and repetition, focus on yourself, what you are looking for in a college. Tell them about your interests, strengths, passions, and preferences.

For the last quarter or so of this essay, you will need to make the match, the connection between you and each particular university that shows how and why there is a logical fit between you and them. Once you have laid out what you are looking for, it is a matter of being specific and directed about how Georgetown, Vanderbilt, Penn, or any other school fits your criteria for the right college. You can explain how you found out about the college and what impressed you on a visit, during a conversation with current students or alumni/ae, or after additional research. You can point clearly and specifically to programs, majors, courses, or activities that suit your interests. Our advice here is to avoid spending much time, if any, holding forth on the pretty campus, the fabulous traditions and alumni connections, the wonders of the city around the university, or the fact that your mom, dad, sibling, or cousin always raves about the place. Instead, concentrate on what you will study at the university, what you will bring to campus as an involved student and member of the community, and why this particular college or university fits the model you have identified. Show the college that you have done your research, that you know what you are looking for, and that you understand how the institution fits your interests. Be concrete and explain the ways in which you first discovered and then learned more about the school, from interviews to discussions with students to campus visits to conversations with faculty.

Meaningful Activity

The Meaningful Activity (or work or volunteer experience) essay is found on the Common Application and many individual college applications. This essay ranges from a short paragraph (about 100 words) to a half page (about 200 words). We encourage students, especially when filling out the Common Application, to take the opportunity to attach this essay as a half-page statement on an additional sheet of paper (when filing by regular mail). You should not take this essay lightly, scratching out a few thoughts as you rush on to the main personal statement. This short essay is an opportunity to be clear and specific about which of your involvements has had the most meaning for or impact on you. Again, this essay is about what you learned from your work, volunteering, or participation, not about how the software company produces CD-ROMs, the hospital admits patients, or the soccer team selects its captains.

The college reader will be interested in the activity you choose to discuss and how you present its meaning for you. In answer to a question we often receive, you do need to make a choice and to discuss one activity or experience. It is best to avoid trying to cram a discussion of multiple activities into this short answer, in an attempt not to leave any of them out. This only suggests indecisiveness and failure to answer the question posed. Consider this overdrawn example:

> While I have played baseball for ten years, earning several MVP awards and being elected Captain for my senior year, an honor which I cherish deeply as a sign of my coaches' and teammates' respect for my quiet leadership, and I have traveled extensively on international service projects, which have taught me humility, respect for other cultures, and independence, I believe that my peer tutoring program has had the most meaning for me.

We hope you get our point.

Perhaps you have been significantly involved in several important school activities, employment opportunities, or volunteer projects. That is excellent. You should list them, along with the extent of your participation, in the activities, volunteer, and employment sections of the application. You may also submit additional résumés, documentation, or references to help bring these aspects of yourself to light (see Chapter 5 for our discussion of supplemental application materials). For this short essay question, you will need to pick one major involvement and discuss its meaning to you. The reason you chose this activity should be clear from your answer. And the fact that you have selected it will in no way diminish the time you spent or lessons you learned elsewhere.

We suggest you approach the Meaningful Activity question as follows:

- Provide a brief description of the activity: this does not have to occur at the beginning of the essay.
- Avoid beginning your answer by repeating the question, "The activity that has the most meaning for me in high school has been . . ." Jump right in with statements about the activity itself, a description of doing the activity, dialogue, or some other active phrasing that catches the reader's attention.

- Avoid repeating basic information about the length or amount of involvement in the activity, since that information is listed elsewhere in the application.
- Bring the activity to life by describing action (scoring a goal, reaching a student you are tutoring, witnessing a birth in the hospital for the first time, rebutting the final argument in the debate championships). Show the impact of the activity on you.
- Consider discussing how and whether you will continue this activity in college.
- Draw some lessons you learned from this activity and discuss how your outlook on life, goals for the future, approach to learning, or personal values changed as a result of your participation.

Significant Influence

Presumably, you have been influenced by many things during your lifetime. That influence may have originated from an experience you had, a person you knew, a teacher you encountered, a book you read, or a combination of some of these (a teacher teaching an important book, an instructor guiding a wilderness expedition, a parent taking you on an eye-opening journey). What the colleges are looking for is your discussion of one major influence in your life. We often hear students fret, "But I have had a perfectly normal life. Nothing terrible has happened to me, so I have nothing to write about!" In addition to the fact that not having anything terrible to write about is a good thing, we emphasize that significant influences need not be bad to be interesting and valuable. Consider the people you have known, the major and minor experiences you have had, the books or teachers you particularly remember. What has made them important, special, meaningful, and memorable to you? What would talking about any one of them imply to admissions readers? When they consider why you have chosen your particular topic, will it make sense to them and will your essay communicate what you want it to in your application? Can the topic you have chosen be developed? Can you capture the person, experience, or influence well in the prescribed length?

There are a number of things to avoid in the Significant Influence essay:

- If you are writing about a significant person in your life, it is not a biography. Your ability to capture the essential elements of someone, be it a teacher, parent, grandparent, coach, or friend, and to show his or her impact on you is what matters.
- If you are writing about a significant experience, the essay is not a travelog, simple play-by-play, or, as we discussed in relation to the Meaningful Activity essay, a description of what you did as a Sunday school teacher all those years. Your ability to bring the reader there, to capture narrative detail, and to show what you learned from the experience through your descriptive lens is what is important.
- If you are writing about a significant book, the essay is not a book report or a plot summary. Show the reader what you got out of the book, and how it changed the way you think about life, academics, friendship, or any other topic that is important to you.

The Significant Influence essay is a personal statement. It is about you and what has been of major importance to you in your life. As such, realize the statement you are making, explicitly (directly) or implicitly (indirectly) in your writing.

The Significant Influence essay, in the form of the Significant Experience or Significant Person topic, is probably the most common college application essay. Yet students can still write original and interesting essays in this genre. In addition to our general guidelines, we suggest these additional points:

- Try to avoid getting stuck on identifying the one *defining moment or person* in your life. Choose one influence that has helped to make you who you are today.
- Walk backwards from what you want the college to know or learn about you, and then consider what experience or person or other influence might help you to show this point.

- Upon choosing a potential topic, think about all the other applicants who may have selected a similar focus. What will make your approach unique and different? How will you make your essay stand out?
- If you have had a tragedy or significant struggle in your life, avoid dismissing the topic outright. Although handling such topics is difficult and sensitive, consider the ways in which discussing a powerfully negative experience in your life could help you to show some very positive qualities and personal development to the colleges.
- Get specific. The best way to avoid sounding like hundreds of other essays is to avoid generalizations and to bring in details that make this influence and its impact decidedly yours.
- Consider writing in another voice than the first person "I." Might you write more creatively and originally in the third person "he/she" narrative voice? Could you write in the second person "you" voice and use a lot of dialogue? Which voice would help you most effectively get across your message?
- Remember what year it is. Unless you can make a very persuasive argument, and your influence from long ago really is arguably significant in your life today and in the future, more recent experiences, people, and influences are better candidates for this essay topic.

Powerful Idea

Many different essays can represent the Powerful Idea topic. The colleges are looking for you to engage an important concept. They want to see how you address it, what conclusions you draw, how you use the idea to reflect on your own values and beliefs, and how you make and defend an argument. Whether you are reacting to Thoreau's belief in civil disobedience, Roosevelt's defense of the Four Freedoms, the challenge to build a new monument in Washington, D.C., or the opportunity to present your views on how to promote interracial tolerance, you will need to show a firm grasp of the ideas at hand, an ability to write a clear and well-reasoned essay, a sense of the importance and relevance of the ideas to the world and to you, and a knack for moving from the general, abstract level to the specific, personal domain.

Choosing to write an essay that allows you to engage a powerful idea may set you apart from many other applicants. If you have something important to say, consider writing an essay in this area and follow these guidelines:

- Have your facts straight, and avoid outrageous or overly provocative claims. Stay within your area of knowledge.
- Be careful about offending a reader when you are writing on a sensitive topic, such as religion, race, or abortion. You will want to show that you can take a stand and defend a position and your values while simultaneously engaging in tolerant, reasoned debate.
- Think about your answer. This is not a time to rush off a response without considering your argument and the ramifications of what you are saying. Have friends and adults you respect react to your essay and play devil's advocate, offering alternative viewpoints on the issue.
- Remember that this essay is about you, even though you are engaging a bigger idea. You may talk about how you have reacted to or learned about this idea. You may discuss examples of studying the topic, engaging in debates on the issues, or having experiences related to the challenge posed by the essay question. Indirectly, your ability to synthesize the debate and organize a coherent response will show the reader a great deal about your intellectual and personal strengths and orientation.

Sample Essay Questions from the Common Application and Applications from Top Schools

Here we present some long and short essay questions from some selective university application forms for the fall of 2001. The forms often change yearly, so consider these ones models, and make sure to obtain the most recent application packet for each college or university to which you are applying. Today, most of these applications are available online at the schools' websites or through a number of online application services, including review.com and embark.com. The Common Application is also available online at www.commonapp.org. You may choose in many cases to submit the applications online, or to download them, view them on your computer, print them out, and mail them.

In studying these essay topics, you will note both originality and commonality among the colleges. Use these topics to trigger ideas, provide templates, and illustrate the type of thinking and writing you will need to do for multiple applications. Though many colleges and universities accept the Common Application, many do not, and many others add their own supplemental essay questions to it. Every year, additional colleges begin accepting the Common Application. In 2002, public universities will for the first time be invited to join the list. If you are using the Common Application, make sure to check each college's requirements and the Common Application materials or website to find out whether you need to fill out a supplemental form and/or essay. Some colleges expressly use only the Common Application forms—for example, Harvard, Wesleyan, and Williams—with or without a supplement. Others, like Dartmouth, accept the Common Application, but have their own application that is longer, more involved, and more revealing. In such cases, we often recommend that students use the college's own application, as it allows them to express more about themselves and indicate stronger interest and commitment to the college. The rule of thumb is, if the college's individual application is significantly different from the Common Application, and asks you to write additional essays, then you should use the college's own application, given time and resource constraints on your ability to produce well-written and carefully completed applications.

If you want to get a head start on your applications, choose a few topics from the following list and begin your writing during the spring of junior year or the summer before you begin senior year. Many high schools are now offering English or college preparation classes geared toward helping students write their college applications. These essay examples will provide models for some initial essay drafts and generating discussion.

The Common Application

After filling out lists of activities and volunteer and work experiences, students are asked to provide more detail on one of them. This can be an essay from about 100 to perhaps 250 words on an attached page:

> In the space provided below, or on a separate sheet if necessary, please describe which of these activities (extracurricular and personal activities or work experience) has had the most meaning for you, and why.

PERSONAL STATEMENT

This personal statement helps us become acquainted with you in ways different from courses, grades, test scores, and other objective data. It will demonstrate your ability to organize thoughts and express yourself. We are looking for an essay that will help us know you better as a person and as a student. Please write an essay (250–500 words) on a topic of your choice or on one of the options listed below. You may attach your essay on separate sheets (same size, please). Also, please indicate your topic by checking the appropriate box below.

1) Evaluate a significant experience, achievement, or risk that you have taken and its impact on you.
2) Discuss some issue of personal, local, national, or international concern and its importance to you.
3) Indicate a person who has had a significant influence on you, and describe that influence.
4) Describe a character in fiction, a historical figure, or a creative work (as in art, music, science, etc.) that has had an influence on you, and explain that influence.
5) Topic of your choice.

Duke University

The short answer and essay provide you an opportunity to present your ideas to the Admissions Committee. We are eager to learn more about your intellectual and personal interests—to get to know you better. We urge you to give careful consideration to the form and content of your answers to the short answer and essay questions.

1. Please answer the following in the space provided. You may attach a separate sheet of paper, but limit your answer to no more than one-half page.

   a. Consider the books you have read in the last year or two either for school or for leisure. Please discuss the way in which one of them changed your understanding of the world, other people, or yourself.

2. Please answer one of the following questions. Circle the letter below for the question you have chosen to answer. Attach your essay to this inside page. Be sure to include your name and address on the attached sheet. If your essay is typed or computer printed, please double space. Please limit your essay to no more than 2–3 pages.

   a. According to Stephen Carter, we can admire those with integrity even if we disagree with them. Are there people you admire even though you deeply disagree with them? What do you admire about them? How do you reconcile this apparent contradiction in your assessment?

   b. What has been your most profound or surprising intellectual experience?

   c. Please write on a matter of importance to you. Any topic is acceptable. If you have written something for another purpose—even an essay for another college—that you believe represents you particularly well, feel free to submit it here. As a guideline, remember that we are especially interested in issues of personal significance.

We recognize that all good writers seek feedback, advice, or editing before sending off an essay. When your essay is complete, please answer the following: Whose advice did you seek for help with your essay? Was he/she helpful? What help did he/she provide?

University of Chicago

This is your chance to speak to us and our chance to listen as you tell us about yourself, your tastes, and your ambitions. We have offered an array of topics, each of which can be addressed with utter seriousness, complete fancy, or something in between—it's your choice. Play, analyze (don't agonize), create, compose—let us hear the result of your thinking about something that interests you, in a voice that is your own.

Instructions. Respond to Questions 1 and 2 with a paragraph of about two hundred words each. Then choose one of the four essay options and respond to it in a page or two. Be sure to write your name on each of the sheets and attach them to the application form.

1. How does the University of Chicago, as you know it now, satisfy your desire for a particular kind of learning, community, and future? Your response should address with some particularity your own wishes and how they relate to Chicago.

2. Tell us about a few of your favorite books, poems, authors, films, plays, music, paintings, artists, magazines, or newspapers. Feel free to touch on one, some, or all of the categories listed or add a category of your own.

ESSAY OPTION 1

The Golden Gate Bridge in San Francisco, the Gothic architecture of the University of Chicago, Mardi Gras, the Great Wall of China—all are highly visible landmarks, characteristics, or events that are emblematic of a particular place. In a more subtle way, there are other "landmarks " that are less recognizable but nonetheless suggest a specific place. Perhaps it is the local mall, or spring tulips in your garden, or abandoned warehouses, or an annual Fourth of July parade or October pumpkin festival. Write about a landmark, characteristic, or event that suggests to you a specific place.

ESSAY OPTION 2

At a crucial point in his career, the writer James Baldwin withdrew to a secluded spot in the Swiss Alps. "There," he later wrote, "in that absolutely alabaster landscape, armed with two Bessie Smith records and a typewriter, I began to try to recreate the life that I had first known as a child and from which I had spent so many years in flight. . . . It was Bessie Smith, through her tone and her cadence, who helped me to dig back to the way I myself must have spoken . . . and to remember the things I had heard and seen and felt." Inevitably, certain things—recordings, household objects, familiar smells—help us to "dig our way back" to our past. Write about something that has enabled you to return to a forgotten part of your past.

ESSAY OPTION 3

We recently learned that scientists have decoded the protein sequence of human DNA—that beautiful braid first described by Chicago alumnus James D. Watson and his colleague Francis Crick. Thus, we have witnessed another great achievement in the history of human endeavor and now wait—as citizens, as theologians, as poets, and as politicians—to see what will be done with this new knowledge. Imagining a future in which our nature is revealed (or is it?) by the order of the three billion or so elements of human DNA, describe your hopes or fears . . . clarity or confusion . . . resulting from this scientific breakthrough.

ESSAY OPTION 4

In the spirit of adventurous inquiry, pose an untraditional or uncommon question of your own. The answer to your question should display your best qualities as a writer, thinker, visionary, social critic, sage, sensible woman or man, citizen of the world, or future citizen of the University of Chicago.

Bowdoin College

Bowdoin asks the following as a supplement to the Common Application (one to two pages):

Who is the secondary school teacher who has had the greatest positive impact on your development? Please describe the ways in which this teacher has influenced you.

George Washington University

Essay for Freshmen (approximately 500 words)—The Committee on Admissions will use your essay to determine your ability to organize your thoughts and express yourself clearly. Please answer the following essay question combinations: A and B, or A and C . . .

A. Please explain briefly (50–100 words) how you learned about The George Washington University and why you decided to apply for admission.

B. In no more than 500 words, describe how you would make the best use of each of GW's strengths: the classroom experience, the campus, and the city. Rank them according to your view of the ideal college experience, and expand on the "ideal" as it relates to your college plan.

C. In lieu of responding to question B, you may choose to submit a graded creative/fiction writing sample. No term papers, please.

Yale University

1. There are limitations to what grades, scores, and recommendations can tell us about any applicant. We ask you to write a personal essay that will help us to know you better. In the past, candidates have written about their families, intellectual and extracurricular interests, ethnicity or culture, school and community events to which they have had strong reactions, people who have influenced them, significant experiences, personal aspirations, or topics that spring entirely from their

imaginations. There is no "correct" way to respond to our request. Write about what matters to you, and you are bound to convey a strong sense of who you are. We ask that you limit your response to a page of text, single-spaced . . .

2. Now write the essay you would have written if you were not trying so hard to say just the right thing to the Yale Admissions Committee. Perhaps you felt torn, wondering which of two topics to discuss. Regain your equanimity by writing about the one you didn't choose . . .

Stanford University

Stanford's short answer questions are as follows:

Sharing intellectual interests is an important aspect of university life. Describe an experience, book, class, project, or idea that you find intellectually exciting and explain why.

Jot a note to your future college roommate relating a personal experience that reveals something about you.

Of the activities, interests, and experiences listed above, which is the most meaningful to you and why?

The following are Stanford's one-page essay questions:

a) Attach a small photograph (3.5 × 5 inches or smaller) of something important to you and explain its significance . . .

or

b) If, for a period of time, you could live the life of any individual (fictional or non-fictional), who would you choose? How does this choice reflect who you are?

Colgate University

As a supplement to the Common Application, Colgate asks,

What three words best describe you and why?

University of Virginia

All first-year candidates must apply to one of the four undergraduate schools listed below. Please indicate clearly which school you have chosen, and please answer the question for that school in half a page, or roughly 250 words. If the school you choose differs from the one you chose on the Basic Application, we will assume that you have changed your mind and will switch your application accordingly.

College of Arts and Sciences. What work of art, music, science, mathematics, or literature has surprised or unsettled or challenged you, and in what way?

School of Architecture. If you could change the current architecture of your school, what change(s) would you make?

School of Engineering. What experiences have led you to choose the School of Engineering?

School of Nursing. What experiences have led you to choose the School of Nursing?

Answer one of the following questions. Limit your response to half a page, or approximately 250 words.

   a. Look out any window in your home. Given the opportunity, what would you change about what you see?

   b. Besides the computer, what technological development has had the greatest impact on human society?

   c. "The past is never dead. It's not even past." So says the lawyer Gavin Stevens in Faulkner's *Requiem for a Nun*. To borrow Stevens' words, what small event, either from your personal history or the history of the world, is neither "dead" nor "past"?

   d. Does discrimination still exist? What experience or event has led you to your conclusion?

   e. What is your favorite word, and why?

Please submit a final piece of writing on any subject you choose. Limit your response to one page, or approximately 500 words.

Georgetown University

In the space available discuss the significance to you of the school or summer activity in which you have been most involved.

Compose and attach on separate pages two brief essays (approximately one page each) on the topics given below.

All Applicants: The Admissions Committee would like to know more about you in your own words. Please submit a brief essay, either autobiographical or creative, which you feel best describes you.

Applicants to Georgetown College: Please relate your interest in studying at Georgetown University to your future goals. How do these thoughts relate to your chosen course of study?

Applicants to Georgetown School of Nursing: Describe how your experiences or ideas shaped your decision to pursue a health profession and how these experiences or ideas may aid your future contribution to the field.

Applicants to the Walsh School of Foreign Service: Briefly discuss a current global issue, indicating why you consider it important and what you suggest should be done to deal with it.

Applicants to the McDonough School of Business: Briefly describe the factors that have influenced your interest in studying business.

University of Pennsylvania

Your intellectual abilities, your sense of imagination and your creativity are important to us. With this in mind, please respond to one of the following three requests. You may use the space provided or enclose an additional sheet of paper.

Your essay should not exceed one page.

   a. You have just completed your 300-page autobiography. Please submit page 217.

b. First experiences can be defining. Cite a first experience that you have had and explain its impact on you.

c. Recall an occasion when you took a risk that you now know was the right thing to do.

Dartmouth College

Four questions, with shorter space provided, are required.

1. What was the highlight of your summer?
2. Which of your pursuits, in or out of school, do you find most fulfilling? Why?
3. The character of the College is a mosaic formed by the life experiences of its students. Share with us aspects of your background that you believe would add to the Dartmouth Community.
4. What else should we know? Tell us more about yourself, explain an interest, describe a talent, or raise an issue of concern. Anything goes!

Princeton University

Four questions, with shorter space provided, are required.

1. One of the highest compliments that can be paid someone is that he or she has "good character." What's your idea of what "good character" is? Give examples if you like.
2. If you were given the time and resources to develop one particular skill, talent, or area of expertise, what would you choose and why?
3. What one person, class, book, or experience would you point to as having had a significant effect on the way you think about something? Explain.
4. Those of us in admissions are often asked what are the two or three things in a student's application to which we give the greatest weight. If you were in our shoes, what are the two or

three things in an application to which you would give the greatest weight? Explain why.

Northwestern University

Applicants choose one of four 400- to 500-word essay topics. Also included are a "Northwestern Statement" and several short statements.

1. "Fear," it has been said, "is a great motivator." What is the most afraid you have been, how did you conquer it, and how did it contribute to making you who you are today?
2. To what degree should schools limit their students' freedom of expression on campus? Persuade us of your view.
3. Where does your mind wander when you let it? Analyze what that says about you.
4. In his poem "The Love Song of J. Alfred Prufrock," T. S. Eliot said, "There will be time to prepare a face to meet the faces that you meet." What is one of the masks that you wear for others, and why do you wear it?

Optional: If you have done any research or independent study outside of school, please include an abstract or summary of your work.

Reading between the Lines of Essay Questions

Note that many of the preceding essay questions are actually veiled or modified versions of one of the four major essay types we have identified. For example, Northwestern's "fear" essay is actually a Significant Experience essay with a particular twist. Northwestern's "freedom of expression" topic is a Powerful Idea essay. Their "wandering mind" option presents an opening for a Significant Influence essay, a personal statement that uses a significant person or experience to illustrate one or more of your passions, or a Powerful Idea essay that allows you to dwell on an intellectual interest. Northwestern's fourth option, responding to Eliot's notion of wearing different masks to represent yourself to others, opens the door to a similar Significant Influence or Powerful Idea essay, or a longer Meaningful Activity essay. When you see what initially appears a strange, complicated, or difficult essay topic, ask yourself whether it fits one of the main essay categories. Consider also essays you may have already written for other colleges, for a class in school, or in free form to evaluate if they may fit this topic.

Adapting Your Work: Using the Same Essay for Multiple Topics

Let us say that you are applying to eight selective colleges and universities. You will be faced with the task of filing eight applications. It may be that you can cover half of them, for example, by using the Common Application and the main personal statement and shorter Meaningful Activity answer you have written for it. You may then have supplemental essays to complete—for example, Bowdoin's and Colgate's—as well as topics to cover for universities that do not use the Common Application or for which you prefer to use the college's own application. You will not have to write eight or more separate essays. You will start from this standpoint: "What do I want to say to the colleges in my writing about myself?" Your core essay will react to this imperative, and you will try to express this core idea to every college to which you apply. You may need to write three or four different essays to cover applications to eight of the colleges we sampled above, as well as some short responses here and there, but you will be able to excerpt and adapt your essays to fit seemingly disparate essay questions.

It is often compelling to the reader to encounter an essay that is seemingly "off topic," but which responds to a unique essay question in a more circumspect or indirect way. Imagine you have written a Meaningful Activity essay about your dedication to soccer. You are tough, committed, a team captain, a leader. You train year-round and attend summer sports camps. When you go out onto the field, you become a different person, exhilarated by the challenge of the sport and your victory. You have learned to lead by example on the field, and this has helped you to focus in your classroom work as well. You know how to put on your "game face" when you need it, on and off the field. Now you sit down to complete the Northwestern application, and are dismayed to see those four original questions. Think carefully about each one. How could you adapt your soccer essay, for which you did a lot of work and of which you are quite proud, to fit one of those topics? Your greatest fear could be facing your toughest soccer opponent, or overcoming a career-threatening injury, or competing in a premier league trip abroad. There is not a great connection to the "freedom of expression" topic, so you may skip this one, but your mind may wander to the smell of freshly cut grass on the field at the beginning of the fall season. Perhaps most intriguing of all, your "game face" represents one of those masks to which Eliot was referring. In class, you are a mild-mannered chemistry student. On the field, you are World Cup material.

Even though you are applying to multiple colleges, *you* do not change from school to school. Try to conserve your energies and use as much of your good work as possible. Address each college and question individually, and make sure to answer the topic appropriately. As some of the colleges explicitly note, you may submit samples of writing to them which you wrote for another college or project, and you may even create your own topic.

The Additional Writing Sample

Some colleges specifically require or offer you the opportunity to submit a graded analytical essay with your application. Take advantage of this opportunity. The graded essay should typically be an analytical paper you wrote for an English or history class. Work with your teacher, parents, and counselor to choose an example of your best work. It need not be an A+ paper, but it should be well-written, coherent, and an example of the kind of work you do on a longer-term assignment. In addition to the teacher's grade, constructive comments and margin notes from the instructor help to indicate the quality of your paper relative to the teacher's expectations, your classmates, and your past writing. The additional writing sample helps colleges to compare your application essays to some of your best school work.

The two forms of writing, while different in style and substance, should be consistent in ability and quality.

Another type of writing you may submit is a research report or independent study piece. You should usually do this in summary or abstract form, especially if the paper is very long (over five pages in length). Perhaps you have completed a scientific research project that you have written up on your own or with a teacher. Maybe you have even published your work somewhere. Perhaps you did an independent history project or attended a creative writing workshop.

Asking and Answering Your Own Question

Each year, a few colleges seem to offer students the opportunity to ask their own question and then answer it. This can cause paralysis in the applicant. With no guidance from the college, you wonder, "What are they looking for? What should I write about? What if I ask a stupid question?" Go back to the beginning. You should be asking yourself, "What do I want to tell the college? What is important for them to know about me?" You may write your essay first, then worry about the question later. Put yourself in our soccer player's shoes again. You have that great "game face" essay, but now you have no topic to guide or constrain you. Now is your chance to add an extra dimension to your essay by creating a question that is interesting, provocative, humorous, deep, or personal. Without being offensive, arrogant, or foolish, try to pose a question that is original, revealing, and which shows that you have given the task some thought. Avoid copying the question from another college application or too closely imitating a cliché. Imagine that others will be confronting and answering your question, and try to pose one that will make sense to them and which they can answer to help the colleges learn something about them. Consider beginning your question with a favorite and meaningful quotation. Do not ask, for example, "Why do you love soccer so much?" or, "Who do you want to be when you grow up?" or, "What is one of the masks you wear for other people?" Try something along the lines of "Each of us competes in different arenas. What is your field, and how do you play the game?" or, "It has been said that great leaders are made, not born. When have you exercised leadership, and what have you learned from the experience about yourself?" or, "What have you done forever? Why have you stayed with it, and what does this say about you?"

Dos and Don'ts of Good Essay Writing

We think it useful to repeat, adapt, and expand here some of the essay writing guidelines we mentioned in *Making It into a Top College*. Here we divide the dos and the don'ts of essay writing and presentation to help guide your efforts.

Do

1. Start early. Save potential source material through junior year (good papers, creative writing, journal entries, notes on ideas and phrases you like). Begin a draft application in August before you go back to classes senior year.

2. Set your own deadlines and take control of the writing process. The more you write, the less "they" nag. If you take it upon yourself to govern your essay-writing process, and to complete your essays and applications well in advance of college deadlines, your parents will likely hassle you much less. Talk with your parents about mutual expectations for writing your essays, and let them know the extent to which you will want to share your work with them.

3. Share and share alike. Try to share your work with those who will give you constructive feedback on your writing and encourage you to do your best. Do accept offers by your parents, counselor, or a friend who knows you well to review and react honestly to your writing. They may be able to tell you how your essay reads to an outsider, and whether your language is readable and well-organized.

4. See multiple essays as individual pieces of a thematic puzzle.

5. Know thyself better than anyone else, before you begin to write. Make a list of the personal qualities that make you special. Review your list of strengths, which reveals the asset you will be on campus.

6. Be honest and maintain your integrity.

7. Be relaxed. You are relating your story, and you are in charge of your presentation. You select the theme, the setting, the style and tone, the message, and the spirit of your story.

8. Trust your own instincts. The message you have decided to send to the admissions committees is important and right, because it matters to you and should be shared if a group of strangers is to know you.

9. Take risks. Try a topic that may be considered slightly offbeat or unusual, even controversial in nature if it has relevance for the selection process. Dare to talk about yourself and to believe you can write on a sensitive issue that brings insight to the committee.

10. Be humorous and demonstrate your ability to laugh at yourself or at least not take yourself too seriously.

11. Show who you are through an incident, a major event, a crisis, or a tragedy rather than tell a committee who you are and what you stand for.

12. Develop a strong introduction to catch the reader's attention and interest. It makes all the difference. You cannot ask over-worked admissions officers to wade through half your statement before they comprehend what you have in mind to tell them.

13. Keep your story simple, keep it brief, and keep it focused on one theme or point.

14. Keep it yours. You own it; it is about you and by you.

15. Know that there are many kinds of essay writing. Your theme should determine the style and tone of your expression. You can create a serious, lighthearted, dramatic, reflective, or straightforward story. The choice is yours.

16. Focus on one or two major points about yourself. Focus on the primary idea that expresses the essence of who you are.

17. Choose a personal topic. Though you may have a concern such as world hunger, overpopulation, or gun control, you will find it more difficult to describe yourself—as opposed to the problem—unless you have a personal connection and commitment to the issue.

18. Make your voice heard in your writing. Use your natural style and language to communicate your thoughts.

19. Proofread your final draft several times to be sure you have not made any errors.

Don't

1. Embroider or shade the truth.
2. Try to shock the reader for shock's sake.
3. Be overmodest. It is not appealing and often comes across as false modesty or insincere coyness.
4. Leave the admissions reader guessing what your real point or meaning is.
5. Try to be someone you're not.
6. Let others tell you what you must write about and how to write it.
7. Attempt to relate everything you have experienced and are interested in.
8. Sound pompous, arrogant, bombastic, all-knowing, or smart-alecky. The committees will immediately wonder why they would want you in their community.
9. Try to impress the reader by showing how privileged you are: how much you have traveled, what great jobs your parents have, how big your house is, what a nice car you have.
10. Engage in self-hype and hucksterism. Let your accomplishments and record speak for you. Overselling will make the committee suspicious of your genuine worth.
11. Fall into too casual or colloquial a style.
12. Use clichés.
13. Send an essay or application that is sloppy or contains misspellings and grammatical mistakes.

How You Know When You Have Written Your Best Personal Statement

You have completed your best essays for college when you put down your pen or turn off your computer and say to yourself, "That's it. I have given the essays my best effort. I have shared a major piece of myself with a group of strangers so that they will know me better. I believe in myself and what I have accomplished. I know that I have some special features I can bring to the college campus, and I believe I have conveyed them clearly and honestly to the admissions committee."

To help you start writing your own best personal statement, read the examples of what other applicants have created in Chapter 4. Each of the writers we feature struggled at first with his or her choice of topic. The final products in these pages went through several drafts before these writers knew they were done. Each of these pieces displays the qualities that make admissions committees say, "This is a student we want to have here next year."

In Chapter 4, we present a number of essays, divided according to different types of students. View these as models for how you might cast yourself as one or a combination of these types, and begin to see how you can present yourself successfully.

CHAPTER FOUR

Types of Students and Examples of the Essays They Have Written

We divide the model essays in this chapter by student types. Our intention is to help students categorize themselves in order to better see themselves in some of these examples. Of course, all students are different. It is our hope that you will see a piece of yourself in one or more of these types and realize how you might begin to represent yourself in your own writing. There are more types of students than those represented here. Selective colleges look for students who define themselves by their passions and experiences while they simultaneously transcend classification. Avoiding clichés and stock essays, students can say, "Yes, I am an artist (or an athlete, or a scientist, or a volunteer); I need to show that through my writing as this applicant did." You will not be perfectly captured by one of these types, but they may help to organize your thinking and guide your drafting, even as you try to break out of the category.

The All-Around Kid

Many students feel that they do not have one particular talent or interest to discuss in their essays. Or, they prefer to let the colleges know that they are involved in many different areas and want to continue that balance and diversity in college. There is nothing wrong with being an all-around young man or woman. It is important for you in your presentation to talk about the multiple skills or interests you have, and to talk about the role they play in your life.

Thomas: Painter, Pianist, Physicist, Runner

Thomas was admitted on Early Decision to Dartmouth after submitting a wonderful essay that brought together his many interests and talents. He responded to the question, "How do your interests relate to each other? (or) What is a common thread among your interests?"

With calculated strides and carefully timed gasps for air, running through dense forests and remote pastures is both a science and an emotional high. But despite the physics behind aching legs and the chemistry of my rapidly disappearing wind, the exercise is always a transcendental experience. The striking scenery takes my mind away from computing my pace as I enter a realm of deep reflection. And when I roam the twisting trails and vast valleys, I am endlessly inspired by my surroundings. Even as I hit a button on my watch to record my split time, the emotional trance persists despite all the inevitable technicality behind the sport. As with my other passions, when I tread through natural settings I reach a mental niche where both systematic rationality and intense feeling exist in dynamic combination.

Although the image of a reserved scientist shedding his lab coat to paint a picture, play some jazz, or run a few miles might seem unlikely to the general eye, this is my conception of an ideal day. While my interests may be diverse, they are all connected by a common and essential element: a certain mix of science and emotion. Juggling beakers and paintbrushes with sheet music and dumbbells is not always simple, but the balance that exists within each fulfills me.

That important combination of objectivity and expressiveness always arises when I create art. Although I enjoy scrutinizing technical details that make my pieces more realistic, the unlimited opportunities to present emotion and creativity make the experience complete. The paintbrush becomes a tool whose careful strokes will produce not only subtle shades and highlights but also deeper statements and emotions. When I paint a portrait, that spark of titanium white that I dab in the pupil of the eye fills the face with conviction, depth that defies the concrete layers of oil upon canvas. There is something exhilarating about carefully analyzing a subject and then producing an image that is even more powerful than what I see in reality. And while I maintain a scientific mindset of analytical precision with color and value, often the content of my work spans from serious statements to even satirical atmospheres. Nearly two years ago I began integrating the image of a frog into a large series of paintings, sculptures, and drawings. The green creature invaded the otherwise ordinary still-lifes, landscapes, and abstractions, bringing a light and facetious theme to them. Currently I am working on a series of oil paintings depicting a hand grasping various objects, each representing a profound concept. While I continue to strive for realistic portrayals in my art, I also need to maintain that sensation that comes when I create something striking.

Music, with its combination of scientific logic and emotional expression, is immeasurably important in my life. I am intrigued by the mathematical theories behind the progressions, chords, and rhythms; they are all rationally linked in an analytical scheme of intervals and cadences. But the most exciting aspect is that a simple line of symbolic notes can translate into the most energetic sambas or poignant sonatas. On paper, the transition from a diminished chord to a major seventh merely describes a shift in tonal frequencies, but in our ears we are struck with a comforting feeling of resolution. Playing the piano is so fascinating to me because when I study the logical theories I learn to create sounds of great emotion and meaning. Although the piano is a mechanical machine of hammers and wires, its sounds are anything but concrete and scientific. I find it thrilling to place my hands upon the extending rows of harmonic levers and produce tones and feelings that elude verbal description. Works from the strictest classical pieces to the loosest impromptu jazz possess certain indescribable emotional tones. In this way, the piano offers an opportunity to combine technical mastery and artistic expression into a single auditory product.

I also find this balance of mind and soul in the academic realm. There is nothing more pleasant than quickly shifting from complex mathematical differentiation to impassioned Shakespearean verse at the sound of a bell. And once the meaning of Hamlet's soliloquies sets in, I eagerly move on to cellular respiration or Newton's laws of motion. Even in the math and science courses that I have taken, the understanding I acquire is never entirely objective and methodical. The theories of calculus and implications of physics satisfy a certain human curiosity about the nature of things. When I discover a hidden connection or a surprising realization, I have an unmistakably emotional response. There is something beyond those worldly variables and calculations— something of greater truth. For me, the intellectual experience is the sum of all the grammatical, technical challenges and the deeper, more relevant concepts.

I desperately need this sense of balance between science and emotion in my life. Whenever I grow restless working with mechanical calculations or vocabulary lists, I place my notebook upon the stand of my piano and simultaneously improvise and study. By some amusing circumstance, I feel more at ease pondering methodical, ordered information when hitting the heartfelt tunes of the blues. And when I am weightlifting, a lasting, scientific pursuit for me, in between sets I usually work on sculptures and paintings that accompany me in my basement. And though my fingers may tremble from the systematic process of muscular fatigue, those intermissions of artistic expression restore that crucial equilibrium that fuels my motivation.

Derek: Athlete, Actor, Musician, Mechanic

Derek was the kind of student who was involved in just about everything. He crossed many lines at school, but persevered in being himself. In his writing, he tried to send a message to the colleges that he fit many types, and understood the difficulties of moving between groups in high school. He wrote about a typical day, and was accepted at Bates, Vassar, and Skidmore:

I am a defenseman on my high school's varsity ice hockey team. Today at 5 a.m. I woke up and went to practice. In the locker room I sat quietly as the conversation turned to the performing arts class at my school.

"That acting class is gay."

"Only girls and fags take performing arts."

I didn't contribute. Instead I quickly got undressed and went home to shower and get ready for school. I had performing arts during first period today. I learned about contact improvisation in dance.

The rest of the school day passed quickly and I arrived home around 3 p.m. Following a light snack of Lucky Charms I headed out to the garage. Opening the door I saw a 1970 MG Midget, my car. The car is white with two fat black racing stripes and a black roll bar to complete its racy image. When I first bought the car nearly two years ago it was a total basket case, barely running and not really stopping at all. Since then the car has been under extensive restoration, completed almost entirely by me.

I spent the next two hours searching for a leak in the brake lines which was emptying the car of brake fluid far too quickly. I took both brake assemblies completely apart then put them back together without finding a thing. Seeing that it was nearly 5, I dejectedly put my work aside.

After washing my hands with a gritty degreaser in the laundry room I sat down at the grand piano in the corner of my living room. I played for about an hour and a half, playing pieces ranging from rock and blues to pieces of my own composition. Finishing up at the piano I went to my room, completed my studies for the night, and went to bed.

Lying in bed and thinking of the day I just lived, I am happy. I spent it just the way I wanted to. I fulfilled every interest I could without making sacrifices for the narrow-minded kids on my hockey team or the cleanliness of the ivory keys of the piano.

Derek's Meaningful Activity short essay continued the same theme. It violated the tenet of not choosing one activity to discuss, but it further elaborated on Derek's perceptiveness and maturity:

The most meaningful activity that I do is learning and experiencing life. Everything I do and everywhere I go I try to experience something new. Each activity I participate in is varied in both subject and the people I associate with. My activities create relationships for me with people ranging from beer-guzzling jocks to theater-is-life dramatists to ignored-by-the-school-population techies. Each conversation I have with any one of these people allows me to see the world a little better from their perspective, which in turn leaves me with a better understanding of life.

From the rough and tough hockey players I find that besides simply enjoying the sport as I do, they just want to fit in, be well liked, and to avoid at all costs being the one everyone laughs at, not with. From the theater folks I learn that again, although they enjoy it, this activity is used as a device to elevate themselves above the jocks who are always laughing at them. By knowing that they are really doing something important and profound it is easy to look down on people and call them insignificant. From the techie "losers" come the most obvious insecurities of the bunch. Not having any real device to combat the jocks laughing at them or the intellectuals looking down on them these people surrender to the attacks and just deal with it until they can get out of high school. So where does that leave me? I am a member, a victim, and culprit of all three groups, and countless others. I live my life with the sole purpose of understanding people, learning from them, and understanding myself.

Andy: Sports Participant and Sports Writer

Andy wanted to let the colleges know that he was involved in and excited about many different activities. We encouraged him to do so, but also to focus one of his essays on a particular interest, sports writing, which he had developed during his years at boarding school. This is one of the pieces he wrote for Dartmouth, responding to the query, "Which of your pursuits in or out of school do you find most fulfilling?" Andy violated the rule of not writing about more than one activity in a Meaningful Activity essay, but he did so in a way that worked for him, given his theme of school participation and athletics:

> Many of the activities I do at school bring me great pleasure. I cannot imagine, for example, not playing sports. Though I have no great amount of athletic talent, I revel in athletic competition. There is no place I would rather spend my free time than on the hockey ice or the squash court or the golf course. Community service is also a fulfilling commitment of mine. Habitat for Humanity was something I was persuaded to try by a friend, and it has become one of my favorite parts of the week. Working with my hands, building something concrete, I really feel like I am making a difference in someone's life. It is a great feeling to know that the children of this house will grow up kept warm by the insulation I installed and kept dry by a roof I helped to build. Of all the activities I do, I think the one that means the most to me, though, is writing for the school paper.
>
> I have been on the staff of the paper since my freshman year. I signed up to write about sports, and initially I got small assignments about low profile teams like sub-varsity football. I kept at it, eventually getting tapped to write about big varsity teams like lacrosse. Then one day I got an article on the front page, with a photograph to go with it. I was really excited when the issue came off the presses and there was my name, front and center. I thought that as a junior I had gone as far as I could. There was only one more prestigious position available: columnist.
>
> The columnists are those few privileged seniors who are told only to "write an article on the topic of your choosing." In fact, they are asked for at least 500 words. Everyone else is given a stern warning to keep things short, but the columnists are given free rein. They also got their pictures right above their articles! I was determined to get one of those columns by my senior year. I lobbied ceaselessly, and offered to help out with whatever menial jobs the editors had. At first, the editors were unsure. I was only a sportswriter, after all. So, the sports editor gave me a little editorial to write about baseball as a trial run. By this time, the mighty

exploits of Mark McGwire and Sammy Sosa were big news. I handed in my editorial, and it appeared in the paper, but I was unsure if it was enough to get myself a column. To make matters worse, that was the last assignment I got for a long time. I was worried that I had upset the editors somehow. That was why at the end of my junior year, right after the new editorial staff took over, I was shocked to see in my mailbox a letter with the words, "Please submit an editorial on a subject of your choosing for the upcoming issue. Minimum 500 words." My months of involvement and hard work had paid off.

Writing columns, however, was far more difficult than writing about sub-varsity football. Everyone reads the columns, and with my picture right above my name, there would be no mistaking who wrote mine. Columns take a lot of time to write. In fact, I have to rewrite them, which is something I never had to do with my normal assignments for the paper. The rewards for a well-written column are great. I got more feedback from my first column than I ever had for all of my previous work. I even had my article picked up by the local newspaper, which was a big thrill. The most fulfilling part, though, was when I noticed that one of the kids in my dorm had cut out one of my pieces and hung it on his wall. It really caught me off guard to see that something I had written had touched someone enough for them to do that. That little gesture is the reason I write for the paper, and it means more to me than any goal I will ever score in a hockey game.

The Athlete

The athlete is someone who focuses his or her personal statement on the impact of athletics in his or her life. The athlete may or may not be going through the active recruiting process for colleges. If you're an athlete, you may go in any of several directions in writing about sports: from coaching others in your sport to volunteering with the disabled, from winning the state championship to facing a serious injury. Your writing will indicate your intense commitment to one or more sports in your life.

Jake: A Yale Scholar-Athlete

Jake was an A student in an Advanced Placement (AP) curriculum at a small private school. He played soccer and baseball and had won multiple academic awards. He chose to write his essays for Yale on soccer and an old friend, revealing his personal attachments and values, and not just his athletic commitment. His descriptive details are wonderful, and Jake meshes the personal reflections with active narration to let the reader into his world:

THE BONDS OF SWEAT AND BLOOD

Playing soccer has been a blessing to me because it has given me the opportunity to come closer to my grandfather. I never could connect with him very easily until I started to talk to him about my passion for the sport. I have rarely felt comfortable beneath the down-turned corners of his mouth, or the sharp, angry angles of his furrowed eyebrows. He shatters the Hallmark card stereotype of the doting grandparent who sneaks candy into his pride-and-joy's pocket behind the back of an unsuspecting parent. On the contrary, when he visits for dinner, invariably it is he, not my mother who says, "I think you better remove that," frowning and pointing at the baseball cap perched on my head. At every visit he gives me a new lesson in manners. Meanwhile, my progressive-thinking, hippie-generation parents smirk because he plays the role of "the enforcer" with such aplomb. Even more of a pitfall to our relationship than his "old school" discipline is his stubborn nature. I vividly remember arguing with him once for fifteen minutes over the capacity crowd of Fenway Park. I could not press my position too hard for fear of touching off a diatribe on respect. Ultimately the discussion was punctuated by his emphatic, "No, that's wrong!" Though I have always resented his rigidity, and am frequently exasperated by his stubbornness, four years ago I finally discovered a way to punch through his leathery skin and make a strong connection with him. Only after I started playing high school soccer could I offer him something to share with me that no one else in my family could. Finally we could relate to each other.

I found this common bond with the grizzled old patriarch not through any calculated plan to smooth out our relationship; but rather through pure serendipity. My mother, his own daughter, did not even remember that he had been an avid athlete in his prime. His fanaticism had long lain dormant while he raised four girls, none of whom displayed any interest in stepping onto a playing field. Similarly, my own passion for soccer did not reach maturity until my Freshman year. Though the sport was not new to me (at six my parents introduced me to the obligatory rite of passage known as Youth Soccer) I suddenly felt an inexplicable love for it. I liked to play because it was fun, I was good at it, and it allowed me to be part of a team, something bigger than myself. Yet my parents could identify very little with this. My father knows the Latin roots of most words that an ordinary human could not even spell, yet I can not remember him to have ever watched a tele-vised sporting event. My mother loves to pass judgment on my analysis of British literature, yet she honestly believes that hockey players wear cleats and soccer players wear skates.

As I spent more and more time and energy on soccer, going to camps, training, cutting caffeine and carbonation from my diet, I began to mention my new interest in phone conversations with my grandfather. Much to my surprise, my enthusiasm for soccer and my desire to be a Varsity athlete tapped into a long hidden well of emotion in him. Almost overnight, our conversations transformed from ten-minute courtesies to two-hour long affairs. At first, we talked about almost nothing but soccer. He was thrilled to be get-ting more than one word responses from me (he once asked me if "yup" and "uh-huh" were the only words I knew). At the same time, I was overjoyed to have a truly interested savant listening to my accounts of a recent game rather than two parents who had little sports background. I could feel his quivering joy through the telephone receiver when I mentioned the excitement I felt during my first Varsity start. When I tell him how I burst with pride every time I bury an important goal, his stern persona cracks and I can hear him reminisce about his days backing the line at Shelton High. It matters little that he played football and I play soccer. It is the common experiences of excitement, perseverance and camaraderie that help to relate the two of us. He has often told me that "football is just something your mother refuses to understand," while I have confided in him that nobody could comprehend my love for soccer as well as he does. Our conversations about my exploits on the soccer field have opened the way to even more discourse. He often tells me stories I have heard before, but I never grow tired of his wistful musings on growing up a Brooklyn Dodgers fan and always playing the underdog to his two Yankee supporting older brothers. My connection to him through soccer has benefited our relationship so much that I now prefer talking to him rather than anybody else about stressful subjects, such as applying to college. He is clearly my greatest advocate, and while I think this was always true, he could never communicate it to me until I communicated with him about something we mutually love and no one else could share.

It came as no surprise to me that when I broke my leg during one of my team's games this fall, he was the only person who could understand my pain. The school nurse asked me daily if my leg bothered me, and I invariably answered that it did not. My teachers showed pity that I would have to struggle to get to my upstairs classes while trailing a shattered fibula. I insisted that I could manage. My mother cried that I had suffered a traumatic injury, but I reassured her it would heal quickly. I spoke to my grandfather that Friday after I broke my leg and he immediately said, "You must be disappointed that your season is over. I remember sitting out a broken shoulder while my team continued on without me . . ." *Finally,* somebody got it.

I sit on the sidelines now, and watch my team winning game after game. We are defeating opponents that we have never beaten before in our school's history, and we are poised to compete for our first league title. I am disappointed because in my senior year, I lost the sport that I love. Yet it is not the excitement of soccer, nor the camaraderie that it provides me with, that has changed my life. Soccer has been a pastime, a diversion, just a game. I love soccer because it is fun, because it provides me with a source of companionship and a lesson in dedication. But I love it even more because it was the catalyst for a powerful and much improved relationship with my grandfather.

Here is Jake's second personal essay:

It was not so much the house itself that I loved, that weathered and creaky eyesore atop the hill on Walter Street. Rather, it was the good times it represented, the fun that took place there, and the caring people who inhabited it. The Edwards, those eccentric but exciting people always vaguely reminded me of some comic-strip family. Yet to me, the only child of two orderly parents, they symbolized all that was positive about a family, the best of what a household could be. Every time I came to their house, every cold evening that Neil and I reposed there after a hard day of sledding, or every summer morning when we walked off to ride our bikes or play in the woods, I was invited to partake in the looseness and din that always appeared to be a way of life there.

Neil's house was old, generally in disrepair, and not at all what I was accustomed to. There was occasionally a curious smell: a mixture between the dogs that they owned and the various pet lizards in the house, and the baby that they always seemed to have. Yet the house was not dirty, just a bit cluttered; perhaps this even added to the fun of going there. They were the type of people that did not mind a few imperfections like peeling paint or a few appliances held together with duct tape. I vividly remember the kitchen having a tiny pantry which was stuffed with non-perishables to the point of bursting. On Saturday mornings, after I had slept over, Neil and I got up at 6:00 a.m. to watch cartoons as six-year old boys tend to do. We would scale the precariously stacked cans of Grand Union–brand strained beets to reach the Cinnamon Toast Crunch (a forbidden item in my house). Even going to the bathroom became an Indiana Jones–esque adventure. It was located at the extreme corner of the house, off the landing of the staircase. One literally had to turn his body sideways to fit through the door, which barely opened. After creating a portal of a few inches, the door struck the bathtub, as if the architect did not have the benefit of depth perception when designing the house.

On Friday afternoons, Neil and I would ride our bikes endlessly around the secluded cul-de-sac on which he lived. We eventually came in, and climbed the pantry-palisades to find our snacks before we hunkered down in front of the television. After a short time, Neil's father, Sam, came home. I can easily picture him now the way I saw him then. Always after work he would enter dressed the same way: black dress pants, white oxford shirt with the tie removed, tragically thick glasses, and no shoes. Never shoes. That was who Sam was, and Neil too. Though the path up to the house was covered in gravel and stones (as well as the off shard of broken glass left from who-knows-when) Neil's dad always entered the house without his shoes.

"Come on you goofs, kill it," he exclaimed, pointing to the television, which simply was not enough fun for him. Rather he thought up millions of games and activities for us, often participating himself. He turned the house into a mini-amusement park. Frequently, not only would he allow the kids to amass all of the pillows and sheets in the house to build forts, he actually encouraged it, even suggested it. When we were done, he would clean the disastrous mess we had left behind, always without a complaint.

In our early teenage years, Neil and I went to the movies every Friday and Saturday. We stayed up late into the night on the internet or laughed stupidly at *Saturday Night Live.* The "Goat Boy" skit always seemed to win a chuckle. We then tried to sleep away most of the next morning. However, we were rarely successful. Neil's younger brother John could only contain himself for so long before he either bounded on top of our prostrate bodies until we woke up, or else yelled like an air-raid siren for minutes on end. Waking up like that usually put me in a foul mood, but occasionally the morning revealed a pleasant surprise. I remember arising once to discover a freshly made crepe by my head.

It has been a year now, since Neil moved away and the house was shut up to me forever. Neil's mom, Alice, got a job in Cambridge last year. They moved a few months later. They sold that ramshackle old house, which they had made seem not quite as old, and not quite as ramshackle.

In many respects, the move worked out far better than I expected. We still keep in close touch. I get to Boston about six times a year, and Neil comes and visits me here every so often. Things are not the same though. It is true, I enjoy visiting Boston and Cambridge. But I miss sliding down the crumbling third floor stair case in a laundry basket. I miss every quirk of his home that made it refreshingly different from my own.

Whenever he comes down to stay with me in Connecticut, we always bandy about the idea of taking a stroll by that old house up on the hill. We never do, though. I could not bear to see the cracked stone walkway that Sam had laid with his hands replaced by a garden, no matter how lovely. I could not stand to see a new fence put up around the yard where the sagging one had been. It might drive me mad to see a car in the driveway other than the Dodge mini-van with the half-eaten bagel under the seat and apple juice poured in the radiator.

It was the imperfections of the Edwards' home and the free and easy spirit of the family that made Neil's house so special. Neil was that best friend in the neighborhood, and his house was the one I walked to every day. In a way, it seemed to be a scenario more typical of my parents' generation than of mine, a throwback to the days of close-knit communities and suburban America. Nevertheless, he was my closest friend, and his house was where I liked to be.

Andrea: An Athlete and Volunteer Admitted to Columbia University

A talented equestrienne, Andrea was an AP student at a large suburban high school. She discovered through her college search that she wanted to continue riding, if possible, at an urban college. In addition to submitting the essay below, which showed how she had combined her love for horses and riding with a sensitive commitment to helping others, Andrea talked with college riding coaches and included with her applications a résumé of her equestrian accomplishments. You can find her résumé in Chapter 5.

The summer sun was beating down on the dusty driveway, and occasionally a light breeze would sweep through the barn and cool things down. Despite the oppressive heat children were still coming to ride. Except these children were different. Some had to be gently lifted out of their cars, while others quietly made their way to the ring. These children at first seemed alien to me. How could I relate to a child with cerebral palsy, multiple sclerosis, or Down Syndrome? I felt unsure of myself and nervous as I stood in the barn grooming a pony that would soon carry one of these children on its back. As I took the pony's reins and walked it into the ring, I saw a teenage girl being lifted by two volunteers from her wheelchair. As soon as she saw me enter the ring with her mount, an immense smile spread over her face. At that moment I realized that I had something in common with these children who initially had made me so nervous. We all loved horses, and the Pegasus program gave them an opportunity to learn to ride and me an opportunity to teach them.

While riding has always been a large part of my life I have often wished that riding competitively was a sport where each rider could be part of a team; instead it is a very individualized sport; there are not many opportunities to share talents and work towards a common goal. When I began to volunteer at the Pegasus Therapeutic Riding program, I saw an opportunity to be part of a team. This program utilizes the tender relationship between a rider and a horse, to help the children better relate to others and expand their self-confidence.

Riding is a challenging undertaking for anyone. It requires hours of training, personal courage and poise. A rider must be sympathetic, persistent and mature. The teenage girl who had minutes ago been confined to her wheelchair and was now mounted on the pony I led around was a true rider. As we walked and did exercises and games, I learned that her name was Stephanie, that she was fifteen years old. Often she would laugh when the pony would turn around to nip at a fly and in the process give her a little nudge. Other times she would tell the pony to "Whoa" so she could rest and adjust her position. Her stiff legs ached, and she would have to stop every six or seven steps. For the next few sessions, I eagerly awaited Stephanie's arrival. Gradually she began to increase her riding time. Her legs would relax and lower. Persistence was Stephanie's special quality. She kept riding and worked hard. The other children on their ponies would begin to trot, and even though it was almost an impossible task, I would see Stephanie straighten up and squeeze her pony, urging it to go forward into the trot. I asked her one day why she always wanted to do more than anyone predicted she could ever do out of her wheelchair. She smiled at me and gave her pony a pat.

I knew that Stephanie and I had the same high level of ambition which keeps us going even when obstacles are placed in the way. After every session, Stephanie carefully dismounted as her wheelchair was brought over. One day Stephanie dismounted as usual, but chose not to look for her wheelchair. Instead she grabbed my arm. She wanted to walk. I was alarmed. I didn't want to hurt Stephanie mentally or physically. If she fell would she be able to get up again? I knew that if I asked her to sit in her wheelchair, she would have her confidence undermined, and she might never again feel the courage and strength to walk without her wheelchair. As we walked down the dusty driveway to her car everything became silent to me. I focused ahead using all my strength to support her. I knew that she was trying as hard as I was. Finally we reached her car and turned slowly around to face the riding ring. Everyone had been watching us, and they looked proud of both of us.

That day Stephanie and I both learned something. She had developed the trust in me not to let her fall. I developed trust in myself. Now, when I am at an important horse show and I enter the ring I experience the same fear as when Stephanie first gripped my arm. All the jumps in the show ring look so formidable, and I always desperately want to do well. When Stephanie dismounted and saw the long driveway ahead of her she desperately wanted to show everyone that she could do well. Stephanie demonstrated her true horsemanship by reaching for her goal. As I eye the jumps I always hope that I can try to take some of the trust in myself that Stephanie gave me to reach my goals.

Jennifer: A Soccer Fanatic and Teacher

Jennifer was an A and B student and star soccer player at a suburban public high school. She took an advanced curriculum, played for the school team and premier travel teams, and competed for the state championships. In her applications, she was able to present her incredible enthusiasm for soccer, her personal exuberance, and her interest in working with children. Her personal statement started with active scene-setting:

Picture this:

The whistle blows as the clock winds down to the last two minutes of the championship game. The score is tied 1–1. Playing against your rivals, you want nothing more than to beat them. You are exhausted, having played 88 minutes of an intense, fast-paced, physical game. You receive the ball, dribble, faking left, then right, going past defenders, hearing the crowd cheering for you to "Go to Goal!" Your teammates are by your side, supporting you, your coach yelling from the sidelines, "Shoot!" You respond automatically and quickly take a right-footed shot into the corner, hardly believing your eyes as you see the ball hit the back of the net just as the whistle blows, signaling the end of the game. It is like a dream; you can hardly imagine that all of it is true. YOU HAVE WON!

I get a natural high. Not from smoking crack or pot or drinking alcohol. No, I receive a natural high by playing soccer. Ever since I was five years old and my mom forced my chubby little feet into soccer cleats and dropped me off at my first day of practice I have loved the sport. I have to admit that initially I dreaded going to that first practice. However, I am so thankful to my parents for introducing me to the sport that has become my greatest passion.

I graduated to the intramural level over the next two years, made my way up to the travel team, qualified for a premier league and eventually earned a starting position on the high school's varsity squad. My ten years of experience have taught me that my teammates and I, as women with different and distinct personalities, share one passion: our love of soccer. This common thread brings us closer together as we bond and form cherished memories. Soccer is something that gets inside of me, gets my adrenaline going, makes my heart beat faster, pushes my body to accomplish things I never imagined I could do. When I play, I leave every part of my personal life, school, friends, all of my worries and stresses behind me and just focus on the game.

The kind of feeling I get when I score the winning goal or know that I have played an outstanding game is what I call a natural high. It is a feeling that rewards me for all of the commitment, hard work, and dedication I put in every day for three hours of practice. It can only come from within, when I know I have pushed beyond my limits and cannot possibly go any further. It is a feeling that comes along only once in a while, to remind me of how important it is to go to practice every day, to lead the team to victory, and to work my hardest. When I have sprinted until my lungs burst, dribbled until my feet ache, and stayed with the best of them, only then can I experience a natural high.

I was not born with a natural amazing athletic talent. However, I was born with a highly motivated attitude that forces me to work for every accomplishment I have achieved in my lifetime. No matter what it is I take on, I am determined to excel. My success does not come easily to me; I always push myself to my limits and never give up or let down. Capitalizing on my gifts of passion, a high motivation to succeed, and hard work has helped to improve my skills not only as a soccer player but also as a student and volunteer. The high I feel when I receive an A on a test and the pleasure I get when looking at the grades on my report card are rewards for the many hours of studying and commitment I put into my school work. The benefits I gain from teaching first graders religious lessons at our local church come when I begin to connect with the kids. I feed off of the excitement emanating from my students and that natural high comes back again as we form lasting relationships. I apply these characteristics of my personality to every area of my life: personally, academically, and athletically.

The Performing or Creative Artist

Are you a dancer, artist, actor, musician, writer, or other performer or creative individual? Then you might fit this category and write in a way that showcases your talent and individuality. Writers often face the pressure of living up to their declared strength in this area by having to write the world's greatest essay. Musicians, painters, and photographers will struggle to find words to portray their art. The students here showed their talent with words and painted verbal pictures to reveal the process and impact of their creative work.

Kim: Writer, Actor, Singer, Leader

An A student at a large public high school, Kim revealed her knack for writing without ever saying that she was a good writer. Her essays jumped off the page as creative, different, and unique portraits of her daily life. Powerful and mundane events were given life and descriptive detail, and Kim's voice, humor, and empathy shone through.

My waffles peep their heads out of the toaster as the phone rings. 7 a.m.? This doesn't usually happen. Maybe it's someone looking for a ride to school. It's not. Mrs. M's on the line. She sounds very far away. Two kids on the parkway, she says. It was wet last night. And cold. Out of control. Two kids killed, she says. She tells me their names, and a wave of momentary but false relief crashes over me. I don't know them. They are faceless. My mom looks at me strangely, and sees trouble in my eyes. I hang up the phone. The Eggos are getting cold, but I'm sick at the sight of them. The yearbook upstairs can tell me who they are. I take the stairs two by two, and lug the book out from under the bed. I'm embarrassed that I don't know them by name. There they are, two smiling faces. Did one of them hold the door for me yesterday? Maybe other days, too. I never would have noticed.

Tomorrow arrives, and a fog has descended over us all. My trigonometry test was a joke. Difficult to focus on cosines right now. The auditions were canceled, due to the funeral. I don't know if I'm going to try out for the play, anyway. My monologue is in dire straits, crumpled up in the trash can. "Art thou?" "Oh me!" "Dost proclaim!" Language is confounding. I pull on my skirt and sweater. Glancing in the mirror, I appear perfectly normal. I think I'll pretend I'm from Manhattan, where it's typical to be wrapped in black. Professional, that's me. Yoko and I are going to drive to the church together, to stand in the back and not be seen. We didn't know them, but our friends did. We need to be there. It gets dark outside so early in the winter. Only two weeks until Christmas. I wonder about the boys' presents waiting on high closet shelves, out of sight. I hope their parents won't forget to put them under the tree.

We join a long procession of headlights, backed-up for miles down the road. Late already (trouble starting the car again). After ten minutes of crawling, we're rolling into the driveway. The white breath of dusk assaults our faces. Stinging, red, and afraid we huddle inside the crowded doorway. We manage to find some familiar faces. Loud music is playing, pulsing through the pews, down the aisles, flowing into me. U2 wailing in my soul. The song is no longer the same. I look around me. Becky is standing nearby. In History class I usually see her scowling at someone, her nostrils flared in annoyance. But not tonight. She is staring at the ground, hands clasped, head dropped. In prayer she seems small, even peaceful. I may try to talk to her. We're all here together, in one giant lifeboat.

The service floats by, and my friends and I hug good-bye outside. The still night is shattered by sobs. One man is very close to me. I notice his dress tie, a black so deep it melts into the shadow of his winter coat. Maybe he's the boy's uncle, his cousin, his dad. A part of me wants to understand his pain, but I cannot be a spectator to his sadness. I turn away and head back to the car.

At the dinner table that night, the cat rubs against my leg. I reach down to pet him, feeding him from the table, although I'm not supposed to. He purrs with delight, and my mom smiles. By 11:00 I'm lying on the bed upstairs. Trying to think about nothing never works. I go to the trash can and dig around for the balled-up artifact. Helena's soliloquy, Act 1, Scene 1. I'll leave it on my desk and try to rework it tomorrow. Maybe Shakespeare and I can manage to get along. I haven't written in my journal for a while, and I suppose this is as good a time as any.

December 10: Today was so strange. I think I've lived it in slow motion. I don't feel like writing much right now, but I'm a little bit better. I'm not too afraid anymore. James Dean, what dost thou say? "Dream as if you'll live forever. Live as if you'll die today."

Here is Kim's second essay, which shows her talent with her words, her sense of humor, and her ability to capture every nuance of one of high school's most common challenges:

"Gore's environmental policies have been his greatest attributes in the primaries." Save me, Al, I don't know if I can go through with this. Am I insane? Yup, that's it. Insane, just like Steve Forbes. He spent HOW much on his campaign? Oh well, no winter vacation in Bali with the kids this year, Steve. What time is it anyway? 2:10. Five minutes before I take the dive. I'm definitely turning a pale shade of green. I can feel my vital organs collapsing. It's just like that story I saw on *Dateline* last week about an exotic disease a tourist picked up somewhere. It made his liver shrivel up to the size of a Skittle. What did she just say about the Environmental Protection Agency? Oh, who am I kidding? It's no use anyway. Taking notes is supposed to help you focus, but I'm too far gone for that. Here we go. I'm going to look at him again. Why can't I stop? I'm such a stalker. Aren't there laws against this kind of behavior? I can see it now: "Police Blotter—Issue of restraining order." Won't Mom and Dad be proud. I know why I'm magnetized. It's that little gleam in his eye that makes my heart palpitate. He's got a young Robert Redford thing going on. All right, that may be true, but that little gleam may not be so cute in three minutes when he turns you down. Oh wait, that's right! He *can't* turn you down! The scientists at *Seventeen* have proved this negative outcome to be mathematically impossible. What did the article say? "Guys like it when girls ask them out. They are usually too nervous, and it takes the pressure off of them. Chances are he'll be extremely flattered. Go for it, girl!" And, if I remember correctly, that article was on the same page as the scintillating exposé, "Oops! She bought it again! Britney Spears takes us on a shopping spree at the Armani Exchange." I really have to cancel my subscription.

The bell is going to ring any second now. With my luck, we'll have a spontaneous fire drill and I'll be forced to sit through class like this on Wednesday. Finally! It rang, or something to that effect. The "bell" sounds more like a dying elephant. Great, now try to remember why you're doing this. Why are you doing this? Why? Because you can, because you want to, because you care about him, because you'll never forgive yourself if you find out he accepted a last-minute invitation from someone else, because you're completely out of your sweet little mind, and in a minute, he's going to get up, stuff his textbooks into his backpack and walk out of your life—at least until tomorrow. Quick, check the hair. I can hear Vidal Sassoon crying for me. And, to help matters, my trusty comb is sitting at home by the sink. I even put a Post-it on my mirror last night to remind me, and is it in the bag? Nooooo. What the hell am I wearing? Teal? Do I WANT him to run screaming? What happened to the earth tones this morning? They must have been in the wash.

Yes, dear, he's leaving the room now. Just a few careful steps in your platforms and you can catch up. Is this going to work? At least I'll have the satisfaction of knowing I tried. Like the great philosopher Mick Jagger once said, "You can't always get what you want, but if you try sometimes, you might find you get what you need." Mick, I hope you and Keith were right. He's well within range. Just say his name and you're on your way.

"Hey, what's up?" He's smiling at me. "Are you going to the prom?" No? He's not going. But why? He's not really into those kind of things? OK, we can work with that. Stop walking and look him in the eye before you say it. "Well, I'd really love it if you'd go with me. I know it's short notice, but it took me a while to decide whether to ask you or not." Too much information, genius. What are you going to do next, divulge the fact that you've been living this moment over and over in your head for the past two weeks? Maybe I'm in the clear. He looks surprised, but not repulsed. The ball is in his court now. I hope he'll decide to lob it back instead of letting it fly into the net. Wait, what did he say? I was thinking about tennis, not paying attention. Did he say yes? He must have, because I'm lifting off the floor. My internal organs are regaining life and I'm floating slowly toward the hideous white cardboard ceiling tiles. I'm suspended in pause, but he's still standing there, shifting his weight from one foot to the other, awkwardly. Play: "Great, so I'll talk to you tomorrow about the details, then." He flashes the old "nod and smile," then slips back out of my life, like Gatsby after a party, igniting something warm and familiar inside of me. Am I still standing in the middle of the hallway staring into space. Yes. Yes I am. I'm walking out the doors now, into the real world. I have to write that paper tonight about the EPA and I'm going to need the notes. Maybe I could call him. I mean, how bad could it be, right? I'm the most amazing woman in the world. Never underestimate the power of teal.

Lena: An Artist at a Crossroads

Lena was a strong student at a large, diverse New York City public high school. A talented artist of Russian descent, she was torn between the applied arts and other disciplines in the liberal arts curriculum. Trying to find the balance between her interests and deciding on her college path formed the basis of her essays. Lena chose to apply to art schools within universities and to design schools. Admitted to Washington University's school of art and the Rhode Island School of Design, she chose Rhode Island, with its greater concentration on studio art. This is her short answer about art as her most meaningful activity:

To which activity have you made the greatest commitment? Why?

Artists are not only born: they are made. My mentor, Mr. Douglas Potter, taught me this lesson when I began studying with him 3 years ago. Now, as I devote more and more time to my artistic pursuits, I find myself leaving school at 6 p.m., only when the janitors kick me out. I have realized that art is a major part of my life and there is no other course but to dedicate as much time to it as I can. Art is an extension of my mind and myself; the more time I spend creating, the more I understand what I feel about myself as a person. Simply stated: I love making things. I love thinking, planning and doing. Expressing myself through art is something I was born to do. I can't refuse, so I welcome the opportunity to let my creative abilities flourish.

Here is Lena's personal statement, a tongue-in-cheek play on food and academics, using a Muppet as her foil:

Miss Piggy once said, "Never eat more than you can lift." I must concur. The most famous of all pigs knew that in life, one should find balance. Following Miss Piggy's example, it was impossible for me to eat all the food mommy piled on my plate when I was younger. The importance of this statement goes beyond my dietary habits, however. Now, I am the one to decide what I should eat for dinner and I find myself at a fork in the road (mind the pun): how can I satisfy my intellectual cravings without spilling over the sides of my plate?

This omnipresent question involves deep thought because all my educational experiences have made me excited. Challenging my limits was always what I did best, but as senior year rolled around I knew it was time to focus on my goals. With humanities always being my love and major interest, it was a given that I would focus on art and language classes. I couldn't pass the chance to conquer an Advanced Placement math class, however, and decided to invest in AP Statistics. Statistics was the perfect way to combine math with my real world knowledge. Suddenly, formulas weren't the only key to solving life's problems and my artistic viewpoints aided me in forming valid conclusions. Statistics is connected to my humanities orientation by a very thin thread, but I know when to hold on to a good thing; my calculus-adept father can finally listen to me say "I love math!"

When I indulge my artistic expressions, you can be sure dad will ask me why I'm not studying theorems. If only there were a simple answer. There isn't and this is where my personality might become a bit complicated. Simply stated, I am an artist; to dig deeper, visual expression is connected to my thought processes. To render my face is to illustrate my inner inhibitions. When no words will express my joy or my anger, I can put charcoal to paper and reflect my emotions. I think in terms of sensation, like a character from the world of Anaïs Nin, and reflecting my moods on paper is my release.

Feeling so strongly about art, I might not be so determined to continue along the framework of a liberal arts education. However, discovering subjects that entice me, like statistics, sheds light on the fact that I might be missing my true passion in life. Continuing on a path that strictly leads towards the academic would be a great blunder: my intellectual curiosity is matched only by my love for self-expression through visual arts. How can I choose between the academics and the arts? I have come to a fork in the road, and my decision is clear: I will take it.

Maybe listening to the wisdom of a Muppet scholar is a far-fetched notion, but I am only truly able to find happiness by productively combining my artistic side with my structured intellectual side. If high school was about self-discovery, then college will be my time for indulging my passions and aspirations in order to focus on my future. Give me the opportunity to question the greatest professors and let me discover how the Internet affects artists in the late twentieth century. My desire to learn everything I can and put it to use in a prolific manner is a top priority. I want to be able to use a well-rounded education to someday start a business in the art world. Give me opportunities to function in ways I never thought possible. I would never pass up the chance. My appetite has been whetted, so please, may I see a menu?

Douglas: An Artist and Creative Thinker

Douglas was admitted to Dartmouth after composing a set of essays that revealed not only his artistic side, but also his penchant for thinking visually and creatively. He told about his passion for art, but through all of his essays, he showed that he thought in pictures and colors. Here are several of his essays, beginning with one specifically about art as his most meaningful activity:

Creating art is the oil for my engine. It helps me to live life more smoothly and richly. Through painting, I express the swirling figments of imagination locked inside my head. Composing works of art provides a tremendous release for the tensions and passions pent up inside me. Every piece I complete is a self-portrait in that I commit more than just my paint and brush to the canvas. I put some of who I am there.

I sit in my room, paint-smeared brush in hand, with no idea how to fill the virgin canvas in front of me. I may sit here for hours waiting for that crucial breakthrough of conceptualization that will pour forth like a spring-swelled river and fill the canvas with the feelings and impulses that spill forth. Suddenly, I picture a dramatic seascape full of marmalade-orange colors. My brush dips swiftly into the patches of oil on the table and begins to transform the concept into reality. In a matter of hours that seem like moments, dramatic light sources and swift lines of pine trees fill the void in front of me.

My emotions and thoughts have been translated into colorful images. What was formerly transient thought has been frozen in oil, forever a testament to the myriad concepts and colors constantly zipping through my brain. I smile at the calm tangerine sky and delight in the bright red bushes in the foreground. Painting provides me with the chance to catch fleeting images and mental thoughts that normally go unnoticed.

I love to paint because it allows me the opportunity to express those thoughts and feelings that are beyond words. I like to write, but I love to paint. Regardless of how dramatic an essay is, or how free-flowing a short story is, words have their limits of expression. It is at this crucial boundary of the pen where the paintbrush takes over. Even this essay, an attempt to explain my passion for painting, barely throws a candle's worth of light on the mysterious art of art. My only regret as a painter is my ultimate inability to explain the magic of painting in words. My only regret as a writer is the impossibility of making my words as eloquent as my brush strokes.

In this next essay, Douglas talked about his interest in history through the window of the process of math:

I love to study history more than any other academic pursuit, which is why mathematics is the most meaningful subject to me. While not always easy, math problems are approached with the forethought of getting them right. Math is full of concrete absolutes. There is definitely a solution for each equation: the right answer. Solving arithmetic problems is like nothing in history. The experience of knowing for sure that you have completed a math problem perfectly delights me. Two plus two can never, ever equal anything except four. Whether my history theories are very good or quite poor, they can always be debated, rehashed, and improved. I enjoy the qualitative aspects of history, but doing a math problem completely right provides me with an important break from the fogginess of historical analysis.

Primarily a social sciences student, I find that working on math provides me with something I never find in history class: truisms. In this way, quantitatively assessing math questions provides an essential contrast to history, which is full of moving targets and ever-changing schools of thought. But there is something unsatisfying about truisms. Math is, in a sense, the lemon juice on my cantaloupe. Its absoluteness makes me savor history all the more.

Without this sour citrus bite, the sweet meat of the melon would not taste nearly as satisfying or invigorating. Personally, I feel that math is full of constrictive rules and regulations on what you can and cannot do with the numbers, whereas history's never-ending theories and contradictory interpretations restrict you only if you let them do so. It is precisely the study of sour math which allows me to more fully appreciate the tender taste of my social sciences. While I do not always enjoy the actual doing of math work, I find the contrast of numbers to words invaluable in fostering appreciation of more esoteric subjects in history. I love to dislike math.

Finally, Douglas posed his own question about problem solving, and then answered it. In this essay, he included a drawing of the mechanical device he described:

What defines people is the way they solve problems. How do you solve problems?

I do not think like a typical person. When faced with a problem, I often approach and solve it in a way that others would never consider. What is obvious to me sometimes is never even conceptualized by others. I seem to have a strange ability to tackle a problem from such a new and different angle.

A prime example of my defining characteristic occurred when Mr. Edwards, my physics teacher, handed my class the problem of protecting a falling egg. We were instructed to build any device we could imagine which was smaller than a six-inch cube and would prevent a chicken egg, when placed within it, from breaking. Each student's invention would be entered in a contest. Naturally, as everyone set to work concocting various cushioning systems for their eggs, I went in the opposite direction and gathered some wood, nails, glue and a hammer. While I was busy sawing, nailing, and epoxying my egg module together, the rest of the class was looking for more bubble wrap.

I think outside the box. What enables me to approach and solve complex problems effectively is my ability to consider each new challenge with a blank slate. This enables me to consider dilemmas large and small without any preconceptions. While in this naturally creative mode, I crafted a device to save my egg. When tackling such a problem, it is important for me to keep the goal in mind. The goal of my device should not be to slow the egg down, but rather to keep it from breaking! The goal of any solution is not to evade the problem, but to solve it. I instinctively analyzed the egg dilemma and saw through the obvious method of nesting the egg in soft materials, as seeds are nested in an apple. Instead of figuring out how to build the juicier apple, I thought it would be better to figure out how to keep the apple on the tree. Fortunately, the apple fell on my head and I decided to harness the force of my accelerating egg to keep it from breaking.

My device consisted of a small wooden platform supporting a perpendicular mast with a ball-and-socket hinge at the top. Onto this moving part, I placed a windmill-like circle with two arms coming off of it. Guy-wires supported and stabilized the mast. The contraption resembled a wood and metal pinwheel. An egg was placed on the tip of each arm, so that they counterbalanced each other. Employing a rubber band and nail, I wound up the arm and set a mousetrap, glued to the wood platform to release the tension of the rubber band when the sudden force of impact was applied to the mechanism. Rube Goldberg would have been pleased. Instead of protecting my fragile eggs, I placed them out in the air. If the thing had fallen the wrong way, I would have been left with a small pile of yoke, splinters, and bent nails. The entire notion was based on harnessing downward force and employing it to lift the eggs upward. The idea was this: when the bottom of the platform hits the ground, the shock of impact should snap the hair-trigger mousetrap that releases the restraint on the rubber band. The band would unwind, setting the egg-covered arm in motion. This arm begins to turn just as the shock of impact ripples throughout the entire device. Thus, the energy is diffused by the centripetal force as the pinwheel spins around, eggs moving with the force. In other words, I used the momentum of the descent to reverse the motion of the eggs. Much the same way, astrophysicists use this sling shot technique when they harness the gravity of a celestial body in order to propel satellites into space.

The fact that I won the contest proves that the most obvious or common solution to a problem is not always the best. However, the results should not overshadow the technique. How I approached the problem has more lasting value to me than how my module performed. I was saddled with a falling egg and used the intrinsic qualities of that problem to solve it. The solution was drawn from the goal.

My friends, family, and teachers have been noticing my different perspective on problems for years. Only recently have I begun to self-analyze and understand my own thought processes. In life, I always try to approach a problem by finding the seeds in the core—the goal. Sometimes that goal is surrounded by a lot of apple meat and the seeds are hard to get at. This, of course, makes it all the more fun.

Valerie: A Teller of Tales

Valerie took a creative direction in formulating a successful Dartmouth question-and-answer essay that helped her to weave her writing, art, and crafts work together:

What are you?

I am a teller of tales. I am a creator of magic. I craft stories that paint the world in colors of my imagination. I draft the dreams that lull my sleep with form and texture, in ink and clay. My role as artist and wordsmith is defined by a way of seeing life as a collection of inspirations and media. For me, the world exists as a reincarnation of objects, situations, and ideas, where a tree may return as a story, and a ship lives again through a painting. My job is to stir this cauldron, to be the writer, the artist, and the craftswoman of reinvention.

I believe that artist and writer are synonymous, because, as each writer's work is a form of art, each artist's work is a form of storytelling. Expression has the same goal in both of these fields, to inspire, to engage, to soothe, and to weave a tale of the artist's soul. Artists are often like philanthropists, awake in bed each night until some burning of the soul is healed through goodwill and funds by the philanthropist and through a new creation by the artist. The artist's particular burning comes from a discrepancy between how she sees herself, and how the world views her. This chasm of opinion exists for many, but it is the artists who are defined by it.

I, too, am compelled to bridge this gap, because I am an artist. I live in my own world of shifting images and turning phrases, immersed in observation and creation. This world is special in that it is mine, but my ownership isolates this world. I have built my bridge to others through writing and the arts, using each opportunity to speak my mind. Everything surrounding me provides grounds for reinvention; yet each creation does not necessarily carry a unique meaning. Rather, the collection of projects combine to articulate my philosophy, and often these collections are prompted by unexpected meetings. A red kayak that crossed my path kindled a series of paintings and sculptures focusing on a lonely boat. A shapely, yellow gourd prompted me to craft candles nestled in gourd skin. A certain shade of blue influenced me to design and sew my own prom dress from navy silk and layers of chiffon.

Clearly, everything that touches me does not inspire a classical oil painting, and I love this variety. This love leads me to value a new recipe for spice cake as highly as a finished sculpture, because they are both my children, crafted by my own hands. The practice of such lesser-known arts as sewing, knitting, candle-making, and woodcarving by no means degrades my role as an artist. These crafts actually enhance my artistry as they provide new media and translate my philosophy into a way of life, making everything I do a form of creation.

Writing, like painting, sewing, or sculpture, is a form of creation, but it is more upfront than other art forms. There is a fear in writing. The expression necessary to all artists, for a writer, rests entirely on the ability to craft a coherent whole from abstract feelings and ideas. Writing is standing up in a crowd and shouting, "this is me!" There is also an egotism in writing, because, by standing up in that crowd, you have already decided that you are worth listening to. When asked what I am, I say first that I am a writer. Although I am an artist and craftswoman as well, my most beloved and labored articulations are crafted with ink on paper. I write, because I have fear, and have egotism, and I have this world of my own.

The Liberal Artist

There is nothing wrong with wanting to study a broad range of subjects in college. That is what the liberal arts are all about. Most students do not know what they want to study entering college, and most will change majors several times during their education. There is nothing wrong with not making a clear choice of major in your application writing. The trick is to write about your strengths and passions in different subject areas, and your desire to pursue those and other academic disciplines as part of a balanced curriculum in college. You may even make the match between your interests and the options available at particular schools.

Kim

We have included one of our writer/actor Kim's essays as a strong model for how to write about the liberal arts while being clear about particular interests and experiences. Here is Kim's "Why Georgetown?" essay, adaptations of which she used for Penn and Northwestern:

> From the beginning of my college search, I knew that Georgetown University was a great match for me. Although it took me a while to narrow down my choices, Georgetown stood out in my mind as an institution that could offer me not only a wonderful liberal arts education, but also all of the countless benefits of living within the Washington, DC and Georgetown communities. In the last year, I have become very interested in politics. My AP US Government course opened my eyes to the ways our government works, to the problems it has faced, and most importantly, to how little I knew about the political process before. I decided that I wanted to learn more, and jumped at the chance to participate in Connecticut Girls' State and a Week on Washington program last summer. My trips exposed me to people who shared my interest in activism and political work, and inspired me to become more involved. This fall at school, I joined a club called Students for Political Action, which, among other things, helped me "get out the vote" in my town during the November rush. This year was as explosive as any in the history of American politics, and I was given ample opportunity to learn about the changing face of our political system. I know now that I want politics to be a part of my life in one way or another, even if it simply means voting in every election, discussing my views with others, and being knowledgeable about the issues affecting us as Americans. I am not sure what major I want to pursue, but I do hope to study politics, government, and social sciences on a higher level. I am particularly interested in the way the media affect society and political views, and Georgetown College offers a minor in social and political thought that could be a perfect undertaking for me. I am also interested in pursuing English, American Studies, Psychology, and Theater, and ultimately I hope that I will be involved in a career that encompasses my love of creativity, self-expression, and political activism. Georgetown College has many diverse courses in these areas which would allow me to expand my world views, and

help me decide what sphere I want to focus on. One of the greatest benefits of Georgetown is that, although it is a university with an unbelievable amount of resources, in the spirit of the liberal arts it does not strictly limit them to students involved with a particular school or major. I would pursue an undergraduate education primarily in Georgetown College, but I am excited that the University would also give me the chance to take some business or foreign service courses in the other schools.

One unparalleled benefit of Georgetown University is the degree of access students have to the resources available in the Washington, DC area. For a student interested in government, the media, and the arts there is no place better. In the future, I would like to work on Capitol Hill or at a news network, possibly during summer internships that Georgetown supports. Aside from the educational benefits of the city, both downtown Washington and Georgetown offer great artistic and cultural outlets. From the museums of the Smithsonian Institution, to the Kennedy Center, to the coffee houses, I know I would never be bored. Georgetown also has a strong commitment to community service in its Jesuit heritage and character, and the large number of volunteer programs in the Washington community would provide a good way for me to continue humanitarian work, possibly in a new capacity, such as at the Capitol Children's Museum, or the American Red Cross. Clearly, Georgetown also realizes that its resources extend far beyond the boundaries of its campus or the Washington area. The University encourages its students to become acquainted with the cultural diversity and richness that other countries can provide by offering study abroad opportunities, and by creating a diverse student body on campus.

It was its outstanding academics and resources that first attracted me to Georgetown, but I realized that the University goes far beyond that: it also develops character. The alumni and students I have met displayed a rare enthusiasm and passion about Georgetown, and explained how their experience there had helped them grow academically, socially, and personally. After considering all of its merits, I have no doubt in my mind that

Georgetown would provide a perfect atmosphere for me to pursue my passions and transform them into a rewarding profession.

Peter: Writer, Historian, Philosopher, Sailor

Peter, a strong and balanced student at a suburban high school, was an excellent writer. He loved historical research, journalism, and government. An active participant in his school and community, he was an avid sailor from an early age. Peter's Common Application shows two sides of his personality and pursuits. Peter was admitted to Vanderbilt, Carleton, Bowdoin, Michigan, and several other colleges that appreciated his intellectual interests and ability to present them in a compelling and thoughtful way. His first essay originated as a history research project that Peter then developed into a newspaper article and an award-winning essay at school:

I paced outside the VFW weighing ideas of aborting or going in. I did not have an appointment and had only a vague idea of what I would find inside as the anxiety rumbled inside me. I finally tugged the heavy metal door open and a rush of cigarette smoke, wet canvas, and beer permeated my nose. Blatantly underage and out of place in my corduroys and oxford shirt, and feeling as if I were invading the turf of the real men, the gritty guys, and the grunts, I reddened as every voice fell silent in the room and eyes stared through me. Pool balls ceased to crack and roll, and one voice called out, "You're in the wrong bar, sonny." I asked if anyone knew the VFW historian. A vet named Jimmy, who I learned had been in an artillery fire-support group in Vietnam, and whose leg had been shattered by a mortar round in Da Nang, rescued me. He gave me a few names and some phone numbers between puffs on the glowing piece of cigar in the corner of his mouth.

I wanted to make my contribution to the Millennium Issue of the school newspaper by telling the stories of the clean American faces under the steel helmets I had seen in books and documentaries. I made twelve phone calls to veterans who had fought in the Second World War and had gone to my high school. I was struck with a sense of pity at how many of them, our ancient warriors, anxiously asked me what I was trying to sell them, nervous about being scammed. They had been reduced to paranoid hermits, yet one man seemed interested in my offer for an interview and I found myself two days later sitting in Mr. Allen Andersen's living room on Andersen Lane.

I wanted to get out of the libraries in which I had sat glancing through books of combat pictures and meet the real people. As a lover of history, especially military history, I was interested in the real story; I wanted to know what being in the war felt like. I sat with Mr. Andersen and his son, Roger, in Mr. Andersen's living room long after the sun had gone down and I had stopped questioning. I listened to his stories. After thumbing through old newspaper clippings and patting photos from the war with the tips of his fingers, Mr. Andersen told me what it was like to be there, how it felt to be in such stressful conditions, where he and his men slept, and what the nights were like. Mr. Andersen recounted story after lonely horror story, telling his son and me about his fear, his lonesomeness in the infantry, and the trauma and stress of combat life.

Suddenly the Europe I'd seen in *Saving Private Ryan* did not seem so far away or so long ago. Mr. Andersen rubbed his feet against the carpet as if to warm them as we listened about the many winter nights in Germany he lay restlessly in a foxhole in icy hay fields unable to sleep, waking up with stiff boots and frost on his mustache. Though the experiences must have been unbearable, Mr. Andersen never once lost his sense of duty while telling his stories. "We had a job to do, and it was a very difficult job, but it had to be done."

Most men who fought in the Second World War came home and went to work. Their sons and daughters did not know about the horrible experiences they had gone through. Our country pushed their sacrifice into the pages of history. Mr. Andersen's demeanor had eased when he shared the burden of war with his son and me. So much of World War Two is shrouded in honor and glory when in reality, self-preservation was the ultimate objective for most soldiers. "It wasn't all glorified, we were just doing our job and I happened to be in a unit that did its job exceptionally well," Andersen said of the First Infantry Division. "But you would never hesitate to preserve your life; you wanted to at least get out of there alive."

Months after our interview, Mr. Andersen sent me a letter thanking me for what I had given him. The writing of the story was second in importance to the telling of his history. The article had become much larger than expected: it was eleven pages. I felt that all he had said was too precious to cut out; I could not sell him short and I felt I needed to pass his story to my generation. Mr. Andersen was the young face under the steel helmet, the blank visage gaping into the camera, the soiled finger resting on the trigger, and I needed to give him a voice. In the telling of his history, I became part of it.

I pass the VFW driving home from school and as I sit glancing at the beige building resting atop the Little League Baseball fields, I think about all the men inside, sitting at the bar, who so long ago laid down their weapons and came back to the world, with so many stories to tell. Volumes of exciting and horrifying stories are sitting on stools, needing appreciation. Perhaps it is time I opened more of these books, because the human connection is far more satisfying, far more enlightening, and far more important than the faded photographs.

Peter's second essay, a supplemental "what else should we know about you?" piece, shows his personality, writing skills, and reflective nature, while simultaneously providing the admissions reader with a great amount of knowledge about Peter's background:

THE MIGHTY SEA

My mother was sifting through the piles of papers that accumulate during one's life and found an old pew card from our church. On it, was a series of questions, and somebody, in almost illegible writing, had penciled in answers. One in particular, read, "*I would like to hear a sermon about* . . . tall, wooden ships." It was my second-grade handwriting.

Since I was very little, I have always been fascinated with boats and ships, especially sailing ships. I have no recollection from where this fascination grew; perhaps I have always been called to the sea. Neither of my parents are sailors or boaters. I grew up in a New York City apartment until moving to the country near the water. My mother would often take my brother and me to the Natural History Museum in New York, which had a powerful smell of things that were very old. It was a smell I came to love. It was a primal smell, and stepping inside, it was like crossing to the other side of nature, I had passed through the boundaries of time as the great wooly mammoths stood high above me. And that huge blue whale, suspended as if in mid stroke, smiled at me with its bristly teeth. The whale frightened me. It frightened me as it was from the unknown, the unexplored, and the uncontrolled. It came from a vast, deep and dark place, on the fringe of the world. It came from a very powerful place. The whole museum held this same mystique for me, and this feeling would come to me continually.

The great wooden sailing ships that traversed those dark unknown waters caught my interest and I used to borrow picture books on Spanish galleons from the library, or listen to Robinson Crusoe read to my brother and me. I found in these books the element to sailing that has remained in me the most enticing, though the competitive spirit of sailing has often shaded it. The quest to understand the dark unknown, and thus ourselves, was a continual theme as every man and explorer had to rely on his own intuition, the inner strength of his own soul, to overcome the fears of the unknown.

After a time, my passion for sailing and the sea grew to a point where I needed to shape it in my own hands. I began to build model sailboats out of long strips of wood I found in my father's workshop and outfitted them with "rigging" I found around the house. Pushpins made excellent winch drums, and a staple could be easily bent into a pulley and hammered into the deck. String and thread became the lines and sheets on my boats, which were not for show. The rough, wood boats were for play. I could no longer watch sailing; I needed to start to experience it. Each sail could be raised and lowered, and each line served a function that could be demonstrated. After I began to sail myself, these models could perform just as regular sailboats, although only on our blue living-room carpet; they had no hope of floating on the real blue sea, but my imagination allowed them this flaw.

It has been many years since I first started to sail myself. I have moved on to more complex boats, and more complicated skills like navigation and seamanship, yet I have still retained my fascination with boats and my love for the sea. I find myself staring at a picture of a sailboat, following the sheets and lines from the hands of the sailors, along the intricate paths to the sails, attempting to figure out how they are rigged.

Four years ago, I sailed my first overnight race and this September, crewed with a boat on the Vineyard Race from Stamford to Martha's Vineyard, and back. The experience had a major impact on me. It renewed my love for the sea and the peace that sailing brings me. Racing, though a healthy complement to my sailing experience, has always come second. The pressure of school and the college process had begun to build and the race was a good respite. Sailing has always been for me, a good respite. It is a time for me, protected by the nature of the sea, to reflect and to have peace, to be with God, yet it has also been a medium for self-searching.

The Vineyard Race also had a strong emotional impact on me. The sailing itself was exhausting and a trial of the body, the mind, and spirit. It was my first time in the ocean, and, as the boat sped along toward the Vineyard and then back home, my own fears of the ocean and storms had to be put to rest. I was sailing into the great unknown, as my material knowledge of the sea was limited to the area of Long Island Sound around my home. It was a total immersion into a life of sailing, and that had the biggest impact on me.

Sailing has been the ultimate test and measure of my existence. It is simple, yet enriched by its simplicity in not being distracted with the congestion of human living. Though one can learn much of the world by sitting on a street corner in New York, watching, one can learn far more about the soul, about humanity, the human condition, from being at sea. One is forced to cope without the security of land within sight, with the limited space in which to work, and in close quarters with other people. You really learn how to appeal to a person's nature when you share the same forty-by-seven feet for days on end. Sailing is a constant test. It requires a person to complete several tasks drawing from many different skills and emotions in order to complete those tasks, all at the same time. Learning how to solve a problem on the water helped me solve many problems on land.

Sailing is the ultimate test of character. When you are out at sea, and the waves start to build and the wind is howling louder and louder, what is happening on land is inconsequential. You are there for survival almost. Books like *The Perfect Storm* and *Into Thin Air* have become popular today because these are books about experiences that men and women no longer have much in their lives. How many times a day is our existence challenged? We feel the need to be scared as it reminds us that we are alive, like riding the Great American Scream Machine, or driving at unsafe speeds, or watching the numerous scary movies that have come out in the last five years. We do not fight for life every day, and these experiences remind us of what the human body and mind are capable. They give us some measure of our limits.

The few storms I have experienced have all contributed to my insight into the force that is present at sea, that draws me and dares me to follow. There is no way to know how you will act when the wind blows out of control and beyond the limit of the boat, or what you will think when the sky suddenly turns black, and the water is as gray as death, save the white crests of swells blown by the howling wind. When the lightning cracks with a thunder a few yards away, louder than any gunshot, than any conventional sound you experience in daily life, the fear begins to build, yet you always seem to rise to the occasion. If God is going to challenge you, you had better be ready to stick to your guns, and each time you come out alive, you are the better for it and it gives you a strength and resilience that no ordinary activity could provide. What does not beat you can only make you stronger, and you learn to appreciate the beauty of it all.

There is something very beautiful and romantic about a sailboat, out there sliding silently with the sun setting in brilliant colors with the rhythmic bounce of the boat over the waves. I am sure one has a similar feeling standing at the summit of a tall mountain, blanketed by white snow. Sitting on the side of a boat, heeled over to weather, with the wind whipping your face and chilling your nose while your body sits warm on deck, covered in layers, you feel the beauty of being perfectly in tune with nature, without a worldly care. You get away from life, from land, and it all goes away. You are as far removed from cares and problems as you could be, out on a boat. You are protected by the inaccessibility of water, yet there is also something out there in the ocean. It is a force to be reckoned with. It is simpler than many things, yet it is powerful, and I feel it now every time I step on a boat and get beyond safe sight of land. Perhaps this force is the face of God. Or perhaps it is a force like a mirror that reflects our own feeble humanity staring back at us, urging us to push the envelope and see if we are really as strong as we believe.

The Research Scientist

If you have been seriously devoted to an academic pursuit during high school, have taken courses at their highest level in school, and then studied during the summer and engaged in additional research, you might fall into this category. If you have published a research paper, worked in a professional lab, competed on the math team, or read everything available on nuclear physics or quantum mechanics, then think about how you might convey your passion for research—in the sciences, history, literature, mathematics, psychology, or another area—in your college writing.

Greg: Scientist, Technology Buff Admitted to Dartmouth

Greg was a student at a small high school who knew very early on that he wanted to specialize in computer science and technology. Beginning in ninth grade, he took university-level courses locally and during the summers to expand his knowledge and skills in computer science, engineering, and high-tech fields. Greg used the four questions on the Dartmouth application to showcase his personal and intellectual pursuits, conveying his passion for knowledge and enthusiasm for a variety of activities:

What was the highlight of your summer?

"Yes, that's my car parked out there, and yes, it's a 1999." I had just arrived at Friendly's Restaurant, my place of employment for the summer. I had been there only five minutes and already I felt uncomfortable. Rob, the grill man on duty, was a large imposing black man questioning me about my lifestyle and my "story." I quickly caught on and told him that I was a preppy, wealthy white kid, and I knew it; but I felt that I had been unfairly stereotyped as a rich white kid. To be honest, I had also unfairly characterized Rob as just another one of the black grill workers.

As someone who was 29, had three children, worked two jobs and had been in jail, Rob was as different from me as anyone I had ever met. Quickly, Rob and I got over our obvious differences and talked about things that we had in common. We were both amazed to see how similar our opinions, families and values were. While I went to a preppy private school and he had not, while I lived on a quiet tree-lined street and he had not, we thoroughly enjoyed one another and eventually became good friends. I taught Rob how to play chess and he taught me how to change the oil in my car.

In the past, at school and camp, I had been somewhat friendly with people from different backgrounds than mine; however, Rob and I became true friends. Through Rob I leared to respect perseverance, personal struggle, and resilience in a new way. I discovered a measure of tolerance for those different for me that I did not know I had. Rob gave me a chance to connect with someone different from myself and to know myself in a new way. I am indebted to him.

Which of your pursuits, in or out of school, do you find most fulfilling? Why?

People tell me my enthusiasm is contagious. Spreading passion for my interests, especially science, has always given me enormous pleasure. Whether the topic is physics, economics, the current political scence or a recent scientific breakthrough, I want to know about it and I want to debate it. In and out of class, I enjoy talking about the application of theoretical principles and problems with my physics teacher. My economics teacher and I have different political views; however, we enjoy debating the current business and economic climate. I am stimulated when I have the chance to talk seriously with one of my friends or parents about anything scientific. The opportunity to teach one of my friends about Newton's Second Law or about the International Space Station forces me to test my knowledge as I share it.

A few weeks ago I explained to my best friend how an internal combustion engine works. And while we were watching the World Series recently, I was talking to my mother about the physics of baseballs and footballs and why they travel the way that they do. Now my mom knows why a curveball curves! I regularly tutor my classmates and on occasion I have been lucky enough to fill-in for an absent teacher.

For me, the world is my classroom. I learn as much being in front of the class as being in the class.

The character of the College is shaped by the life experiences of its students. How would you contribute to the Dartmouth community?

I experience life as a scientist. I try to do more than scratch the surface of the mysteries of life. I prefer to dig more deeply into the wonders before me. I enjoy the theoretical aspects of my studies, but I also enjoy applying my skills and pursuing my interests outside the classroom.

As the Technology Editor for both my school yearbook and newspaper, I am responsible for all computer issues relating to either of these publications. These responsibilities give me a chance to apply my computer knowledge while helping out my school. My additional role as the Layout Editor for the newspaper allows me to act as the intermediary for the articles and the completed newspaper. I have the opportunity to be creative as I convert hand-written and typed articles into the newspaper, which ends up in the hands of the students and faculty. Working on school dramatic and musical productions, doing sound and light work, has given me the chance to blend my technical know-how with my interest in the arts. And believe me there is plenty of drama behind the scenes!

I have also used hands-on technical knowledge from university courses I have taken by assisting my school Registrar with computer problems related to course scheduling and record keeping. I have been fortunate enough to be able to apply my knowledge to a variety of situations during Middle and Upper School and look forward to sharing my know-how through involvement in the Dartmouth College community over the next four years.

Did we miss anything? Please feel free to convey anything significant that you think we should know. This could be an anecdote or essay related to an interest, talent, experience, issue of concern, or aspect of your background or qualifications. Anything goes!

Carpe diem? Carpe millennium! My family has taught me that to succeed I have to seize every opportunity. My mother started a new career in her forties. My father ran for Congress while running two successful businesses. My brother, who attends Dartmouth, was a Congressional Page. I have been taught always to question what I am doing and to strive for more. After exhausting my school's computer science program I went to Fairfield University and took twelve credits in Computer Science. At age thirteen I was in college courses with adults two and three times my age. My upbringing helped me to succeed and to excel in this environment.

I have had an ongoing campaign to educate my school community about the fact that the millennium will start in 2001 not 2000. As a scientist, I approach life logically. As a result I was interested in researching the technicalities of this issue and putting together a logical argument defending my view. Last year I gave a speech at my school about the millennium. Recently I was asked to give it again as an introduction to a visiting scholar at my school. The week before that, I had the opportunity to do a small workshop with the fifth graders at my school about this topic.

Even as a young child I was interested in logical and tactical pursuits. This interest led me to pursue chess as a hobby. I pursued this passion at home and at school, eventually winning an after-school chess tournament. In the years following, my friends and I put together an informal chess club, often meeting on the weekends to practice and talk strategy. Eventually we moved onto the national level, playing in an American Chess Association tournament in New York. We all learned a lot about chess as well as competing and interacting with people from other parts of the country.

My knowledge and understanding are always evolving. Why seize the day when I can seize the millennium?

Roberta: A Research Scientist with a Passion for Solving Problems

In her application to Dartmouth, Roberta was able to convince the admissions committee of her academic preparation and her commitment to science in the broadest sense. Her writing conveyed spirit, intellectual curiosity, and a natural style. Showing that length is not the best indicator of good content, Roberta kept her responses short, with all working together to present a complete picture of herself. Here are portions of her application questions and answers:

What academic subject is most meaningful to you? Why?

I love science. Throughout middle and high school, science courses have always been my favorites. The teachers are always the most enthusiastic. They seem so excited about what they do. The material is fascinating to me, whether it involves drawing parallels between experiments others have done, or conducting experiments where you do not know the outcome. The juxtaposition of exactness and uncertainty, and the elusiveness of the answer, with all the twists and turns that research can take, excite me. One of the reasons I am applying to Dartmouth is because of the Women in Science Program, which sounds like an ideal way to become more closely involved with people who have made science their life's work.

Please indicate which activity is most meaningful. Why?

For my sophomore, junior, and senior winters I have volunteered every Wednesday from 2:30 to 5:30 at Person to Person, a local outreach organization associated with my church. It was started in 1968 as a response by the parish to the assassination of Martin Luther King, Jr., and the need to reach out to the less fortunate in our community. My responsibilities there include folding and sorting clothing donations, organizing food, and preparing baby bundles that are distributed to our clients. During the time that I am at Person to Person each Wednesday, clients come in and find clothing and food for themselves. Often, I am in contact with them, helping them find the items that they need. I value the work I do there because I can see the difference that the organization makes in the lives of people. As awkward as it sometimes is for me, I realize how much more awkward and difficult it must be for the clients.

Please list any college courses in which you have been (or currently are) enrolled.

I studied Genetics as part of the 1995 Center for Talented Youth at Johns Hopkins University. The course met for three weeks, five hours per day, five days per week. There were between 100 and 110.5 contact hours with the discipline. The course covered all the material offered in a one-semester college class. The textbooks used in the course were *Basic Human Genetics,* by Mange and Mange, and *Genetics Laboratory Investigations,* by Mertens and Hammersmith.

Briefly describe any scholastic distinctions or honors you have received since tenth grade.

At the end of eleventh grade I received four awards:
- The Harvard Club Book Award which is given to "an outstanding junior in overall excellence, leadership, character, and service."
- The Connecticut Governor's Scholar Award for outstanding academic performance.
- A Society of Women Engineers Award which is given to "juniors with high achievement in science and mathematics."
- A Bausch and Lomb Award which is given to "the junior with the highest average in science subjects."
- In twelfth grade I was named a National Merit Commended Scholar on the basis of my October 1996 PSAT scores. I have achieved the High School High Honor Roll, which requires a 3.7 GPA every quarter of high school thus far.

What was the highlight of your summer?

This past summer I attended a program at Tufts University Veterinary Medical School. This program allowed me to explore the fundamentals of veterinary medicine by shadowing fourth year students, observing clinical and surgical procedures, and attending lectures. The most interesting part of this experience was a lecture given by an animal behaviorist. Dr. Nicholas Dodman described his research on compulsive behaviors in horses, dogs, and cats, and what could be done to prevent it. What was exciting was that much of his research involved new thinking. One comment stuck in my mind. He said, "I have all sorts of new ideas bouncing around my head all the time. All day, all night. Many times I'm up at 3:30 in the morning just thinking. It never stops." That kind of enthusiasm is contagious.

You have been asked many questions on this application, all asked by someone else. If you yourself were in a position to ask a thought-provoking and revealing question of college applicants, what would that question be?

What do you love?

Now that you have asked your ideal question, answer it.

I love to laugh. Fits of giggles, loud guffaws, silly grins—I love them all. A laugh can cure even the worst case of stress. I try to laugh and make others laugh every day and I have found that it is not hard.

I love my dog. He makes me laugh. He loves me without reservation. He brings me presents: large sticks, dead ducks, slippers, half-eaten socks, and dead mice with moldy tails. He greets me every day with such exuberant joy. He grins when I rub his belly.

I love hard problems. I love the feeling I get when I finally solve the puzzle. I call it the great AH HA! Once when comparing favorite classes with a group of friends at lunch, I said I couldn't decide whether I would rather take eight periods of science or eight periods of math. Both subjects are satisfying because they challenge me and I can succeed. Being a member of the JETS (Junior Engineering Technical Society) team is one of my favorite activities because it presents difficult, real-world problems that require cooperative thinking.

I love to try new things and see new places. As a family, we are corporate nomads. We have moved all over the country. While it has sometimes been very hard to be the "new kid," I am more confident and less apprehensive about new situations as a result of moving. I have learned to rely on myself. I have also learned what it takes to make new friends. Our family vacations have involved travel throughout the country and overseas. I have had the opportunity to experience a variety of cultures from the Anasazi to the Dutch.

I love to be organized. From multi-divided binders to color-coded pushpins, from computerized homework schedules to project boxes, I am organized. It just happens that Staples and Hold Everything are my favorite stores. This is not obsessive; it just makes me happier to be organized. It also helps me manage a very busy life.

I love to help people learn. I get enormous satisfaction from helping my friends understand homework problems. This year, I am also a peer tutor for the "A Better Chance" program in our town. One of the activities at Dartmouth in which I am interested is "Reading Buddies."

I love answering questions.

What I Stand For: The Student with a Passion and a Statement to Make

In this catch-all category, we put those students wishing to make a strong statement of purpose. We have in mind religious students giving indications of their faith (as Jason and Karen did in Chapter 3), volunteers, Eagle Scouts, environmentalists, political activists, and other students with a cause. We include examples of particularly strong Powerful Idea, Significant Influence, and Meaningful Activity essays that convey a major sense of purpose.

Alicia: An Environmental Activist Accepted at Bates College

Alicia was a student at a small private school. She had developed an increasing passion for the outdoors, the environment, and animal rights issues during high school, and was looking for a college where her individuality, commitment, and experiences would be appreciated. Her personal statement for Bates was passionate and honest without turning into a polemic:

> I agree with Dr. Jane Goodall, the renowned primatologist, that "every individual matters, human and non-human alike. Every individual has a role to play. Every individual makes a difference." This principle coincides with my own philosophy and passion for animal rights and the environment, and is the driving force behind the actions that I take to make the world a better place for all beings. In the future, I will continue to pursue this passion by developing my role as a champion for animals and the environment. I believe that everything I do (and that everybody else does), no matter how small an action, truly makes a difference in the world.
>
> My understanding of the impact of our habits, as humans, on the welfare of all creatures and ecological balances, led me to embrace veganism. This practice encompasses all aspects of one's lifestyle: the food one eats, the clothes one wears, the products one uses, and the practices one supports. Therefore, I abstain from eating or otherwise using products that contain animal ingredients, and I do not support practices that exploit animals (including animal experimentation, circuses, dissection, horse and dog racing, and rodeos). I have found my philosophy and altered lifestyle surprisingly liberating. "Our task must be to free ourselves . . . by widening our circle of compassion to embrace all living creatures and the whole of nature and its beauty" (Albert Einstein).
>
> I have acted on my convictions about protecting animals and the environment by replacing traditional products in my household with animal and environmentally friendly ones, riding my bicycle instead of driving a car whenever the destination is close enough to do so, composting, conserving energy, and changing my family's source of electricity from fossil fuels to renewables. Not only do I believe that the principle "reduce, reuse, recycle, buy recycled" is extremely important, but I also practice it whenever I

can; I collect the plastic that my family uses (but is not recycled by my town) and take it to a nearby factory that makes this plastic into new products. I have expanded my efforts by writing letters to legislators about such issues as a restoration plan for Long Island Sound, the use (and need for labeling) of genetically modified foods, the treatment of circus elephants, deer population control, animal experimentation, and Mitsubishi's proposal (which has, fortunately, been abandoned) to build the world's largest salt factory that would damage the surrounding ecosystem. I have also brought my dedication to my school community, where I lead the Conservation Club. In all these ways, I have chosen to "live deliberately" (Henry David Thoreau).

My desire to preserve our natural resources was invigorated by my participation in the Maine Coast Semester of the Chewonki Foundation in Wiscasset, Maine. As a part of this program, I enjoyed a two-day solo, during which I challenged myself to become more aware of my surroundings by telling time by the sun and the tides, acquainting myself with the natural darkness of night, and listening to the birds I had learned to identify. In addition, I discovered the power of collective effort. The students and faculty in this inclusive community maintained the campus: together we accomplished all of the cooking, gardening, construction, cleaning, and other work that needed to be done. My experience at the Maine Coast Semester strengthened my confidence and ability to act within a community to attain goals.

Although I feel proud of the self-initiated evolution of my philosophy and my contributions to the ideal of a sustainable future, I believe there is a great deal more that I can do. I will not only continue to learn about animal rights and environmental issues, but I will also do all that I can to make the world a better place for all beings, because "we must be the change we wish to see in the world" (Mahatma Gandhi).

Alicia's "Why Bates?" essay explicitly made the match between her beliefs and interests and what she believed to be the mission and personality of the college:

I wish to attend Bates for numerous concrete reasons, but the most compelling one is intangible. When I initially visited the campus last Spring, I had the instinctive feeling that Bates was the most appropriate college for me. As I continued to research colleges during the Spring and Summer, none of them came close to matching the feeling that I experienced when I visited Bates. I therefore saw Bates as my first choice and resolved to apply Early Decision. Besides the abstract sensation that I had, and the fact that Bates is located in Maine, a state I admire, there are various other factors that intensify my conviction that Bates is an excellent match for me.

I believe that my own philosophy and that of the school are complementary. I am drawn to the college's inclusive philosophy, exemplified by the friendly and outgoing student body, and the fact that Bates has never had fraternities and sororities, and that standardized test scores are not required for consideration in admissions. I believe this inclusiveness is extremely important for the growth of the individual as well as the community. From an academic standpoint, the Environmental Studies program will provide me with the opportunity to expand my knowledge and understanding of issues relating to the Earth. The Short Term and internship opportunities at Bates also appeal to me because I believe that it is important to go beyond the classroom to work and learn. In addition, I value the Service Learning Program because I wish to learn from and contribute to my community. Beyond the intuitive feeling I had when I initially visited the campus and the various tangible aspects of the school that I am drawn by, I feel at home on campus and would really love to attend Bates.

Cindy: A Student with Strong Faith Who Lost a Loved One

Cindy was able to combine in this essay two major components of her perspective on life: her faith and experiencing her cousin's loss to cancer. Her sincerity and empathy are clear in the way she references her service through a religious organization, her realization of the loss that a fellow student had experienced, and her conclusions about life. Cindy was admitted to Columbia.

When I call to mind experiences that have shaped my life, two major events stand out as having had the most influence on who I am today. They are my participation in Emmaus, a youth retreat organized by my church, and the death of my cousin Carol.

I serve as a team member for Emmaus twice a year. This retreat is organized by teenagers and adults for other high school students. I was a candidate on this retreat in the fall of my sophomore year, and began to serve as a team member in the fall of my junior year. Emmaus is one of the best things that I have ever done for myself. It is a chance to actively participate in my faith by passing on God's word to my peers. It is also a chance for me to gain insights into aspects of my faith. I am surrounded by people who have found God in their own way, and, throughout the weekend, I get to meet new people and hear their stories. Classmates of mine, with whom I may never have spoken, are willing to share their experiences with the entire Emmaus community, and I get to see sides of people that I never knew existed. This Emmaus weekend has time and again destroyed any preconceived notions I may have held about certain classmates, and I have learned that there is no way I can judge a person by what they show me in school alone.

As a team member I am able to hear each talk given by either a student or an adult in advance. The speech that has meant the most to me was a speech entitled "Self-Awareness," and was given by a popular senior boy named Tom. He was the "big man on campus," popular, confident, self-assured, well-known and well-liked. He stood at the podium and quietly, openly and in a matter-of-fact way proceeded to talk about his struggle to come to terms with his father's death from cancer, to find a sense of self and to make friends. He spoke particularly about the conflicting feelings of anger, grief, and love that he experienced after his father's passing, and his words struck a personal chord with me as I listened.

The summer before Tom's speech my cousin Carol succumbed to the cancer she had been battling for several years. Her death and her struggle with her illness remain imprinted upon my memory as much as my memory of her alive and healthy. While I recall her long hospital stays, her debilitated physical capabilities toward the end, her weak appearance, and her chronic exhaustion, what strikes me most of all is the way she kept up her spirits. What is always present when I think of her is the image of her in her hospital bed during our last visit with her, the last time I would see her alive. She had been undergoing grueling chemotherapy in what would be a futile attempt to shrink the inoperable tumor on her spine. The treatment made her incredibly sick and tired. It made her voice raspy and her hair fall out, but the minute we walked through the door she brightened up, looked right at me and said "How've you been, babe?" Her room overflowed with flowers and cards and balloons sent by loved ones, and she had amassed a vast collection of "angel on my shoulder" pins, as her fondness for angels was well known. But she wore only one of those pins, one that the nurses had presented to her after a particularly difficult radiation session. She smiled and joked, made fun of the doctors and herself. "They hate to talk about death!" she exclaimed. "Do you know what they say? They say, 'I'm not God.'" She laughed as she imitated the deep voice of her doctor. Although she could not stop the cancer from claiming her body, she never allowed it to claim her mind or her spirit. She always put up a brave and cheerful front, although we heard from her husband, Les, how she used to privately cry over her inability to do the things she used to love to do, like cook Thanksgiving dinner for her family, or invite friends over to the house for a Christmas get together. She was selfless and brave, and will forever be my model for handling adversity with grace. She taught me the value of living fully every day, and telling the people I care about how much they mean to me. I hope that I will be able to emulate her courage and personal strength, and she will always remain in my mind and my heart.

In his speech Tom revealed a very personal side of himself and his words helped me to realize that he and I, for all our different activities and friends, were in fact, very similar. He reassured me that I was not alone in my struggles to fit in and to deal with the death of a loved one. He helped me gain a sense of direction in my daily life that would bring me not only closer to God, but closer to myself as well. He gave me hope that as time went on, the conflicting feelings that were still milling about inside would subside, and that while I would always feel cheated that Carol was taken from us, I would gradually learn to accept her death and embrace her memories.

Tracy: Active Volunteer and Writer

Tracy was admitted to Harvard, Princeton, and Dartmouth after submitting beautiful and varied writing samples and essay responses. Here are some of her pieces:

How far can one hundred yards of road take you? It sounds like a trick question, one that needs a wise old man from a fairy tale to answer, but I have a picture framed in my room of a little old Greek man who showed me the answer. I don't know his name or his age, only that he wore a soiled shirt whose bottom button couldn't stretch across his stomach, and he leaned on a warped wooden cane as he smiled at us without his two front teeth. We called him Papou, the Greek word for grandfather, and while we paved a road under his crude concrete balcony this summer, he joined us with his own tool and bucket of cement to show us exactly how far his narrow road could carry us.

One hundred yards, I remember thinking on the day that we walked the dirt road for the first time. What's the point? Reaching the end of the road, I realized it wasn't even an ending, the road just stopped. There was no destination, no real purpose, the dirt just crumbled away into a field of yellow scrub and goats, and that was the end. We were told that by paving this road, the yiayia's, the Greek word for grandmothers, would not have to worry about slipping in the mud when it rained on the dirt road. And so we began, with bandannas and shovels, and gloves and little Greek children who gave us round green fruits that they collected in the folds of their shirts, to pour cement for the one hundred yards of road that had no destination.

As if the grinding of the primitive cement mixer beckoned him, Papou climbed down from his balcony that first morning and propped himself up against the side of his house, and watched as a wheelbarrow dumped the first load of cement in front of him. He disappeared back inside for a minute and returned with a plastic bucket and small metal scraper. For the rest of the day, he scraped the remaining cement from our wheelbarrows into his own bucket, and paved his own piece of the road alongside us. He smoothed the cement with his bare hands as if he were patting his own child, and we wore gloves. He thrust his knees into the moist cement and hunched over the road as if to bless it, even though he was ruining his best, maybe his only, pair of pants, and we washed off our own filthy legs with the hose in the barrel. Papou didn't see that the road was *only* one hundred yards long. He saw that it was *indeed* one hundred yards, and he showed us a pride that gave each one of those yards a purpose.

Towards the end of the first day, as Papou grew tired and slumped once again against the wall of his house, the sky over the village turned a violent green, and we all crowded inside the doorway of Papou's house just before the storm hit. We watched as the wind tore branches off trees and ripped clusters of shingles off the rooftops of nearby houses. Then the rain came. It fell twice as hard as the wind blew, and we all watched in horror from the threshold as our road washed away down the hill. The yiayias would have to be careful not to slip, I thought.

The storm never let up that day, so we abandoned Papou in his doorway and trudged down the hill toward the center of town, letting the rain wash us away with our road. However, something about the rain following Papou's work made us angry, somehow determined, and so we decided to start over again early the next morning at five o'clock. In the dark that morning, the familiar grinding of the mixer was the only sound that gave us our bearings as we groped up and down the road with the wheelbarrows. Our silhouettes against the lifting darkness were colored with the excitement that had seeped through our skin with the rain the day before, and *we* had a road to pave. Hours passed and eyes grew accustomed to the dark, and shoulders hurt, and blisters throbbed, and *we* were paving one hundred yards of road. We worked mostly in silence, racing against the dark, and when the mixer finally shut off, we collapsed in a heap on the ground, dirty, exhausted and cold, with one foot of road unpaved.

When we heaved ourselves off the ground moments later, the first light of morning had broken, and we could see each other's faces again. We stared at one another first, and then lifted our heads slowly up the road. In front of us lay one hundred yards of smooth pavement. And at the top of the road, at the point where the dirt once crumbled into the scrub, Papou stood in the soft cement with his back to us, looking across the field to the warm pink light of the rising sun. And it was at that moment that I realized exactly where our road led. It led to that undefined place where the filmy coating of sunrise blurred with the scratchy points of yellow grass, to form a haven where pride is simple, and yiayias never slip. I've never gone farther in one hundred yards.

Here is Tracy's second essay. Notice how she connects with the reader and the person she helped:

Small details can have a large impact on the course of a day, a year, a life. In what way has a small event had an impact on your life?

In second grade I decided that I would grow up to live in a small house in the country and become a well-known author, and I began to write stories. In sixth grade I switched my plans to moving to California to become a famous movie star, and I took acting lessons. By eighth grade I was determined to be the youngest person to accomplish something, *anything,* and I designed a board game that I wanted to take to New York City to sell for production. As many times as my ambitions changed, the idea that I would grow up and go somewhere in order to do something memorable remained constant. And then I went to Odd Fellows' Nursing Home just down the road from my school.

I started as a volunteer visiting residents at Odd Fellows' on Sunday afternoons two years ago, but it was not until last Fall that I met Mrs. Sarah Olson. She was standing in the driveway of Odd Fellows' as I was leaving after a visit, and I said hello to her as I passed. It wasn't cold, but she wore a hat, mittens, and overcoat, and so I turned around to ask her if she, too, was going on a walk. She said yes, that she went on a walk every day around the circle of pavement in front of us that marked the end of the Odd Fellows' driveway. When I asked if she would like to join me and walk somewhere else instead, she said no, that she just liked to walk five times around. The ring of pavement was no bigger than a generous Duck-Duck-Goose circle, but even on her small walk, Mrs. Olson was happy to have company, and I joined her.

We walked carefully around the outer edge of the pavement, and as we talked, Mrs. Olson kept her eyes focused on the ground in front of her like a new driver. She held a cane tightly in one hand, and a linen handkerchief to wipe her cold nose in the other. Together we talked of collecting raspberries from our respective bushes in the summer, and of sucking the sweet fruit blood from under our fingernails after the picking. We talked until the completion of our fifth circle, and then we stopped at the base of the front steps that led back inside. The way she stood, a little more hunched now than before, her shirt hung off the back of her shoulders, and I could see a name tag reading "Sarah Olson" sewn inside the collar. It was then that I realized we had never introduced ourselves.

With the five circles finished, I thanked Mrs. Olson for the walk, said I hoped to see her again, maybe, and turned to walk down the driveway. I had not made it very far before I heard her voice, thin in the air, call to me, "Wait." I stopped and looked back up the driveway to see Mrs. Olson still standing at the base of the steps. "I'd like to go around a sixth time today," she said. When I asked if she was sure that she wanted to, she answered, "Yes, today I will." And so with a slightly slower step, the two of us made one last lap, then smiled our good-byes and left.

Mrs. Olson is no longer at Odd Fellows', but I still think of her often. I remember the look on her face after she finished her sixth circle, and I remember my own happiness in thinking that maybe I had helped make her that proud. Moreover, I believe that Mrs. Olson probably remembers me. It was a simple, anonymous thirty minutes that we spent together, but even in that short time I think that I left a memory of myself with Mrs. Olson, a mark that I had been there. And I didn't go anywhere. Not to a country house, not to California, not to New York City. Not at all. I just went in circles. My name was not on a front cover or on a movie screen or on a copyright, but I think I accomplished something. And though I may have been going in circles, I didn't end up where I started.

In this essay, Tracy is able to bring in the range of activities in which she is involved:

Briefly elaborate on the activity you find most meaningful.

A prison guard, a clothes washer at a mental hospital, a Burger King employee, a truck driver, a motel chamber maid, an aspiring motorcycle mechanic, an eighteen-year-old runaway father of one, a twenty-three year old mother of three, an alcoholic carpenter, a teacher who has trouble reading three syllable words, and I. They are the Project Second Start class that meets every Wednesday night to earn their high school diplomas, and I am the volunteer who sits in on the class to help explain that the "l" in "would" is silent, and that .9 *is* greater than .100. In the time I have spent with this class, I have taught a man to write poetry to win back his wife who left him, and I have helped a woman spell "abortion" in writing a letter about her week's activities. At the same time that this class has learned from me, I have learned from them that living without judgment on others can be second nature. And just as this class has missed years of its education, so had I missed an important part of my own education before joining Project Second Start. I hope to continue this part of my learning at college.

In addition to volunteer work, I have also been inspired by my work on the Editorial Board of our literary magazine, as News Editor of our newspaper, and as Co-President of our literary society, and I look forward to pursuing literary activities in college.

Lastly, I love playing soccer. After eight years of playing on Varsity, Travel, Select, and Premier teams, and having been awarded All-League First Team recognition on my high school team for the past two seasons, I am serious about continuing soccer in college.

In this essay, Tracy uses detailed narrative to bring forward a powerful idea:

What idea has most influenced your life? Explain.

Standing in my front yard one day this summer, I watched a car creep up and down the road past my house four times before it finally turned into my driveway. Roads in New Canaan are thin and winding, and all the trees look the same, so my parents and I are used to giving directions to travelers who have taken wrong turns. However, this driver was not lost or looking for help, but rather returning at a slow speed deliberately, to a territory whose every bump and twist he knew perfectly. When the man stepped out of his car, he introduced himself to me as the boy who had grown up in the house that I live in now. And though I did not recognize the stranger standing in front of me, I felt I already knew the boy of whom he spoke.

For seventeen years I have collected old glass marbles and matchbox cars as they have surfaced from an abandoned sandpile in my backyard. I connected quickly that the man in my driveway was the child responsible for their burial, and I told him of my collection. He laughed as he remembered his pile of toys in the sand, and when I asked him why he had left them there when he moved, he answered, "I used to play with them every day, and when I was finished playing at the end of each afternoon I would just leave everything there until the next morning."

His explanation sounded simple. When he was young, he would play with his toys when he wanted to, go inside when he wanted to, and return to his sandpile again the next day. However, the fact that the marbles and matchbox cars are still buried today suggests that there was one morning when the boy woke up and decided not to play. There was one exact moment in time when something changed, when he did not return to his sandpile, and he has not been there since.

The idea that there are singular, unpredictable moments in time that divide one stage of life from another has greatly affected my life. I am conscious that something I am active in today may become part of the past stage without my realizing it, and so I commit myself to each project with the belief that I will never do that particular activity in just the same way again.

For example, if I want to publish a short story today, I am not going to worry that I would have a better vocabulary to write it with in ten years. And when I volunteer to teach illiterate adults, I do not question whether I would be more effective after a few more years of my own education. For today I can pursue both of these activities with the capabilities of a seventeen year old, and although the story I write and the class I assist may not be as successful as they would be if I tried them again in ten years, they will invariably be a reflection of my best effort at this point in my life. For as long as I believe that my life comes in stages whose beginnings and endings are invisible, *this* moment is always the right time to write and to work, and I am never too young to try anything.

Finally, Tracy reveals her true nature as a volunteer:

How did you spend last summer?

In fifth grade I was on the Student Council, and that meant that I could meet with the Principal to discuss things like where the new water fountain should be placed. Through ninth grade I was the tallest girl in my class, and that meant that I got to be at the head of the school Chorus line, leading the singers into and out of our holiday concerts. Last spring I earned straight A's in all of my classes, and that meant that I could win an award at the end of the year. Then last summer I worked as a volunteer in the Operating Room of a nearby hospital, and that meant nothing at all. This story is about how a blue uniform and a name tag reading VOLUNTEER SERVICES took me from the top of my class, from the front of the line, to the lowest of job positions, and, most unforgettably, to the bottom line of life and death.

My friends at the hospital were the cleaning crew who emptied our plastic bins three times a day. The doctors were the ones who passed me in the halls and stared at the ground to avoid saying hello. The nurses were the ones who hushed their gossiping voices when I sat down in their lounge. And I was the one who, relegated to the background, learned to find a pride in my simple tasks.

I would pick only the crisp sheets out of the laundry cart to make the beds every morning because they would snap open when I shook them and look cleaner on the stretcher. When I was given a uterus or a gallbladder to carry to the "frozen section," I would run up the four flights of stairs to the lab rather than wait for the elevator, so that the person on the other end might commend me on my speed. And the doctors used to laugh at me when I made medical report packets, because I would collate the papers until at least one pile of forms had disappeared, and then I would replace it with a fresh stack. Stripped of my identity as a competent worker, I held fast to these chores as my proudest accomplishments. And then I met the one group of people in the hospital who had been stripped of even more that I.

The patients walked into the Holding Room, or the "before" room, of the Operating Room where I worked, wearing striped, backless robes and sticky, green slippers. They were each given a blanket, a sanitary cap, and one bed in a line of seven. They were each asked to give up their glasses, dentures, and jewelry. Then I taped a name tag on the end of every bed, and the doctors, who never read the tags, came to me to ask what their patients' names were. Nurses stood over the beds talking quickly, plugging in patients' names to what seemed like a form letter of bedside manner. And when the doctors and nurses left to prepare for each surgery, then it was my turn.

By the end of the summer the nurses had come to trust me enough to leave me alone in the room with the patients, and when I was in charge of the room I would talk to them. The patients would tell me about their homes and their families, and as they were wheeled out of the room we would wave.

In the afternoon of my last day of work I spent an hour talking with the last patient in the room, an old Italian man who told me his nickname was Spaghetti. He told me that he loved jokes, and we laughed together for a while. However, when the doctors came in to take him down the hall, Spaghetti grabbed my hand hard, and we stopped talking. He stared up at me, frightened, and whispered, "Everything *will* be all right." I squeezed his hand. "Yes, everything will," I answered. "Thank you,'" he said and was wheeled out the door. Left alone in the empty room listening to Spaghetti's stretcher roll down the hall, I appreciated the difference between the bottom and the top. For as I stood in that Holding Room in a workplace where behavior seemed determined by hierarchy, my VOLUNTEER SERVICES name tag meant that I was unimportant enough to be caring, and to me that meant a lot.

The Survivor

The student who fits this category in some way has lived through a tragic or difficult situation that has significantly influenced his or her development and outlook on life. If you have faced substantial loss in your life, through the death of a relative or friend, for example, or have yourself survived a shocking or terrible situation, such as a life-threatening disease or violent attack, then you might want to consider writing about it. The college reader will be looking to see the impact of the experience on you and your perspective, the maturity and skill with which you relate the situation, and the relevance of the event to your future development in college.

Amy: A Motivated Dartmouth Applicant Who Lost Her Father at an Early Age

Amy chose to write a Significant Influence essay centered on the loss of her father when she was a little child. She used the tragedy to honor her father and talk about the ways in which she emulated him and saw his memory as an inspiration in her daily life. A straight-A student with diverse interests, Amy was admitted to Dartmouth on Early Decision.

December 29, 1980. My parents, my uncle, and I were flying home from visiting family during the Christmas holidays when I was one year old. We were in my father's Cessna 172 and planned on landing at an airport near our home in upstate New York. There was zero visibility but a light on the instrument panel indicated that we were approaching the airstrip. Everything went dark suddenly, and the plane started shaking as if it were being enveloped by a tornado. My father had miscalculated our altitude, and we had dropped below tree line and were crashing into a dense forest. As both wings were ripped off, the woods clawed at us until we smashed into a tree, killing my father.

Although the death of my father was difficult to come to terms with, everyone knew he had lived each day to its fullest and would not have regretted a minute of his life. He tinkered with electronics in high school, building a robot in his free time. He took a year off from college to devote himself to campaigning for a politician whom he believed in and creating a computer program which helped analyze the demographics of voting districts. He installed a wood stove and built a solar hot-water system on our house, so that we only had to pay two dollars for fuel during the oil crisis. All of these accomplishments are what many people dream about and never get around to doing. If my father had put these things off he never would have had the opportunity to be himself. Also, the warmth of my father's character deeply affected the people he touched. His cheerful attitude, kindness, and forgiving nature put a spark in many lives. His example pushes me to give and to take as much as possible out of my daily life.

At the same time, I have also grown up with a screaming hole in my life, forcing me to take notice. It reinforces how easy it is for someone's life to be so fulfilled one day and over the next. This reality motivates me to live each second to its fullest potential.

Also, by understanding the fragility of life, I realize how important it is to appreciate life while I have it. This is to my advantage because since I grew up with this understanding, I have also grown up being very happy, from being fascinated by sewers at the age of two to loving calculus today. I am exhilarated by hiking and playing the clarinet and by virtually all of the things that I do. When people ask how I can be so cheerful in physics at 7 a.m., or when it is 3 a.m. and I am not yet finished with my history paper, I never know what to say. Should I tell them it's because my father died when I was one year old? I think they would take it the wrong way.

Although I cannot remember my father on a personal level, he has inspired me. I am on a mission to live my life to the fullest, to inspire with my enthusiasm, and to enjoy every moment just as he did.

Stacey: A Cancer Survivor Who Made It to Brown

Stacey was more than just a cancer survivor. A strong and involved student, she chose to relate her battle with cancer by focusing on the loss of her hair and how that symbolized facing her disease. She then used other parts of the Brown application to highlight her major interests:

In reading your application we want to get to know you as well as we can. We ask that you take this opportunity to tell us something more about yourself that would help us toward a sense of who you are, how you think, and what issues and ideas interest you most. (2 pages, handwritten)

I cut my hair in the first days of September when I found out I was sick. Except for little trims, I had not cut my hair since I was eight years old. For that matter, I had hardly ever been sick. Cutting my hair before it fell out made me feel I had some control over my life, which had suddenly taken an odd turn. My twenty-six-inch-long hair became about eleven in one blow. My new cut pleased me as I began the tests to determine the stage of my sickness, Hodgkin's lymphoma, and I enjoyed looking in the mirror even through the stress of my first chemotherapy treatments. Three weeks, they told me, and then my hair would all be gone if it was going to go. But that day, three weeks after Day One of treatment, my hair held on tight as I tugged. For the next week, each day, no hairs would come out no matter how hard I pulled, and I began to imagine myself as one of the lucky twenty percent who would not lose their hair. I congratulated my follicles for holding on so well, for fighting hard despite the drugs that were attacking every fast-growing cell in my body. The next morning, however, four weeks and a day after my first treatment, they gave up.

My hair that Wednesday morning felt limp and fine on my head as I got into the shower, and with every run of my hands a half dozen strands would come out. I was apprehensive, but I tried to be positive about this new experience. Through the school day, I found it entertaining to litter my friends' books with my falling hairs. That afternoon I decided I did not want to have such long hairs falling out all over, though, so I got a four-inch cut. Everyone commented on how attractive I looked the next day, despite the increasing amounts of hair I was losing with each pull. By Saturday, bald patches had developed, and Sunday morning I filled my waste-basket with dark hairs that were falling out everywhere.

Still attempting to have some control, I quickly bought a shaver and went to my best-friend's house where she and my boyfriend buzzed my head. The look was different, but still really stylish. Yet as the fuzz fell out and left white scalp, I began to feel like a sick cancer patient.

My baldness seemed to represent my cancer. I had never had any symptoms, nothing that made me feel I was sick, yet every time I looked in the mirror I stared into the face of my Hodgkin's disease. My parents told me how lucky I was, because when they had been young, it was a death sentence. But the white, round head combined with the puffed-out steroid cheeks made me feel like every one of those ill children I had seen on television and in hospitals. I was unable to escape the reality of having cancer, and my self-esteem was challenged. I have always been quite strong and confident, but left so nude and vulnerable, it was a challenge to stay tough.

I did have a perfectly shaped skull, however, that made my head quite an attraction for artists and photographers, and my friends loved to rub it as if it belonged to a Buddha. I decided it was easier and more comfortable to bare my head than to cover it up, so I avoided hats and wigs as much as possible. I did not care if people looked at me oddly, I still wanted to be myself. Determined to keep as much normality in my life as possible, I tried not to give in to the fatigue and mood-swings I felt and did everything possible to keep up with my full schedule at school. I went to the tennis matches I should have been playing in, intending to cheer on my teammates, but, instead, I fell asleep with my head in my mother's lap.

I wanted people to be comfortable with my illness as well as with my new look. A few people even complimented me on my interesting choice of haircut, and I simply responded, "Thank you," with a smile. To some degree, it was fun to look so striking, but at the same time my baldness was a daily reminder of the cancer I was fighting. No matter how well I carried on and how quickly my tumors receded, I still looked sick.

Finally, in January, about a month after I finished chemotherapy, soft fuzz cautiously began to emerge. I was hopeful, but I discovered that the process of hair growth is frustratingly slow. Yet with every centimeter of dark, soft hair that worked its way out, the more healthy and happy I felt. I was winning, and my appearance showed it, finally. I had never appreciated being able to wear barrettes so much. I felt beautiful and really alive again.

It has been just about a year since my hair fell out, and I have a full head of dark, four-inch, thick, curly locks. My check-ups continue to be clear, and I have no reason to doubt that I will be healthy from now on. I have my hair, I have my health, and life is better. I am not yet sure how this experience has affected my life, but I am getting to the point where I can think about it and begin to try to understand.

Here is what Stacey wrote about her academic interests, and her reasons for choosing Brown:

I enjoy learning in all disciplines, especially language, visual arts, mathematics, and science. For my future education I see myself focusing on science and medicine, especially areas involving the human mind. I have a passion for learning about people: their thoughts, their behaviors, and their health. I hope to work in human health care in the future. I am especially drawn to Brown because of my interest in its science and health majors, particularly Cognitive Neuroscience, Psychology and Community Health. Also, Providence strikes me as full of volunteer opportunities in these areas. I appreciate Brown's flexibility in terms of curriculum and concentration because this would allow me the opportunity to explore more than one of my interests.

I have talked to some of my favorite teachers who are alumnae of Brown, other graduates, and a close friend who is currently a sophomore about their experiences at Brown. During my interview and while walking around the campus, I felt comfortable and at home, as though Brown would fit me well. All I have experienced regarding Brown University has been extremely positive, and that is why it is my first choice of schools.

Brown's "activity" page allows students to create a more narrative description of their involvements:

Throughout High School, I have been involved in a variety of activities, mainly in three areas: community service, theater, and athletics. My activities, in general, reflect my long standing interest in people.

My primary activity this year is HITOPS (Health Interested Teens' Own Program on Sexuality). The time commitment is considerable (six hours a week on average), but the rewards are great—learning and teaching about vital matters such as HIV/AIDS, homophobia, and dating violence. I am developing leadership and team building skills that will serve me for my entire life.

Two summers ago I volunteered at a renowned day-school for autistic young people. I worked 14 hours per week with three- to seven-year-olds, teaching them as well as learning from them. These kids were fascinating to me, and the relationships I formed with them were unique. It was there that my interest in the psychology of the human mind developed.

I have worked with people from diverse backgrounds in my community and elsewhere for several years. Three years ago I traveled to Browning, Montana to live on the Blackfeet Indian Reservation for a month. I assisted in activities to improve the community and was educated about their American Indian lifestyle. Their culture made an enormous impression on me. I volunteered 17 hours per week this past summer at a shelter for battered women and their children and my mother and I have been tutoring a little girl from Haiti for the last year.

Another activity that has been important to me is the Amnesty International group at my school (2 hours per week). I have been a member since tenth grade, and this year I am co-head of the group. We work in close contact with the national organization and focus on international and local human rights. I value being able to make a difference in people's lives.

The Performing Arts Program at my school has been an important and exciting part of my high school experience. We have a wonderful Performing Arts Program and director, and the shows are pure fun for me. I was on the stage crew in *My Fair Lady,* was in *Once Upon a Mattress,* and most recently participated in a tap dancing performance for our school's centennial celebration. The rehearsals take about 12 hours per week.

I have participated in sports throughout my high school career. In middle school, I swam competitively for a United States swimming team, and I continued to swim at school my freshman year. I played tennis freshman, sophomore, and junior years and lacrosse freshman and sophomore years. I was co-captain of my lacrosse team in tenth grade and last year won the Sportsmanship Award for my participation on the JV tennis team.

I have received several other awards in the past few years: the Prize for Excellence in Character and Scholarship in my freshman year; the Spanish Prize that same year; the High Honor Roll and the Honor Roll in all marking periods; and scholastic recognition as a National Merit Commended Scholar and an AP Scholar.

The International Student

International students may live in or outside the United States. We include in this category students who are applying from abroad, as well as those who live in America but want to emphasize their international and cultural background as being of great importance to them.

Amy: An International Student Applying to Architecture Programs

Amy, a strong student of Chinese background living in Hong Kong, had a major interest in architecture and design. She attended a summer architecture program before her senior year in a British system school. This helped her to focus her applications on undergraduate architecture programs in the United States. Amy and her essays fit into both the International Student and Artist categories. In addition to a design portfolio, Amy submitted this essay to Cornell, representing her personality using three objects that best describe her:

Chopsticks come in pairs. One complements the other and together they can do marvelous things. In a similar manner, the creative aspect of my personality complements the practical side of it. Anything associated with the fine arts appeals to my senses. My creative aptitude is complemented by a deep sense of commitment and a conscientious mindset. I feel that these two traits, in tandem, bring out the best in me; just as chopsticks, when well balanced by the user, can perform amazingly dexterous tasks. I see myself capable of facing new challenges with imaginative resourcefulness together with a sensible pragmatism.

A compass is unpretentious yet, indisputably, has a definite mind of its own. It neither makes a lot of noise nor begs for attention, but it makes its presence known in a significant way. It is dependable and unwavering in its direction. The compass leads quietly, confident of its bearing. The projection of quiet confidence is one of my more prominent traits. The strict discipline instilled by swim training, ballet workouts and piano practice has helped me forge my strong sense of commitment in the pursuit of things that I have a passion for. I set about working towards achieving my personal best, both academically and in extra-curricular activities, by staying focused and continually raising the bar for myself as I strive to become better at what I do.

Much like a kaleidoscope, I am the eclectic reflection of the colorful and cosmopolitan cities (San Francisco, Singapore, Tokyo, and presently, Hong Kong) that I have lived in. The international exposure during my formative years has yielded an individual who is not only aware of, but also sensitive to, the indigenous cultural diversity in each place. The ever-changing environment has heightened my curiosity to explore what is around me. These experiences are often exciting, and sometimes offer unpredictable results, similar to the kaleidoscope's randomly-formed and pleasing images.

Living overseas has accelerated my appreciation of the political, economic, and social dynamism in a city like Hong Kong. In a true kaleidoscopic sense, the invaluable opportunities of living abroad in different countries has offered me a chance to capture the brightest source of "light" to reflect the finest images of collective experiences.

The Expatriate

Expatriates are Americans who currently live abroad. Some students who have lived out of the United States but have returned home recently also may fit this category. Expats can present interesting perspectives on America and their foreign place of residence, and often have a great deal to say about independence, intercultural communication and understanding, and diversity.

Jason: A Japanese American Serving the Needy in Hong Kong

An Asian American student living in Hong Kong, Jason was a top student and a strong participant in community service. He wrote about his faith, his academics, and his devotion to public service. He was admitted to Harvard, Georgetown, Michigan, and other top schools. Here is Jason's core personal statement, which he titled "Crossing Over":

I am a skinny, curious, Japanese American growing up on the shores of the South China Sea. Beyond this, I am a Christian traveler. Before me is an uncharted course—another part of my journey across great waters. I have already traveled a long way, sipping vitality from life's turbulent streams. Now, to lead me in the right direction I reach into my rucksack of experience and pull out memories of service in Calcutta, Foshan, and Belilios, which are milestones in my personal quest to learn and to commit. Wherever I go, my faith drives me and will keep me steadfast.

In Calcutta I saw the realities of life in graphic detail. The image of a blackboard at the Nirmal Hriday (The Home of the Destitute and Dying) reading, "24 In, 4 Out, 3 Dead" still haunts me. My path darkened and I hesitated to tread on. The shriveled bodies lying lifeless on cots frightened me. I searched for strength to commune with the summoned in their final moments. We were an intrepid dozen from Hong Kong who merely came to sing but found ourselves immersed in something much more profound. We crossed the invisible boundary that separated us from society's forgotten. The exchange of emotions was moving. I had never sung better. As I departed from this place of sorrow and strength, I placed a canteen of courage in my pack alongside my faith to sustain me on my journey. I then traveled on.

My annual trip to Foshan, an orphanage in Kwangtung province, was another important passage. The cries of one hundred orphans were overwhelming. A sickly blue baby stood out in a crowd of unwanted female infants. She had no chance of survival. I was saddened that this child would miss out on life. Others equally pained wanted to leave. To comfort them I told the tale of my time of trial in Calcutta and offered my fellow travelers a drink from my canteen of courage. Together we lifted the gloom and worked harder to give these children the care they deserved. As I have a final kiss to the orphans, I put a deeper appreciation of my family in my sack. To strengthen me, I carefully bottled the spirit of the blue baby, which whispered, "Live the life that I can't." My journey continued.

During my travels I organized a program at Belilios Public School to teach English to eager, young Chinese. My own experience in studying five languages, equipped me to teach my pupils a new language. Inspired by their thirst for knowledge, I taught them the mechanics of English while sharing my experiences. We laughed and enjoyed the time we spent together. I will always recall my students standing up in the morning to greet me when I entered the classroom. I gave them confidence to put in their own packs, while I placed their gratitude and good cheer in mine.

So here I am at the crossroads. In addition to these perspectives, I draw from my pack tenacity from my years of Kendo, discipline as a Madrigal singer, accountability as Junior Class President, Yearbook Co-Editor-in-Chief, and Vice-President of the National Honor Society. I look upon these experiences and other insights of life along the Silk Road to give me direction in the next phase of my journey. I see before me a life in public service. I dedicate every day of my life to God, who is my compass. Whichever course I choose, the greatest part of my adventure lies ahead.

As a Christian traveler, I know that when I find myself at the end of the road too tired to walk any longer, He will lead me back home. I will then place my burden upon the hill and kneel before the King, and proclaim, "Lord, my journey is over, and this is my story."

Jason was able to adapt this core statement to fit the particular essay questions for several colleges. Some examples follow. For Northwestern's question about fear as a great motivator and the most afraid he had ever been, Jason focused the essay on the fear of confronting the reality of India:

It was my first time in India, it was one in the morning, and it was very dark. I thought I was prepared for this country. Prior to this trip, I was warned of the dangers of eating meat and drinking tap water, but I was not ready for the reality of the vastness and the mass of humanity of India. India doesn't just seep into you, it hits you like a ton of bricks. As I walked out of the airport in Delhi, I was immediately confronted with the chaos of the city. I was frightened; Indians young and old were soliciting their services, some tried to pick up my bags while others attempted to sell me everything imaginable. Others looked at me with haunted eyes. The overall experience was overwhelming. The darkness of the place increased my anxiety. I thought I had made the wrong choice in coming. I wanted to go home.

I was not an unseasoned traveler. I had been to many countries and experienced many cultures. India, however, was an entirely different matter. I can vividly remember the bus ride to the hotel, the cars whizzing by and the lights and sounds of the city daunting. I fell asleep attempting to piece together everything I had seen. It was just a series of horrible visions. The media images of India as a dark, cold continent with people sleeping on the streets, beggars without limbs, and children squatting in sewage seemed to be all true and both frightened and depressed me.

In Calcutta I saw the realities of life in graphic detail. The image of a blackboard at the Nirmal Hriday (The Home of the Destitute and Dying) reading, "24 In, 4 Out, 3 Dead" still haunts me. My path darkened and I hesitated to tread on. The shriveled bodies lying lifeless on cots frightened me. I searched for strength to commune with the summoned in their final moments. We were an intrepid dozen from Hong Kong who merely came to sing but found ourselves immersed in something much more profound. We crossed the invisible boundary that separated us from society's forgotten. The exchange of emotions was moving. I had never sung better. As I departed from this place of sorrow and strength, I placed a canteen of courage in my pack alongside my faith to sustain me on my journey. I then traveled on.

My initial reaction of fear dissipated as I proceeded to look beneath India's ugly face of destitution. I realized to overcome my fear I had to come out of my shell and engage with the Indian people. I talked with the beggar in Agra and through body language learned of his needs. I walked down the streets of Jaipur trying cooked foods from open stalls. I took in the aroma of the open spice markets of Delhi. I danced with a group of young entertainers on the palace grounds in Samode. And from a waiter in Udaipur I learned the nuances of Hindi.

I reached out to the impoverished. Instead of hurrying past the disfigured, I offered them a smile. I befriended the street urchins and they became my scouts to discover countless wonders. What was once so frightening because I chose not to engage myself became less so as I replaced my fear with laughter. A magical transformation occurred as I saw the disfigurement and poverty fade into the background to reveal a country with the face of humanity.

My trip to India taught me that if one chooses to close the gap between people to engage in their lives he or she will be able to see things in a different light. As I travel and experience new people and cultures, I no longer am a transient tourist but rather an active participant.

For Stanford, Jason adapted the essay to fit this question: "If, for a period of time, you could live the life of any individual (fictional or non-fictional), whom would you choose? How does this choice reflect who you are?" He chose an appropriate fictional character who would allow him to stay with his theme of faith and service:

If I could live the life of any person, it would be Christian, the Pilgrim, from John Bunyan's *Pilgrim's Progress.* I am a skinny, curious, Japanese American growing up on the shores of the South China Sea. Beyond this, I, too, am a Christian traveler. Before me is an uncharted course—another part of my journey across great waters. I have already traveled a long way, sipping vitality from life's turbulent streams. Now, to lead me in the right direction I reach into my rucksack of experience and pull out memories of service in Calcutta, Foshan, and Belilios, which are milestones in my personal quest to learn and to commit. Wherever I go, my faith drives me and will keep me steadfast.

In Calcutta I saw the realities of life in graphic detail. The image of a blackboard at the Nirmal Hriday (The Home of the Destitute and Dying) reading, "24 In, 4 Out, 3 Dead" still haunts me. My path darkened and I hesitated to tread on. The shriveled bodies lying lifeless on cots frightened me. I searched for strength to commune with the summoned in their final moments. We were an intrepid dozen from Hong Kong who merely came to sing but found ourselves immersed in something much more profound. We crossed the invisible boundary that separated us from society's forgotten. The exchange of emotions was moving. I had never sung better. As I departed from this place of sorrow and strength, I placed a canteen of courage in my pack alongside my faith to sustain me on my journey. I then traveled on.

My annual trip to Foshan, an orphanage in Kwangtung province, was another important passage. The cries of one hundred orphans were overwhelming. A sickly blue baby stood out in a crowd of unwanted female infants. She had no chance of survival. I was saddened that this child would miss out on life. Others equally pained wanted to leave. This was our Slough of Despond, and like Christian, I refused to permit us to sink into its depths. To comfort my fellow travelers I told the tale of my time of trial in Calcutta and offered my fellow travelers a drink from my canteen of courage. Together we lifted the gloom and worked harder to give these children the care they deserved. As I gave a final kiss to the orphans, I put a deeper appreciation of my family in my sack. To strengthen me, I carefully bottled the spirit of the blue baby, which whispered, "Live the life that I can't." My journey continued.

Throughout his pilgrimage Christian gave counsel to those he met along the way. During my travels I organized a program at Belilios Public School to teach English to eager, young Chinese. My own experience in studying five languages, equipped me to teach my pupils a new language. Inspired by their thirst for knowledge, I taught them the mechanics of English while sharing my experiences. We laughed and enjoyed the time we spent together. I will always recall my students standing up in the morning to greet me when I entered the classroom. I gave them confidence to put in their own packs, while I placed their gratitude and good cheer in mine.

So here I am at the crossroads. In addition to these perspectives, I draw from my pack tenacity from my years of Kendo, discipline as a Madrigal singer, accountability as Junior Class President, Yearbook Co-Editor-in-Chief, and Vice-President of the

National Honor Society. I look upon these experiences and other insights of life along the Silk Road to give me direction in the next phase of my journey. I see before me a life in public service. I dedicate every day of my life to God, who is my compass. Whichever course I choose, the greatest part of my adventure lies ahead.

As a Christian traveler, I know that when I find myself at the end of the road too tired to walk any longer, He will lead me back home. I will then place my burden upon the hill and kneel before the King, and proclaim, "Lord, my journey is over, and this is my story."

For the University of Pennsylvania, Jason needed to transform his essay into a page from his autobiography. He only changed and added a few sentences to make the essay fit this new style. He started the essay this way: "I always have considered myself on a journey. In high school, I was a skinny, curious, Japanese American . . ." The rest of the essay was the same, but Jason added this conclusion: "The idea that in life I was always accountable first to God and then to myself continued to serve me well as I moved on to college. But college is another time and another story." These additions helped Jason give the essay the feel of looking back and continuing a story into the future, which made more sense for Penn's topic.

In addition to adapting his core essay, Jason wrote four or five additional short complementary pieces. For Dartmouth:

What was the highlight of your summer?

As I look back upon my summer, I come across images of my service trip to Foshan orphanage. This summer, I, along with a group of students from Hong Kong, went to Foshan to serve abandoned children. Suffering and sadness were to be replaced by affection and compassion. I chose a club-footed baby and drew her close to me. I felt her heartbeat in my own as we shared the miracle of life. I set my child on the floor and watched in awe as she struggled to stand up and hold on to me. Bracing herself on her deformed feet, she lifted her arms high. Already, as a discarded child she had suffered more than I ever will, yet she still had the courage to stand. Over the week, I saw a dramatic change in the spirit of the orphans, as they transformed from empty, listless beings at the beginning of our stay to effervescent kids when we departed. While I sang to these children and fed them, I felt a deep sense of joy. This once dark orphanage was brightened by the resurgence of life within it. Our group made this happen. Laughter broke the silence of the still compound. The experience was magical and will remain with me for a long time to come.

Which of your pursuits, in or out of school, do you find most fulfilling? Why?

The Yearbook is a demanding school activity. Our organization is entrusted to record faithfully the events of the school year. The yearbook is the one keepsake to which all students will refer time and again. With this in mind, every year from 1997–2001, I have striven to create a yearbook that aesthetically and intellectually stimulates the entire school community. To ensure the success of our efforts, I must run the yearbook as a tightly managed business. We have an annual budget of US $50,000 and I have personally led my team in raising funds of more than twice that amount as an endowment. Everyone is accountable and must be committed. My experience as Staff Member, Editor, Managing Editor, and finally Co-Editor-in-Chief has prepared me to see that everyone does his or her job and does it well. The year is filled with all-nighters, long meetings, and last-minute crises. My duty is to coordinate our efforts so that the drafting process progresses according to schedule. Preparation of the yearbook is the toughest extracurricular job in the entire school. Our reward is the sense of accomplishment at the end of the school year when the yearbook is finally published. The yearbook is the timepiece of the school, and I am proud of it.

The character of the College is a mosaic formed by the life experiences of its students. Share with us aspects of your background that you believe would add to the Dartmouth Community.

In Hong Kong, I have developed a passion for studying languages. In addition to English, I am fluent in Mandarin, Cantonese, and Japanese; and I have begun to study Korean, which I am confident I can equally master. I have used these languages extensively in my day-to-day life. I have lived abroad for fourteen years and have traveled throughout Asia, including the many regions of China; the exotic cities of the Indian subcontinent and the Indonesian archipelago; the rainforests and coastal region of Australia; the countries of Japan, Korea, Taiwan, Thailand, and the Philippines, as well as Europe, Canada, and, of course, the United States. I have witnessed first-hand the historic handover of Hong Kong to China, the collapse of the Asian economies, and the first summit between the two Koreas. My language skills, travel experience, living abroad, and commitment to service have provided me with insight into different systems of government and the underlying societies of Asia. I could bring to Dartmouth a fresh perspective about what life in Asia is really like. Given my background, I feel that I will be able to sensitize others to the coming tidal wave of globalization and make a contribution to the academic and social life on campus.

Laurie: An American in Singapore Accepted to Bowdoin College

An American who spent most of her life living abroad, Laurie was a strong student in an international baccalaureate program in Singapore. She knew she wanted a smaller liberal arts college, preferably in the Northeast. Her Common Application essay focused on her international life and its effects on her worldview:

I stood on the barren and rocky landscape of Inner Mongolia, where it is too cold for the grass to grow, and stared at the endless, cloudless blue sky. It was an eye-opening experience during my junior year when five girls and I went on the "project week" required for our international baccalaureate program. We visited Beijing and Inner Mongolia as a cultural exploration of a country we knew little about.

Our first stop was the train station in the heart of Beijing where we caught the twelve-hour sleeper train to Hohhot, Inner Mongolia. This seemingly routine step proved to be somewhat heartbreaking as we saw the floor blanketed with people, many of whom were most likely carrying all the possessions they had. Mongolian people, by western standards, live in absolute poverty. Their faces illustrate the harsh weather and hard work they have to surmount to survive. Yet these people, destitute as can be imagined, offered the little food they had to us strangers who had nothing to offer them except a mere mention of our gratitude. I found that even though I attend a school whose focus is on the wider world and the services we can take part in to help those in need, the reality of the poverty and our ever growing wealth never really set in until I saw it for myself.

I was born in England, although I am American, and moved to California at the age of two; then I moved back to the same village in England for four years before moving to Houston for two years. I have now been living in Singapore for five years. I feel the experiences of seeing the people of the world, how they live in poverty and in wealth, and how they cope with it, have proved invaluable to my life, as they have shown me infinite ways of thinking. Our trip to Inner Mongolia was not meant to provide anything specific for these people, but to learn what and how we can provide them with help. I learned that to help others, we must first understand their culture, and then try to help within the parameters of their traditions. This forced me to question the standards and beliefs that were ingrained in my mind as a child, and encouraged me to view a situation from more than one perspective. I am learning not to look at a problem only from my Western mindset, but to try to step outside this way of thinking to help someone of another culture. I feel more thankful for what I have, and am always thinking of the poor and disadvantaged in any action or organization I choose to support. As a result, I have helped in service organizations at school, such as Book Recycling and Riding for the Disabled. I hope to continue in many service programs in college, as my high school has taught me that helping others can be a part of the everyday life of an individual. Even if we cannot help worldwide, we can help in our local communities to better the lives of those less fortunate than ourselves.

Laurie's supplemental essay for the Bowdoin application discussed two teachers who had a significant impact on her development:

I feel very fortunate that during my school years I have come across some of the best teachers in the world. These teachers love what they teach. They are willing to go to extremes so that I understand why they love their subject so much. In turn, I have gained an understanding, and a passion, for subjects I knew little about. From elementary school onwards I have had teachers who know how to teach their particular level and subject brilliantly. They know how to capture their students as though they are an audience watching a play.

Mr. H. had the most dramatic impact on my life. He was my teacher in England, a man with a sharp mind and very dry, English sense of humor. He is a History teacher because he loves it. Mr. H. is the reason I love History so much. He opened our class to the realities of the world at a very young age. He took us to Europe to see, first hand, the beaches of Normandy that the allies so bravely stormed in 1944. He made History come alive and made it clear to the modern student. I will never forget the way back to England from Normandy on the ferry. Mr. H. and I had a conversation that lasted the whole way home. I have so much respect for this man as he teaches what he knows to be true regardless of what others think of him. I still write to him and keep him updated on my schooling even though I live in Singapore and he is in England.

In a continuation of Mr. H.'s remarkable teaching, my English teacher, Mr. C. has had the most profound impact on me during my secondary school career. Although Mr. C. has one of the strongest Australian accents I have ever heard, he is actually Greek and has lived in Australia all his life. He adopted part of both cultures. This is something I can relate to, being an American born in the United Kingdom, and having moved four times during my life. It is strange that we should meet in Singapore, a country to which we have no connection.

Mr. C. is an excellent teacher for one simple reason: he loves what he teaches. Not often does one encounter a teacher who wants his students to learn all that he knows, and with so much enthusiasm. In fact, he has so many thoughts and ideas that he wants so desperately to share that he speaks so fast he never actually finishes each word. His area of expertise, and an area he possesses a true passion for is Greek drama. He reads the plays he teaches us in the original language to give us the feel for what the playwright was really trying to say, as so often the literary devices so cleverly composed by the dramatist are lost in the translation.

Since he has so much respect for the playwright and the characters, they come alive in his classroom. Mr. C. is calculating in the manner he teaches. He will analyze a theme or character in a positive light during one lesson, and completely destroy it the next. He does this so that we choose whom we like and what device works for us, as opposed to his students becoming projections of his own ideas. He wants the experience of literature to be a personal one where the choice lies only in each individual's hands.

Mr. C. is one of the hardest English teachers in the school. He will completely dissect our essays and tell us he is looking for an excellent essay, not just a good one. Often we leave the class feeling completely demoralized, but in the end we know we are better for it. We often see him outside of class, where he makes us read our essays to him and then proceeds to force us to defend every line and word. He wants each sentence to mean something. He will discuss everything we want in class without any reservations. Often, he will digress so far he forgets where he started. But I believe his musings are brilliant in that they force us to think. He questions everything and never lets what he believes interfere in the class.

I will remember both of these teachers because they taught from the heart and loved what they taught. Because of these teachers I have a greater understanding of the value of education, as well as a greater desire to achieve as much as possible in the academic arena. I feel I have the tools to become a better writer, and a passionate craving to find historical truths. These teachers made their subject become as alive for me as it was for them.

The Student with a Learning Disability or Special Needs

We often encourage students with a learning disability, physical or medical condition, or other special need to write about living and coping with this condition. This can help colleges to understand your needs, your experiences, and your particular talents. You can discuss how your disability or condition has affected your academic work as well as your perspective on life. You can note its impact on the development of your character and your family life. You can express your thoughts on how your special need will affect your interests and success in college.

Michael: A Dyslexic Student with Interests in Technology

Michael, an A/B student taking several AP classes in a public high school in Virginia, was able to write positively about his learning disability and how it had contributed to the development of his academic interests and personal strengths. His essays helped put his academic record in context and contributed to his admission to Tulane, the University of Colorado, the University of Vermont, and the University of Denver.

I was diagnosed as being dyslexic in the first grade and have had a computer since I was six. I'm not going to go as far as some and tell you that being dyslexic is a gift because it has taught me to overcome great odds, but I will tell you that it led me to an earlier understanding of computers and how they could help me. In my early years my father worked long hours and did some traveling. When I had trouble with my computer I had to either wait for him to come home or learn how to do the repairs myself. When one gets hooked to this lifeline or a game of Quake, time is of the essence. I learned to do a great deal of troubleshooting myself. I grew to become quite knowledgeable in the technical aspect of computers. This form of desperation really led me to my recent job experience.

During the summer of my sophomore year I interned at an Information Technology Corporation that is located in my hometown. For the first two weeks I worked on computers as an intern without being paid just for the chance to learn more about them. After the first two weeks they picked me up as a Junior Tech, which was a great chance for me to put my foot in the Information Technology door. It was now my turn to assemble computers, to run wires, to set up networks, run Y2K tests, research information, and install and set up complicated software.

This was a very valuable experience for me not only because of the extensive amount of information I learned, but also because it was my first job and I finally got to see how a business runs behind the counter. Seeing the ins and outs of this business was very interesting to me and before long I had my own ideas about how to make their business more efficient. Working at this company was a great experience, and was truly an educational summer job. I have since been moonlighting on my own and doing tech work for people in my town. Word of mouth has been my biggest form of advertising.

I believe that I would add to the diversity of the University of Colorado community by simply being me. I have made it a point in my high school career to be open-minded about life and all it has to offer. I am very excited about the prospect of moving across the country and establishing new roots. I have lived most of my life in a rural area in the Shenandoah Valley with an incredible view of the Blue Ridge Mountains. I welcome the chance to explore the west intellectually and to be a part of the Colorado community. I feel that my easygoing personality, appreciation of nature and respect for school spirit and all it has to offer would be a welcome addition to the university. I have a great appreciation for different learning styles and the needs of different kinds of students. I would hope that any college campus would find my knack for the useless fact enjoyable as my friends and teachers have. I know I would add another marble in that jar of diversity.

Here is Michael's statement for another college, in a slightly different form, responding to the question, "What experiences or circumstances have influenced your academic performance?" We encouraged him to send this to every college he applied to, even if they did not ask this specific question:

Being diagnosed with dyslexia at an early age has heavily influenced my academic performance. I think that being diagnosed with dyslexia was a gift, not a curse. It made me work hard and forced me to develop great study habits. I had to work twice as hard to keep up with my fellow classmates. Yes, there were days when I became frustrated, but it made me not only a better student, but a better person. I think my learning disability has made me a more compassionate human being. I don't take things for granted like some students do.

At the age of six I was given a computer primarily for writing and spelling. Tutors as well as my parents helped me daily so I could keep up with my peers. There was not a summer that went by in grades one through seven that I wasn't reminded of my disability. Summer vacations were always planned around my tutoring. I must admit it was not a very pleasant experience. We lived in the country and my mother and I drove great distances to the best people in the area for help. In those days I was not proud to have this disability. I fought my parents all the way when an Individual Education Plan (IEP) was recommended for my new school. I was leaving a small private institution for a large public school and I was sure I could get by. My parents wanted more for me than that. Looking back on it I'm glad I was forced to accept the fact that my teachers needed to understand my situation. I got through almost four years of school now with just teacher updates and no special resource classes. I learned I can never overcome this disability, I just need to learn to compensate for it. I feel as if I can keep up with the best students, primarily because of the amount of time and work I am willing to put into any subject. Dyslexia has helped me so much more than it could ever hurt me.

Ellen: An Equestrienne with Dyslexia at a Small Private High School

Ellen was a B/C student in a demanding private school. She was a competitive rider and had a learning disability that dramatically increased the time it took for her to complete assignments at school. She received some accommodations at school and learned excellent coping skills. She was accepted at the University of Denver. In addition to writing about her major riding accomplishments, Ellen wrote the following statement about her learning style:

"Why can't you read this, Ellen? It is on the third grade level," my fifth grade teacher shouted at me in front of my entire class. Because of my learning differences, reading and writing have been more difficult for me. It takes me longer to read assignments and interpret what I have read. I became self-conscious when a teacher called on me to read out loud; I used to sit in the back of the classroom and hide. Because of this, I started to fall behind in reading and writing skills. Expressing myself verbally was always easier for me. I felt much more comfortable in group discussions. When it comes to writing assignments my ideas flow like a water faucet: they have no organized manner.

I left public school in the eighth grade. I moved to a small private school. After educational testing I was diagnosed dyslexic.

Upon attending my new school, I learned that I have to ask questions, pay attention, and sit in the front of the class. Often, this means working three hours on a one hour assignment.

At my school, I received two forty-five minute learning center sessions for English each week, and two forty-five minute sessions of math. During these English increments I would work on long-term history and English assignments. My advisor and I would create outlines of reading assignments and frequently elaborate and interpret discussions of current classroom topics. These oral and written interactions helped me organize my ideas so I could proceed on my own. I devoted math sessions to correcting tests and working on difficult math problems.

In addition to this support from the learning center, I was allowed extended time on tests in all my subjects. I found this beneficial as I would not have to worry about not being able to finish the test in the allotted time. I also listened to some of the required reading on tapes from the Blind and Dyslexic Society in Princeton, New Jersey. The required foreign language component at my school was waived. These accommodations were recommended by the school and a neuro-psychology specialist who had evaluated me.

Self-advocacy has helped me considerably. It has challenged me to become a stronger individual and empowered me to learn. I now present my opinion in class, ask questions, and assert myself. Additionally, I arrange appointments with teachers to discuss my notes and long-term assignments.

I have learned that it is OK to seek help and that this is my responsibility. Working together with the Learning Effectiveness Program at the University of Denver, I believe I will achieve my educational goals. I am very aware of my learning differences. I have accepted them as being "me." Yet I have learned to overcome these learning obstacles to achieve my personal best. I am determined and confident in my ability to succeed in college. My plan is to pursue my interest in the study of animals, and I am not going to give up. I have a personal commitment to college as I continue to prepare myself for the future.

SENDING A SUMMARY EVALUATION LETTER

If you have a learning disability or other medical or cognitive condition that has affected your academic performance or personal life, and is relevant in evaluating your record and considering your fit for a college's program, then you should consider asking your clinical psychologist, educational specialist, medical doctor, neurologist, or other relevant professional to write a summary evaluation letter to the colleges. He or she may give the letter to you to include in your applications, or they may send the letter directly to each college. Sometimes, the letters will be sent to the admissions office. Other times, the college would prefer that the letter and any additional materials go to a learning disabilities support center. Often, specialists will follow up by sending a full medical or psychological report and speaking with college academic and professional staff, as necessary and appropriate during the admissions process. You should talk with your parents and school or independent professionals about presenting this kind of information to colleges, then contact the college admissions office or learning support center to ask where this kind of information should be sent.

Kenneth Magrath, a clinical psychologist who conducts extensive learning evaluations, offers these two letters as models for the kind of contact he makes initially with colleges:

Date

Director of Admissions
College Name
Address

Dear Director:

I'm writing in regard to Jane Doe, an applicant to [college name] for the Fall, 2002 term. In January of 2001, I had the opportunity to work with Jane and her family in a detailed psychoeducational evaluation. With the consent of Jane's parents I am sending this letter to summarize the results of that work.

Jane is an exceptionally bright woman. Although Jane's *WAIS-III* Full Scale IQ places her well within the high average range of a national sample of test takers her age, this score *underestimates* Jane's potential. Jane has a broad range of above average (≥ 95th percentile) cognitive skills that include: excellent verbal reasoning skills, and well-developed social knowledge and judgment.

Jane has a learning style that strongly favors verbal over nonverbal problem solving. As you know, these learning issues can interfere with a student's performance on standardized testing; the visual-spatial demands of this type of testing create an artifact that may result in scores that do not reflect a student's actual achievement. This is clearly the case for Jane, whose standardized test scores in mathematics significantly underestimate her actual academic achievement.

Jane's strong record in her classroom work is the best measure of her future success as a student. Jane has received no accommodations in her schoolwork. She combines her strong intellect with an intense desire to learn and develop to create a strong, consistently productive academic presence. Jane's strengths as a writer are truly noteworthy. Her writing is fluent, flexible, and grounded in very solid fundamental skills. Her skills and abilities as a writer are uncommon and represent a signal asset in her work as a student.

In summary, Jane Doe is an applicant to [college name] with well above average intellectual functioning and a consistent record of strong academic achievement in a challenging curriculum. A learning style marked by verbal problem solving skills that are stronger than nonverbal skills is present. These issues interfere with Jane's ability to demonstrate the full extent of her academic achievement on standardized tests. Jane is a resilient young woman with powerful academic motivation, and real dedication to her academic efforts. Jane will be a very productive, successful member of your learning community. If I can provide

(continued)

you with additional information, please contact me at [telephone number].

Sincerely,

Kenneth Magrath, Ph.D.

Date

Director of Admissions
College Name
Address

Dear Director:

I'm writing in regard to John Doe, an applicant to [college name] for the Fall, 2002 term. In October of 2001, I had the opportunity to work with John and his family in a detailed psychoeducational evaluation. With the consent of John and his parents I am sending this letter to summarize the results of that work.

John is a very bright young man. Although John's *WAIS-III* Full Scale IQ places him well within the average range of a national sample of test takers his age, this score *underestimates* John's potential. John has a broad range of above average (≥ 80th percentile) cognitive skills that include: excellent verbal reasoning skills, a strong fund of acquired knowledge, superior abstract thinking skills, and well-developed social knowledge and judgment.

John has a learning style that is marked by difficulties with attention, memory, and visual-motor integration. The results of this evaluation also confirm a previously diagnosed *Attention Deficit Hyperactivity Disorder* and a *Learning Disability in Writing*. These learning issues can interfere with a student's performance on standardized testing; the visual-spatial demands of this type of testing create an artifact that may result in scores that do not reflect a student's actual achievement. This is

clearly the case for John, whose standardized test scores significantly underestimate his actual academic achievement.

In summary, John Doe is an applicant to [college name] with
above average intellectual functioning and academic achievement. An attention disorder and a learning style marked by difficulties with attention, memory, and visual-motor integration are
present. These issues interfere with John's ability to demonstrate the full extent of his academic achievement on standardized tests. John is a resilient young man with strong academic
motivation, and well-developed compensation skills. John will be
a very productive member of your learning community. If I can
provide you with additional information, please contact me at
[telephone number].

Sincerely,

Kenneth Magrath, Ph.D.

The Late Bloomer

If you are wondering how colleges will view your poor grades from
freshman and sophomore year, your sudden enlightenment as a junior
or senior, your change of heart, or change of schools, then you may be
a late bloomer who needs to do some explaining. In a positive way,
earnestly, and perhaps with some humor, you may be able to help the
colleges to understand why you were less focused in your early years
of high school, what happened to make you sit up and take notice, and
perhaps why one school worked better for you than another. The
point here is that you will continue your current upward trajectory as
you enter college. You should introduce the past briefly, then move
quickly to what you have learned from it and how you are different
today. Here are some general points:

- Do acknowledge that your early high school performance, in all
  or some of your subjects, was not up to par.

- Do offer some explanation, but not excuses, for why this was the case.
- Do show how you are different now.
- Do express your confidence for the future. You will be successful in college.
- Don't dwell on minor details or get mired in the past.
- Don't try to minimize past poor performance or lack of commitment, or dismiss these issues too casually.
- Don't blame others for things over which you had control.
- Don't blame yourself for things over which you had no control.

Franklin: Gaining Momentum and Focus

A student with 1200 SAT I scores and A and B grades as a junior and senior, Franklin knew he had to account for some C's and inconsistent commitment and performance in his first two-and-a-half years of high school. He chose to convey indirectly his increasingly serious attitude, first in the area of extracurricular activities, and then through reflection on the death of a classmate. With continued focus and persistence, Franklin gained admission to the University of Richmond, Furman University, University of Vermont, and Dickinson College. Here are his two essays:

> The learning process does not take place just through formal academics. My extracurricular activities have been important learning experiences for me. Running for class office and winning an election is an example of a chance that I took that paid off as a great learning experience. I have a lot of close friends, but I am a very laid back person, and I chose not to stand out in a crowd. Recognizing that this was something that I needed to overcome, in my sophomore year I decided to run for a class office—Social Committee, of all things! I won one of the two available slots. I did a good job and in my junior year I challenged myself again by running for Class Treasurer. The election ended in a tie, but I lost the run-off to a close friend. I didn't run for an office my senior

year, but by forcing myself into an arena where I had to risk failure, I gained self-confidence and learned a lot about school government, elections and myself.

I have learned from taking a risk and failing also. Athletics always came easily to me. I started early in baseball, soccer, and skiing. Usually I was among the best players and made all the All-Star teams. My sophomore year in high school brought a rude awakening. I tried out for junior varsity soccer without getting in the proper condition before hand. I fully expected to make the team, having played freshman soccer the year before, but I did not. I was disappointed, but decided I needed to do something with my time and keep in shape, so I immediately joined the Cross-Country team. Although I was not a very good runner, I stuck with it and ran on the team for the rest of my high school career, gradually improving my times. I am proud I turned a disappointment into such a positive experience. This spring I am really looking forward to having a good year playing for the baseball team and I am determined to be in the best possible condition going into the tryouts.

As I contemplate college, I look forward to selecting a school that will help me grow into the best, well-rounded person that I can become, a college that will encourage, even require me, to grow and learn by experiencing new things. I am truly excited by the prospect.

A LIFE LOST

It was 10:15 p.m. when I heard the noise. Bang, bang, bang, bang, bang. The sound rang out like a machine gun going off nearby. It lasted only a few seconds; then silence. I was at a friend's house about a quarter of a mile from home listening to some music. I could never have anticipated what had caused the noise.

My parents were away, but due home that night from a business trip to Mexico. My stepbrother who was home from college at Brown University to watch the house had gone to see a Red

Sox playoff game (Pedro was pitching and he had to be there), so I was alone.

I did not think the noise was anything extraordinary until I saw the flashing blue lights of a police car from a distance. My friend and I decided to investigate. I almost lost my breath when I saw about 100 feet of fence missing from my yard. Rushing to my house we saw that three pine trees, each at least a foot in diameter, were split in half and a new black Honda Accord was tangled high up in another of the pine trees that had lined the property inside the fence. Parts of the fence, trees and the car were scattered across my yard. While I was observing this scene, about 50 of my class-mates came from a party across town. Many of them were crying hysterically. I soon found out from them that two other classmates had been in the car, and one, the passenger, was still stuck in the car. After fifteen minutes of tearing at the car they removed the boy from the car and placed him on a stretcher. While walking with the stretcher to the ambulance the two paramedics suddenly stopped in the middle of the road. Everyone watched as they cut off his puffy coat and tried CPR. He was placed in the back of the ambulance, but was dead before he got to the hospital. I will always remember seeing his white Nikes in the back window as the ambulance pulled away. The driver suffered only minor injuries.

The next day students gathered and the vigil began. What was once our stockade fence, our wall of privacy, became a wall of flowers and candles lit in tribute to the boy who died there. It lasted for days and my parents agonized over how long to leave the scene untouched. It was hard for me to comprehend how quickly the poor judgment of a kid trying to show off had resulted in the loss of a life and the grieving of a whole community. I began to realize how fragile and valuable life is and how we are respon-sible for others. In the weeks that followed the stockade fence was rebuilt, and the steady stream of flowers subsided. Life returned to normal at school and the investigations and search for blame began. I observed the different reactions of those involved. All participants paid a terrible price, but some have displayed true remorse, while others, like their parents, seemed to seek to lay the blame elsewhere. It has been a year now. New trees have been planted that someday will line the yard, and a memorial race has been started, but a boy's life was lost that never can be replaced. I continue to reflect on the event, which makes me even more determined to make the most of my life.

The Fallen Angel: The Student with Something Negative to Explain

Everyone makes mistakes. Some are more serious than others. Perhaps you have been expelled from school, or you failed a class, or you were arrested for possessing alcohol. You do not always need to relate these experiences to the colleges, but sometimes it is appropriate to do so, when personally explaining the significance of the events and their impact on you will help them evaluate your application and appreciate your development as an individual. Talk with your parents and counselor about writing on a potentially risky topic, the expectations for and ramifications of sharing information about a negative incident, and how the tone and content of your essay reflect on you as an individual and an applicant. If you have erred in the past, your hopes for college are not misplaced. Admissions officers have heard from and admitted many students who wandered off the path in many directions and for many reasons. Here are some guidelines:

- Do consider addressing the issue yourself. You can make the best case for what you have learned and why you are still a strong applicant.
- Do talk to others about your decision to share information about a sensitive situation.
- Do stay positive. Focus on what you have learned, how you have changed, and what you hope for the future.
- Do be yourself and let your character shine through.
- Don't "overshare." You may not need to relate information about an arrest, a drug problem, a battle with depression, or a cheating incident, for example. Find out what your school or your teachers

are likely to share. If an incident was school-based or resulted in a school disciplinary action, then the school will be more likely to share information, either in response to a college's application question about disciplinary actions or as a matter of course. Some schools will share nothing at all.

- Don't feel you have to share something if it was "in the past" and has been settled for a long time. If an event or issue has no bearing on your college applications or life, you may want to refrain from mentioning it.
- Don't dwell on the personal or negative details. You may be able to note that you were disciplined for an academic infraction, or removed from school for use of a proscribed substance, or set back by a battle with depression or anorexia, without taking all of your time to talk about the details of the situation or incident.
- Don't be afraid to take a risk and talk about a crisis or lesson that was a major learning event in your life.

Special Circumstances

Often students will ask us how much is appropriate for them to reveal in writing to colleges, and how to go about relating an experience or situation that has significantly affected them in a unique way. You may decide to write one of your essays about such a set of circumstances or write a separate letter to the colleges informing them of what they need to know. Here are a few common situations that you should explain in your writing:

- Poor grades in a particular term due to a serious illness
- Missing advanced courses due to limited offerings of your high school
- Few extracurricular activities because you work after school and weekends to put away money for college, or because your school does not offer such activities
- Living with a single parent and having to help with your brother or sister, leaving little time for outside activities

- Multiple school changes, because of family moves or other circumstances, and thus a confusing transcript
- Experiences as a member of a racial, ethnic, or religious group, and how that identification has affected you
- A very different high school transcript, due to home schooling or a professional athletic or acting career, for example
- A postgraduate academic year, a learning disability, a significant tragedy in your life, an expatriate living experience, an international background, or other particular aspects of your life which fit some of the types we have identified in this chapter

Martha: An Expatriate Returned Home to Boarding School and Then Yale

Martha had a difficult but ultimately valuable task ahead of her. She needed to explain her multiple school changes and life as an international student. She had not participated actively in many extracurricular activities at school, since she had only recently returned to the United States. However, she had strong interests in math and science, excellent grades, and a mature and educated worldview.

"Martha, where did you say you were from again?" was the typical question my first few days at my new American boarding school. Most of my classmates would respond to a similar question with one distinct location that could be easily pinpointed on a map: New York City, Iowa, Hong Kong. My response, on the other hand, was a little bit different. "Well, last year I went to school in Thailand. This year my family is living in Kuwait. I'm a junior boarder in and I spend my summers in Connecticut." While most people's roots are very definite, mine are more abstract. They are not sunk down in one place, but rather are an extensive system, reaching people and places across the globe. Happily though, this has played a major role in molding who I am, how I see the world and what I want to accomplish in it.

I have had the opportunity to experience new places and to meet new people for as long as I can remember. As the daughter of an energy company scientist and executive, I moved all over the United States from the time I was two until I was about nine, when I started moving all over the world. I am convinced that there is something about my many homes that has given me a different outlook on life. Most influential of all was probably my four years in Indonesia from grades 4 to 7. My father once told me about a concept known as Value Programming. The behaviorist quote he liked to use was, "Who you are is where you were when." For me, the when and where were my formative years in Indonesia. If there is any truth to this theory, then I think that being in an international environment, when I was just starting to assess my own values, had perhaps the greatest impact on who I am now. Living in Jakarta, I learned to love not only Indonesia and its people, but also the diverse international community I resided in. We were all "third culture kids." I grew comfortable with not being able to pinpoint exactly where I was from; I was a young citizen of the world, not of one particular place. I think that coming back to a small bedroom community in the States, following my stay in Indonesia, was when I really came to understand how that influence had changed me. I still loved being an American. However, there were times when I realized that my friends and I had different outlooks. They were very locally focused, while I resided in the bigger world.

Since then, I spent my sophomore year in Thailand (another great academic and cultural experience cut short by the Asian Economic Crisis) and then moved to Kuwait shortly before starting at my current school. Because of my internationalization, my strong interest in math and science, and my desire for diversity I find I view the world differently than many of my classmates. I see the world from my background, one where multicultural is normal, good and beneficial. Diversity is interesting not threatening. Globalization is an opportunity to connect with friends. My bedroom community is not the center of the world but a corner. Living, traveling and interacting across borders, continents and cultures is exciting but not unusual. Math and science are not necessarily male domains. They and we do not have distinct definitions.

I have used my Junior and Senior years of high school in America to focus not so much on cultural diversity but more on a deepening intellectual diversity and development. I have learned to thrive on my own as an individual, not only with a diverse geographic background, but also with a distinct intellectual one. While I join the majority of my dancing and theater friends in finding beauty in prose and dance, I also see something special in the structure and order of calculus problems. I am proud and happy to be one of the rare girls in both my multi-variable calculus and my AP physics classes. I have felt free to be my own individual, to work on developing my own passions and to share them with others. Certainly, my experiences and view of the world shape my aspirations and what I want to do in it. Of all the many changes, a constant has been my passion for learning at the most challenging level.

To continue this direction, I am seeking out the most stimulating environment available in college. I want to utilize my strong math and science abilities to explore a major in engineering. I hope that as an engineer, I will be able to carry my love for math and science into my adult career. Ultimately, I aspire to translate that strong technical base into a career in international business, finance or Foreign Service. I hope this will allow me to work, perhaps live, internationally and thus, to be able to share my academic loves and professional capabilities with others, especially my own family. In the next four years, I hope to continue to grow as an individual and to learn more about my chosen field. Just as important, I would like to study at an institution where it is possible to reach out beyond my chosen field and to experience the cultural and intellectual diversity present. To me this is the best kind of learning. I hope that Yale can help me attain my goals.

Anna: A Bicultural Student Living in the United States

Anna was accepted to the University of Pennsylvania after presenting herself in a way that showed her bicultural background and her sense that Penn was the type of environment in which she would flourish. A student at a small school in the United States with many privileges, Anna needed to explain appropriately why she saw herself as different from many of the other students around her, and how this affected her college decision:

"Di me con quien andas, et yo te digo quien eres." As a child, I heard my mother repeat this Spanish proverb frequently. She was saying to me, "You are who you are amongst." I cannot think of another phrase that is more true when I think about college. College is not only an academic institution, but also a place where lifelong friendships are made and personalities are developed. A teenager is molded into an adult when he/she leaves the household in which he/she grew up and ventures into university life. With the cultural opportunities existing in our world, one must understand and appreciate many types of people in order to be successful in any field or profession.

When I began my college search, Penn was the first university that I visited. I walked onto the campus and suddenly was drawn by some inexplicable force. I had not even been on a tour or at an information session, but something inside of me became ecstatic about the university. Going on a tour and sitting through the information session only reconfirmed my gut reaction for Penn. Thus, when asked "what aspects of Penn do you like the most?" I wish that I could write, "everything."

I perceive the University of Pennsylvania to be a microcosm of the world. While walking down Locust Street, I saw many faces of color and many diversely clothed individuals, forming a union, which I had never seen before. There seemed to be so much cultural mix within a mere half mile stretch, and within that mix, I sensed that each student was contributing his/her background to form myriad "outside the classroom" educational experiences. I believe that I, too, have something to contribute to the University of Pennsylvania campus.

Having come from a bicultural background, with a Venezuelan mother and an American father, and having been raised with two languages, I have seen the "best of two worlds." Whether it is learning to ride a bike, or learning how to Flamenco dance, my existence has been formulated from two perspectives. I was raised in a small town with a very high standard of living and attended a private school since kindergarten. As a result, the South American part of me has been most expressed in my home and on vacation trips outside of Connecticut. Now I am ready to share my culture that I have been unable to show freely. I am enthusiastic to speak Spanish with friends outside the classroom and to teach them various Venezuelan cooking secrets. I also want to recite Shakespearean poetry and develop my Anglo heritage to the fullest. Essentially, I am interested in fulfilling the individual within myself.

This past summer, I was able to express the individual within me when I attended the Harvard Summer School for eight weeks. Among all of the freedom and independence, I feel that I benefited most from the diversity of my environment. I was able to find a small piece of "me" within the diversity. I was more apt to socialize with those who were coming from places foreign to me than those who were similar. The impact of each different person affected my overall beliefs, my curiosity, and heightened my intellectual awareness of the world in which I live. I am anxious to explore in college what the world has to offer. I believe that I would be most successful at the University of Pennsylvania given its diversity, renowned educational facilities and faculty, and the environment in which I feel so content.

The Postgraduate or Student Taking a Year Out

Many students take an additional year after they graduate high school before they enter college. They may opt for an academic postgraduate year at an American or international boarding school to pursue higher level academics, improve their athletic skills, or mature personally and socially. Some students may take a more independent year out of school. These students may take classes at a local community college, work or pursue an internship or volunteer experience, study abroad and travel, or focus on an athletic or artistic talent. This situation is different from being admitted to a college during your senior year, putting down a deposit, and then asking to defer your admission for a year. In that circumstance, you will not be allowed to take full-time college-level coursework during your year out, and you will be expected not to apply to other colleges and universities while the college to which you were admitted holds your place. For those taking a true postgraduate year or year off—either before pursuing college admissions or after not being admitted to any desirable colleges during senior year—writing about the interim year choice and experience should be an integral part of a college admissions essay. You will need to explain why you took the additional year, what you are doing with it, how it is helping you to learn about your personal goals and academic direction, and what you foresee as the right college environment for yourself in the future.

Tony: An Actor Pursuing His Passion for a Year

Tony was admitted to the University of Pennsylvania after taking a year to study acting at the American Academy for the Dramatic Arts after high school. In a cover letter to the admissions office and a personal essay about the meaning of acting in his life, Tony effectively explained the substance, grading, and process of the academy's program, and discussed his decision to try the conservatory program and subsequently to apply to liberal arts colleges. Here is his cover letter:

To the Committee on Admissions:
    As I explained on my application, I am taking this year off at the American Academy of the Dramatic Arts in New York City. The

Academy is a conservatory program devoted to teaching actors proper technique for the stage—focusing on voice, alignment, and projection of sound. A trained actor carries no tension in his body and no accent in his speech. He is able to take on characteristics, but not limit himself with any. Thus, the Academy teaches the phonetic sounds of General American Speech (a stage speech from which you can distinguish the actor's point of origin as North America, but nowhere specific.) General American is still the English language, but can seem quite different when compared to our dialects. Mastery comes only with habitual use. The students of the Academy are expected to use the proper sounds in their everyday speech as well as in scene work in Acting class. The Phonetic Alphabet and the correct formation of General American are taught in Voice and Speech class.

The alignment of the actor is also very important. The slightest tension anywhere in the body can hinder not only movement and freedom of expression but the very sound the actor makes. Since actors make their living by expressing and speaking, these sometimes hidden problems can be very serious. The Academy stresses the importance of good posture and a tension-free "instrument" through its classes in Movement. Relaxation exercises, choreography, and Alexandrian technique help the actor find his or her problem areas, release them of tension, and correct any alignment issues. Here, as well, mastery can only come with constant awareness of the physical being and the correction of any issues.

Stage actors also have the added job of projecting the sounds and emotions that they are portraying to the back of any house. Both in Voice and Speech, and Vocal Production classes students are taught how to support their sounds. Since the principles of good speech and singing are the same, Vocal Production class is a chance for actors to make that connection. It is a class where students are assigned songs to experience the musicality of the language through singing. Voice and Speech is a rigorous set of exercises and drills to both make the actor aware of support, and to strengthen his ability to do so.

On top of the technical classes, the American Academy teaches Theater History and Acting Styles in the second semester. Both courses are designed to get actors to read and experience plays of different periods and, in Styles, perform scenes from them. These classes require much outside research. In Acting Styles, for instance, the first assignment was to research and report on Renaissance Italy. The reports helped round out the picture of Italy during the period, thus helping to illustrate the world that gave Commedia Del Arte its material. Then the following assignment was to create a scene using all of the guidelines of Commedia (the Italian improvisational comedy which was the inspiration for most of what we find funny today!).

All in all, the American Academy of the Dramatic Arts is a serious acting conservatory devoted to creating actors. The courses are designed to instruct in proper technique and the standards of the school are set very high. While there is a grading system in place, the letter on the transcript is not nearly as important as the evaluations that accompany them. These grades, also, are not based on any tests but simply on the rate of development of the actor and his instrument. A's are said to be perfection—a student receiving an A has nothing else to learn from the school. Thus very few A's are given during the first year because everyone has something to learn or improve. Native to an acting school, the grading system cannot be directly compared with those found in high school or a liberal arts college. Even though the letters are the same, they are based on and scaled by entirely different elements.

Thank you very much for your time.

Sincerely,

Here is Tony's personal essay on acting, his decision to pursue it wholeheartedly for a year, and his desire to move on to a broader educational program:

I have always loved to act. As children, my sister and I would put on performances during our parents' dinner parties. We would write the scripts, create the costumes, and even charge exorbitant admission prices like the real theater. When not in school I always had some play rehearsal to attend, and during high school, Drama became one of my primary extracurricular activities.

Academics, however, have always taken first priority in my life. I have also always enjoyed school, no matter how "unhip" that is say. So when the time came to think about furthering my education I was torn. Theater had only been a hobby to me before. Did I want, and could I handle, theater school? I filled out several applications to liberal arts colleges, and then later auditioned for the American Academy of the Dramatic Arts. I was accepted at several colleges, but when The American Academy accepted me I decided that I wanted to give Drama a serious try. At this stage of my life there is more room to try new directions and I knew that someday I would kick myself if I passed up this opportunity.

As my first day at the Academy drew closer, I began to doubt my decision. Every night was a different dream about showing up to school naked or trying to explain to a room full of Clove smoking art students that there had been a big mistake. What would classes be like? Surely they would be different than the kind I had experienced, but would we have to pretend to be various inanimate objects? Whenever I was all alone in my house, I could almost hear the teacher's voice: "Now class, become the carrot! Feel carrot from every pore of your being!" Or even worse yet, "Everyone, find your inner child!"

Then the first day arrived and I was truly surprised. The American Academy of the Dramatic Arts is an institution devoted to creating actors and on the first day it was evident that learning is the goal. My teachers are very serious about the craft and approach it from an intellectual standpoint. I am constantly amazed by them because they can break down and explain a large task with ease. They understand the problems that young actors often face and can set about addressing and correcting them. During all of my time at this school, I have never been forced to "become a table" and I have never once heard the words "inner" and "child" in the same sentence.

The program has taught me good posture, proper breathing, and the International Phonetic Alphabet—the building blocks of good technique. In addition I have learned to have the confidence and presence to make changes happen. I have grown since my first day at The American Academy of the Dramatic Arts, and I have discovered what I truly want from my education. I love the theater and I always will. I have great respect for those who devote their lives to it, but I have come to the decision that I feel off-balance in a conservatory program. Theater is one of my great loves, but it is not my only passion. I want to pursue a Liberal Arts degree. I may stay involved in the Theater, but there are so many avenues to travel, and I want to be prepared for every single one.

The Transfer Student

If you have enrolled in college courses after graduation from high school, then you will almost certainly be considered a transfer applicant to any other college to which you might apply. This can be the case if you are taking several classes at a local community college, or if you have studied full-time for a year-and-a-half at a residential college or university. Your job in writing as a transfer applicant will be slightly different from that of a student applying to colleges directly from high school. In addition to covering all the bases of personal description, you will need to explain the rationale for your proposed move from one institution to another. You will need to come across as even more mature, self-directed, knowledgeable, and focused. Admissions readers will be looking for you to have an understanding of the logic of your transfer and to explain:

- Where you are now,
- How you got there and why you chose that direction,
- What you have learned about yourself and about what you want in college personally, socially, and academically, and
- How the specific college to which you are applying fits your needs and interests.

Transfer essays may be slightly longer, and they often take on a more autobiographical and direct tone. We encourage transfer applicants to make an even greater effort to contact colleges personally, directly, and knowledgeably. Since most colleges take very few transfer students as compared to first-time freshmen applicants, they will be looking for you to make the case to them as to why you are prepared to enter their institution, how the college or university fits you, and what you expect to study and become involved in once you join the campus community.

Patricia: A Spanish Student Transferring from a Small College to a Large University

Patricia, a native of Spain, entered a competitive American boarding school in the middle of her high school years. She did well, but it took her some time to adjust and to begin the college admissions process. With such a late start, as well as an academic record and standardized test scores that were steadily improving but not well established, Patricia found herself with few college choices available as a graduating senior. She spoke several languages, was widely traveled, and ultimately wanted to pursue international relations and the study of German in a large, urban, diverse university. However, she chose Macalester College, a small, challenging, liberal arts college in Minneapolis/St. Paul, as an excellent place to begin her higher education. Although she planned to apply elsewhere as a transfer student after a year or two, she put forth her best effort at Macalester to get involved and succeed academically. By the middle of her first year, Patricia had an A– average, strong faculty supporters whom she had met in the small classes available at Macalester, and a good sense of what she wanted in her next university environment. She wrote these two essays for the University of Pennsylvania, where she was admitted for her sophomore year.

> From the beginning life has offered a source of challenge for my father. After the Civil War, life was difficult in Spain and everyone including my young father had to bear the burden of economic hardship. In some way, all of the success my father has gained from life has been the result of his great determination and resourcefulness. But, like him, everyone reaches a point in life when he/she finds someone who opens a door. For my father, this

occurred when he was attempting to pursue an education. And of all his stories, this one has taught me that, like my father, I, too, carry that perseverance and confidence in myself to go after what I truly desire.

After he earned enough money, my father, full of excitement, went to pay the fees for matriculation at a local university in Spain. There, a school official denied his matriculation because of his economic status. Determined to find a way, he set forth to find someone who would help him with this situation. Without hesitation, he headed for the city's mayor. After passing the guards and asking the secretary, he headed toward the authoritative door. At the threshold, he encountered a man coming out of the same door accompanied by two other men. Because he recognized him by his air, my father approached the mayor and resolvedly asked, "Is this the mayor's office? I need to see the mayor!"

Astonished, the mayor replied, "What's wrong son? I am the mayor." Between breaths, my father affirmed that it was an important matter and that only the mayor could help him. Taken aback by the audacity of this intrepid young man, the mayor excused the other two men, and went back into his office with my father. After hearing the story, he gladly agreed to write my father a personal note for the head administrator allowing my father to matriculate in all the subjects he desired. On a final note, the mayor wished him success, mentioning that he had been impressed by his courage.

That letter opened the doors necessary for my father to achieve his goal. Not only did this benefit my father, but it later rewarded the mayor as life made their paths meet again. When the now retired mayor was building his summer residence on the coast, he could not have known that the person he called for assistance was that young man who once stormed into his office, now one of the best known landscape architects in the country.

My father's determination is still easily seen and it is a quality I have inherited as well. Many of the values and standards I hold have come from my father. I feel I am a carrier of the great capacity of sacrifice manifested by my father who taught me that there are no impediments if it truly is my wish to attain my goals. In my eyes, he is an example of success and achievement. He is my source of strength and my most ardent supporter. Although my life is much easier because my father has provided well for me, I chose to embrace challenge by taking the initiative to stay abroad in America and pursue my own vocation, confident that I would succeed.

My father's open-minded views and spirit of determination have affected the course of my academic career. I have learned the importance of embracing challenge in order to improve, and consequently reaching what truly fulfills me. It is my desire to seek admission as a transfer student at the University of Pennsylvania, enabling myself to access a challenging and demanding curriculum in which to grow and excel. I intend on pursuing the study of International Relations, to then later work in the European Union, or in a supranational organization, strengthening relations between countries. But like my father, I too seek any opportunity that will provide me with the means to thrive. I will follow the example of my father's perseverance and work ethic in pursuit of my life and career aspirations.

After this more personal essay, Patricia presented the logical and specific reasons why she wanted to transfer from Macalester to Penn:

As I evaluated my choices of colleges during my senior year of high school, I was attracted by the size of Macalester College and its student-to-professor ratio. Macalester offered a very diverse student body and high academic standards. Among my teachers in school, it was also highly regarded.

Not knowing exactly what to expect from college life, after arriving here and engaging in the school community, I became impressed by the serious academic environment that Macalester provides, but even more so by the seriousness of its students. It is a competitive atmosphere in which students are also close friends and helpful classmates. Another component of Macalester's academic excellence is the availability of its professors. One can always meet with them when one feels the need, either for academic reasons or for simple advice.

After adjusting to the new environment and looking into my majors, International Relations and German, I became disappointed with the International Relations program at Macalester. I discovered that, although it is offered as a major, International Relations is a patchwork from many other departments. There is not the strong, cohesive program I was expecting. While it is necessary to supplement the study of International Relations with other perspectives, I also believe that the core of the major should be a solid one. There are, on average, only four courses under International Relations per term. And through the influence of other stronger departments, this spring three of these courses focus on the social, cultural and economic situation of the same region.

This narrow course selection has been discouraging. I have realized how I would have to bend my personal interests to the course offerings. Many classes are only offered one semester every other year, and typically they have only one section. One can surely acquire a broad International Relations major at Macalester. However, the lack of a strong foundation within the program hinders its students.

In addition to my disappointment with the program of International Relations, the language program at Macalester is small and limited. There are few professors and there is not a wide selection of courses. I made the decision to double major this year because I want to use my languages to further my future career goals. For this reason, I also want to enroll in a strong language program that will allow me to enhance my abilities. After speaking with some of the professors and students in both departments throughout the year, I have reflected upon what I need during my time in college in order to be competitive in my chosen field.

Through my experiences, I have realized that the program at Macalester cannot adequately meet my academic needs. The strong foundation of a Penn education will provide me with the competitive edge I seek. It is my intention to major in both German and International Relations because it is my goal to work either for a multinational corporation desiring to merge and reinforce its international relations, or for the European Union, strengthening relations between countries. The depth of study at Penn will provide me with the skills and knowledge necessary to obtain these goals. Through the program and opportunities offered by the University of Pennsylvania, I will be able to focus my studies and meet my interests.

It is my intention to pursue a major in International Relations, selecting as my field of interest, Western Europe, and security studies. I will also complement my major with courses in economics, business, and political science. Along with International Relations, I plan to major in German. Languages have always been an important element in my life. I have felt the need to learn them from a young age, and they are key in today's society. Learning a language is the most accurate approach to learning about a certain culture and history. For both in International Relations and German, Penn creates the type of academic environment I seek for building a diverse and competitive foundation.

In addition to the classroom, Penn's diverse student body and location will allow me to learn about new cultures, as I share my own cultural traditions and life experiences with others. I also feel that the interrelation between graduate and undergraduate students is a necessary one. It enables all students to work together and learn from each other's experiences. The proximity to Philadelphia and other East Coast urban centers will allow me to experience international issues first hand, and will afford great opportunities of internship programs.

I am also excited about opportunities for a student who seeks to satisfy his or her interests outside a major. I have always enjoyed courses such as acting, literature of the absurd and music outside of my school's requirements. I have a passion for art history, which I have been developing since I was young as an influence from my parents. I find that Penn's curriculum will allow me the time to dedicate to the other areas, outside my majors, which are part of my interests. It will give me a chance to venture into new fields of academia which may not, otherwise, be discovered.

Penn seems to provide the opportunity for students to enhance and satisfy their intellectual lives. This combination of learning both inside and outside of the classroom is a unique way of developing knowledge and enriching myself.

After weighing the possibilities available to me at Macalester and those offered at Penn, there is no doubt in my mind that transferring to Penn is the best fit for both my academic and personal goals.

Miscellania: Other Strong Examples of Writing on Different Topics

This response to Haverford College's question about how the college's honor code will affect the applicant shows individuality and sincerity:

My Latin teacher, Mr. Davison, taught me that integrity is infinitely more respectable than an A in any course. This sentiment always struck a chord with me. If someone does not earn a grade, it is nothing but a mark on paper. With this understood, Mr. Davison proceeded to infuse the classroom with a sense of trust and respect for the student that I never found in any other class. This trust and respect is what I seek in my higher education, which is why I believe Haverford's Honor Code is of the greatest significance in defining the college and my interest in it.

I see myself succeeding at Haverford because every class is based on a sense of trust that is difficult to find in higher education. Not only will I know that my grades are earned and untainted, but I will also know that the grades of my peers are earned. This is not to say that I believe that the Honor Code is infallible, but I believe that it encourages a respect for integrity throughout the campus. The faculty of Haverford continues this trust through its accessibility and devotion to the education of the undergraduate. The individual attention that goes into each student fosters a trust that I have had the joy of experiencing with my Latin teacher and I do not wish to give up. I see the Honor Code as fostering respect and trust between the student body and the administration, whereas Plenary will serve the same function between the student body and the administration.

I am eager to have the opportunity to be an active member of the Haverford College community. At my high school, I found that the students had little or no control. Haverford's Plenary is the polar opposite of the government I have found unproductive at my own school. I see Plenary as integral to the Honor Code because it gives students the authority to change their environment if they feel that change is necessary and to assume responsibility for the changes that are made. This ability for the individual student to change the environment means that the administration must listen to the student because they are working with the student to initiate change.

The Honor Code instills integrity in each student because it makes each student responsible for his or her own actions. Whether it is in the plenary government, in academics, or in my own personal life, the Honor Code will enable me to take the utmost responsibility for each of my actions. Most of all, the Honor Code demonstrates a respect for the student which is the key to education. I am sure that the Honor Code will allow me to be fully accountable for my actions and allow me to enjoy all aspects of my education at Haverford.

This specific and personal response to the "Why us?" essay for one college helped this aspiring public servant gain admission. Notice the detail on both the author's commitment to service and politics and the university's offerings:

I have been fascinated with politics and public service ever since my parents brought me, at the age of seven, to Washington D.C. for the inauguration of President George Bush. Since then, I was genuinely moved by President Bush's "1,000 points of light" speech and General Colin Powell's volunteerism initiative. As a direct result, I have been actively involved in my community either as a coach for younger children on the baseball field or volunteering to help in local political campaigns. My interest in public policy was further enhanced after I was selected to attend a high school's Institute in Politics and Government where I studied political theory and public policy.

Following this, I created a non-profit organization whose dual purpose is to: 1) encourage young people to give something back to their community through volunteerism, and 2) to collect small contributions directly from children and to donate the accumulated proceeds to assorted children's charities. In short, the goal of this organization is to demonstrate to young people that their individual, small steps to better their community can "make a difference." In addition, by instilling the notion of social responsibility at a young age, there is a better chance that as adults, they will continue to help improve society.

The organization has received an enormous amount of support locally and nationally. The endorsement letters from congressmen, senators, and governors have overwhelmed me. Whether it has been Governor Terry Branstad of Iowa, who said, "There are far too many Americans who think that their personal contributions of time, talent, or financial resources don't really make a difference. Your organization attacks this unfortunate myth head-on . . ." Governor James B. Hunt of North Carolina, who said, "'I share your concern that our youth need to develop a sense of social responsibility in order to become socially responsible adults, and commend you for taking on this initiative . . ." or State Assemblyman Joseph E. Robach of New York, who said, "This venture will be challenging but very rewarding, and I may add is quite commendable . . . Your innovation is an example to all, those your age and younger . . .," the extraordinary amount of praise has been most encouraging. I would like to bring our work to my college community to encourage the student body to give something back to those less fortunate in the local area.

Due to my interests in politics and public policy, the university is an excellent match for me. I was especially impressed with the public policy program and the university's commitment to the intricacies of proscriptive analysis: the process that a person should use when determining the best way to solve a problem. It is crucial that our society have public servants in the future with the ability to solve problems in order to lead our nation to greatness. The only way to ensure this is through education. I hope that my college education will provide me with the knowledge and the skills necessary to fulfill this ideal. I have studied assiduously throughout my educational career and have partaken in rewarding activities, such as being a debater and founding a service organization to prepare myself for public service. I have decided to make the university my first choice because I want to pursue a strong liberal arts education with a focus in public policy while simultaneously continuing to make a positive impact on others through community service.

Another bicultural student, this writer used the unique spelling of his last name to walk the reader through his experience of America and his own family in a successful essay for the University of Chicago:

ELEVEN LETTERS LONG

My palms were sweating and my eyes darted nervously around the room. It was the end of the day and soon I would be heading home on the big, yellow bus, but first I had to pass the test! Before we were dismissed each day in kindergarten we had to complete one of the usually simple tasks of either reciting the alphabet or our phone number, or spelling our names. Today was Friday and before we were allowed to go home and dream away the weekend we were told to spell our last names. "Our last names," I thought. How on earth did they expect us to complete such a challenging task on a Friday afternoon? My friend Charlie sat beside me patiently and calmly awaiting his turn. "Smith," he stated and then proceeded to spell it. "S, M, I, T, H, Smith," he grinned happily. Then it was my turn. Everyone seemed to be staring at me as if I were about to tell a huge secret. "Modzelewski," I squeaked nervously. "M, O, D, can I please go to the bathroom?" It was on this Friday that I realized my name and perhaps my whole life was, well, different from that of my classmates.

Since that terrifying Friday in kindergarten I have undoubtedly and proudly mastered the spelling of my name. The realization I came to, however, has not changed. My name and my upbringing have been very different from those of my classmates. My name is quite obviously Polish, and my parents were both born and raised in England. They both possess beautiful, rich English accents, and they insisted on raising me on tea and Monty Python. My mother's parents, my grandparents, epitomize the stereotypical English characters. They both thrive on tea, humor, and tradition. My father's mother, whom we call Babcia, Polish for grandmother, is distinctly Polish. Her English is poor, and she can't resist speaking Polish to my father, even while I sit perplexed and nervously beside her. I mention all this to emphasize the history of my family which has contrasted greatly with the culture I grew into, yet at the same time shaped my personal identity.

I grew up in a small American town that has a culture of its own, but my English parents and my endless trips to England and Poland have separated my identity from my culture. I feel much more comfortable with a cup of tea in hand, sitting around the telly, or riding the "lift," than I do while sitting in front of the TV drinking Snapple in America. I love watching Monty Python's "The Holy Grail," and mimicking the accent that comes so naturally to me. My hometown is unlike any other. The culture I existed in while living and schooling there was a culture that forced me to cling to my historical background. I'd come home from school, and as I entered the door I would receive this strange feeling that suggested I was entering another country. Home was a country that valued family meals, cups of tea, and honorable respect. My home life and my visits to the country that my mum still insists on calling "home" have shaped my identity.

Therefore, my answer to the question of how my experience of culture has shaped my identity is really quite simple. My experience of culture, in America, has not shaped my personal identity.

What has shaped my identity is the simple fact that I'm not part of the culture I grew up in. The culture I experienced in America made me proud of my last name, my dual citizenship, and my accessible English accent. I am relieved that I can go to London and stay in my family's little flat, visit my grandparents, or even go to Warsaw and watch my father rush around the office speaking in Polish. It is in these situations that I feel at home. It is these experiences that have taught me that personal identity stems from life within one's own home and one's background. Now I am proud to spell my last name, "Modzelewski, M, O, D, Z, E, L, E, W, S, K, I!!!"

This student discussed his family and upbringing in an essay about working with his father in the garden, using a lighter tone and detailed narrative to show his respect for his father, his international background, and his sense of character:

THE VEGETABLES OF MY LABOR

The mosquitoes hover around my shoulders, their incessant hum ringing in my ears. Huddled on my knees, I crawl down each row of vegetables, systematically uprooting the gangly weeds with my dirt-encrusted hands. I can feel the overwhelming presence of the midday sun on my bare back and the beads of perspiration slowly rolling down my torso.

Each Sunday morning, I commence the exhausting process of weeding all fourteen rows of my father's vegetable garden, until the vegetables stand alone on the dark brown hills. I begin my task with the disheartening knowledge that no matter how thoroughly I work, for each weed I uproot, another will replace it within a week's time and the garden will look just as chaotic as it looks now. After hours upon hours spent crouched on my knees in my father's vegetable garden, I only know one thing for sure: that there will always, always be weeds.

In our vegetable garden, weeds come in many different shapes and sizes. There are the thick, windy, dark green ones which grow horizontally instead of vertically; the simple blades of grass; the ubiquitous three-leaf clovers; and the large, light green, spade leafed variety. Despite their differing outward appearances, they all strive toward a common goal: to make my position as "Chairman of Weeding Operations," as my father calls my apprenticeship in mud, as difficult as possible.

At first, my interest in my father's vegetable garden came purely through financial encouragement. Each week, my father would give me a small sum of money with the understanding that, when we left New York for our country house in rural Putnam County, I would have to perform some form of manual labor in return. This usually meant a few hours spent weeding in his vegetable garden. After investing so much time and effort protecting the garden from nature's destructive forces, I developed a spiritual attachment to the garden and each plant growing inside it. I wanted to see it succeed. And so I continued weeding and weeding, every weekend.

Dawson's Weed Whacker, Green Garden's weed repellent, Vegetation's Weed Killer—science has bestowed on today's gardener many devices and chemicals to prevent weed growth. And over the years, my father has done his best to ignore the existence of each and every one. Whenever I prod him about looking into some newfangled piece of gardening technology which could save us, or rather me, substantial time and effort, he invariably gives me the same answer: "Those silly things would probably kill off all our vegetables. I never needed them to help me weed when I was a boy. Besides, weeding is character building."

"Weeding is character building." This is my father's mantra. He claims weeding played a role in developing his character as a boy growing up in the English countryside, where he was always around a garden. His mother was a prize winning flower gardener who also maintained a large vegetable garden. The produce of this garden was a crucial piece of the family's sustenance for much of the coming winter. He was forced to adopt a Puritan work ethic at the age of six when his father died. He tells me that weeding in the vegetable garden was integral in establishing the work ethic that has carried him so far in the business world.

What keeps me going in this seemingly everlasting process is a vision that someday in the early fall it will all end and I will have something tangible to show for it. My father and I will walk into the garden and actually pick the vegetables of our labor. The vegetables themselves will be small and somewhat tough, invariably containing a disproportionately large number of seeds. Even though I don't particularly like vegetables, I will sit down at the dinner table with my family that night and eat something of everything—even the Brussels sprouts. They will taste like, well, like hard work more than anything else.

I am not sure I fully understand my father's notion of character or how it is built. I do know that weeding has taught me something about persistence. Who knows, maybe my father is right. Maybe weeding really is character building, or maybe it is not. What I do know is that I will never feel too proud to get my hands dirty.

A successful applicant to Brown, Columbia, Washington University, and other selective colleges, this student is direct and concrete in relating a semester's experience in an outdoor-oriented academic setting:

BUILDING A BRIDGE

In the spring of my junior year, I attended The Mountain School in Vershire, Vermont. For four months, I lived with 44 other students on a small farm. I did things I had never done before—like building a bridge.

A group of nine students and one teacher spent nine weeks building a log bridge over a small brook. I know that it would take far longer to build a concrete bridge spanning a river, but our bridge had more to do with process than with time. With one exception, the majority of the work was done with hand tools. We used a power saw to cut down a huge tree and a tractor to drag it to the work site. Other than that, we built the bridge with our arms and our axes.

You might think that using an axe is easy; well, it's not. We had to flatten the logs with axes so the bridge would have a level surface and notch the timber so the bridge would fit together smoothly. I nearly took off my leg a hundred times by swinging the axe without looking to see if anything was in its path. My arms would get so sore from chopping for hours on end that on the walk home, they would not even swing with my step. After the logs were notched and level, we joined them together with foot-long nails, using a sledge hammer. I personally bent so many nails that Jack, our supervisor, had to buy stronger nails so the bridge would not take any more abuse when the crooked nails were pulled out, taking large chunks of wood with them.

When we finished the bridge, I remember lying down on it and thinking, "I built this myself. I built something that is useful." Even more impressive to me was the fact that I had sweated and used my own muscle to build that bridge. I thought about every person who would cross it and how each of their steps would be a silent, unconscious "thank you" to the bridge builders.

After it was completed, I walked over the bridge all the time. I felt a real sense of accomplishment when I heard my footsteps on the wood. I made that bridge. I felt like a father doting over a child. In all of its simplicity, nothing made me prouder and happier than seeing the bridge do its job, just as I had done mine while building it.

This young woman wrote a compelling essay about handling her friend's suicide attempt, and the impact it had on her. She was admitted to Brown:

I looked down at my best friend as her hair stuck in sweaty clumps to the side of her head. I tried to find her through the green mask that covered her face. I searched her eyes for even the slightest hint of the spark that was usually there, but I just found lifeless, tear-filled eyes staring back. I wanted the room to turn upside down so that I could see her frown transform into the smile I knew so well. I tried to find words to fill in the gap that had so abruptly grown between us, but I could only stare back mutely. I thought she was going to speak as she lifted her head from the overly starched pillowcase, but instead she leaned forward and vomited into the pale green bucket beside her. Reluctantly, I moved myself forward to comfort her, and as my eyes passed over the bucket I saw thirty or so small white pills swimming in the murky liquid. I was scared and shocked, not knowing what to say, think, or do to help her.

Five minutes earlier, she had asked me into her room because she had to tell me something important. Not thinking anything of it, I followed happily. She shut the door and said, "I did something tonight."

"What's that?" I innocently responded.

Without speaking she stumbled to her dresser and handed me an almost empty bottle of Aleve. My skin turned bumpy as I slowly realized what she was trying to show me. Nonchalantly, I asked, "So, how many of these did you take tonight?"

"I just opened the bottle tonight," she softly responded.

I desperately searched the label for the number of pills inside and my heart stopped as I read "100 pills" in bold black letters. I turned the bottle in my sweaty palm and looked down. There were only about 20 pills left. I took her in my arms, half wanting to shake the pills out of her and the other half wanting to reach into her chest and mend her heart with my hands. She begged me not to go to the doctor because she was afraid that he would get angry and her parents would be angry as well. I had to convince her that these people were going to help her and make her better. As she protested, I carried her down the stairs to medical attention.

As I watched her lifeless body, I started blaming myself. "Why wasn't I there for her when she did this?" She had asked me to come and talk to her earlier that night, but I had put her off because I was too busy. If I had only stayed, perhaps none of this would have ever happened. She leaned back and fell onto the pillow once more, her eyes coming to a close with too much effort. "Cindy," she managed to whisper.

"Yes?" I responded, reaching up to remove the beads of sweat gathered on her forehead.

"Please don't tell anyone about this."

"No, of course not. I promise."

"And . . . Cindy," she murmured, "I'm so sorry."

"Don't be sorry. It's okay. We're going to get you better soon."

She went to the hospital that night and then directly home from there, not returning to school for three months. Everything changed that night, both for her and for me. I needed an answer; I needed to talk to someone and to understand what had happened to my best friend. But I couldn't talk to anyone, because she had asked me not to. I was alone with this experience trapped inside of me, eating away at my mind, my heart, and my soul. I finally spoke to her about three days later on the telephone, and I asked her why she had done it. She told me that she took the pills because she did not want to wake up at school one more morning.

Two years later, I know that I will never understand why she wanted to die that night. I cannot grasp the extent of her unhappiness or the depression that lived so strongly inside of her. As a fifteen-year-old girl, I did not know that such feelings existed in human beings. I realized how lucky I am to be healthy and happy, something that I had overlooked. I have learned to escape from situations that make me unhappy, because I fear unhappiness as I saw what it did to my friend. I value the importance of friendships, knowing that I was a friend to her and that is why she came to me when she needed help. I know that I will always be there for a friend who is in trouble, and I hope that they will be there for me. I learned the importance of listening to people, not just hearing them, but being able to read them as well, because I still blame myself for not listening to my friend's cries for help sooner. Every detail of that evening will remain vivid to me, as I have not gone through one day when I have not thought of her lying in that bed wishing to die. I wake up every morning and thank God that she is also waking up.

Secrets are an aspect of life that live within everyone, but are hidden most of the time. My friend and I carry a secret of a significant event in her life, but it seems as if it is still a secret between the two of us. We have never discussed that night after the telephone conversation we had. These secrets sometimes define who we are, yet they remain invisible. No one will ever see my friend the way that I saw her, nor will they understand the complexity of her situation. People are so often judged on their character or their presence, but one cannot fully understand another human being unless the secrets they hold within are released. I feel fortunate to have had this experience for it has taught me the importance of understanding a person completely, not just judging what lies on the surface. I now know that so much exists within everyone that is not seen, secrets that will always be there but not always revealed. I hold a key that unlocks the soul of my best friend, a key that has allowed me to explore and discover an area of human nature that I was blind to before.

Responding to Northwestern University's question about the most afraid she had ever been, this successful applicant used her experience as a surfer to show her adventurous personality:

The cold salt water blurred my vision and stung my sunburned face. My arms ached with pain as I strained to keep paddling out through the unforgiving waves that kept my body in a constant game of ping-pong against my surfboard. I could already feel the bruises beginning on my hips from the fiberglass board banging against my bones. But I could not complain; it was my own 10-year-old, naïve mind's idea to go out surfing during hurricane season. I should have known what I was getting into.

After what seemed to be an eternity of this rigorous, heart-pounding, body-bashing paddling, I thought I had finally reached safety beyond the breaking point. I then weakly raised my dazed head only to see a rogue 10–12 foot wave looming above me, threatening me with its forming white caps to crash down. My heart stopped. An unknown force suddenly took over my body and with energy I didn't think I had left in me, I paddled furiously up the vertical face of the wave. All functions of my body had shut down except my ability to paddle. I safely reached the crest of the wave just in time to see a small piece of seaweed that had been only millimeters behind my board get sucked over the falls of the wave never to be seen again. I relaxed and fell lifelessly back onto my board and started to breathe again.

Later that day after this encounter with Mother Nature I began to understand what unrelenting force had driven me: fear. When I froze in awe at the enormous wave towering above me, I actually stepped outside myself and succumbed to the grand force of fear. The adrenaline pumping through my body at that moment was so intense that I became capable of doing anything, even paddling over a wave that was three times my size and 100 times more powerful. Fear is an overwhelming force, both physically and psychologically, that can work for or against us. Prior to this surfing experience, fear had always been an emotion that I dreaded. I hated the accompanying feelings of powerlessness and vulnerability, and I loathed hearing the sound of my own heart pounding within my chest. On this stormy September afternoon, I truly learned how to harness the power of fear. I learned for the first time that fear could be my friend, not my foe. Today, I feel completely confident in facing all life's difficult situations with the knowledge that with enough courage, drive and persistence, and perhaps a little fear to push me to my limits, I can achieve the seemingly impossible. After all, boundaries exist only for those who believe in them.

Now That You Have Written Your Essays . . .

You are ready to consider adding supplementary materials to your applications. In addition to a résumé, which you may have already completed, you should be thinking about recommendation letters, portfolios, letters to colleges, coaches, and faculty, lists of books you have read, and other means by which you can present yourself more fully to the colleges. In Chapter 5, we offer examples of supplementary materials and guidance on marketing and presenting yourself through the entire admissions process, even after you have submitted your applications.

CHAPTER FIVE

What Else? Marketing and Presenting Yourself through Supplementary Materials and Communication

Your application essays are the core of your presentation to colleges. Completing them is a major accomplishment, but neither the beginning nor the end of the presentation process. During junior year, you may send letters to coaches or music faculty, for example, to alert them to your talents and interest in their college. You will assemble a résumé to summarize your academics and special skills. During the summer, you will contact faculty and other supporters for recommendations and letters of reference. During the fall and winter of senior year, you will follow up with the colleges to report on your progress. In this chapter, we cover the additional elements of a strong presentation to colleges, providing you with guidance on helpful ways to interact with colleges and universities and those who will support your applications, and with examples of résumés, cover letters, update letters, and other forms of communication.

Marketing and Presenting Yourself

There are several major strategies for presenting yourself from junior year all the way through senior spring. You will want to:

1. Put together a strong, focused résumé.
2. Contact relevant supporters, on and off campus, including, as appropriate, teachers who will write recommendations, coaches who might recruit you, coaches who might serve as references, music or arts or writing instructors who might advise you on

where and how to apply and then serve as references, alumni or on-campus interviewers, learning evaluators who will provide summary support materials for you, and faculty on campus who might advise their admissions office of your potential.

3. Assemble and submit appropriate supplementary materials.
4. Report new developments to the colleges as they occur. These developments include winning awards for academics or athletics, being selected as a class speaker or National Merit Finalist, having a proposal for an independent study project accepted, and obtaining new scores on the SAT I, ACT, or SAT II Subject Tests.

THE MANY WAYS TO APPLY TO COLLEGE

Despite the increasing complexity of the admissions process, colleges are making it easier to submit an application to their institution. You have your choice of electronic applications, web-based application organizers, CD-ROMs with hundreds of applications on a disk, and, of course, paper applications. Always try to guarantee that your applications will arrive well in advance of stated college deadlines. If you have to ask whether the college wants the application to arrive on the deadline or just be postmarked by the deadline, then you are sending in your applications later than you should be. Here are some of the ways to apply:

Paper copies of the application can be filled out by hand (or typed) and mailed to the admissions office. Paper copies can be either downloaded from a college's website or ordered by phone, mail, e-mail, or in person. This method shows perhaps the most individuality, and, when combined with registered or overnight mail, can provide the strongest assurance of "it got there in hard copy." Beware of sloppy handwriting, off-kilter typing, your dog eating it, or "it got lost in the mail." If you send paper copies, considering using registered/return receipt mail or a courier service.

College Link (www.collegelink.com) allows students to fill out information on a computer disk. The information is formatted to a college's specifications, printed out, and mailed to the student for proofreading and mailing

(continued)

in to the college. Benefits: right format, computer entry, proofreading. Drawbacks: not all colleges participate, the necessity of connecting to the service, and not "having it all right there in front of you."

The Common Application can be obtained from your school guidance office or downloaded and printed out from "www.commonapp.org," then filled out and mailed in. The Common Application can be used for multiple colleges, some of which require a supplement. Multiple uses and ways to fill it out make this a good option. Our rule of thumb, however, is that if a college offers you significantly more opportunities to write by using their own application, then you should do that.

EXPAN, provided by the College Board (www.collegeboard.org), allows students to access and file applications electronically through software at school guidance offices. Good for electronic filling out and filing, but harder to use on your own at home.

The Princeton Review's APPLY is a CD-ROM or web-based application service available from "www.review.com" and many guidance offices, which allows students to access more than 500 colleges' applications and either file them electronically or print them out and mail them in. Students fill out demographic information once, and it is then transferred onto each application. Unlike the Common Application, the student files each college's individual application, indicating a bit more interest in and commitment to the school.

The College Board's "Next Stop College" is a recently inaugurated online application service that allows students to apply to over 500 colleges and universities, public and private.

Always print out and make copies of everything. Once you have submitted an application, wait at least a week, and then feel free to call an admissions office and ask "is my application complete?" Lost recommendations, SAT scores not sent directly from ETS, and lack of a transcript are common reasons for a delay in reviewing your application. Don't count on the colleges to notify you in a timely manner that something is missing.

Marketing and presenting yourself to colleges is an ongoing process that begins before you complete your applications and does not end after you send them in. Focus on interactive communication with the colleges right through the time you hear a final decision from them. You may have interviewed with an admissions officer on campus. You can continue to be in touch with them through e-mail. If a college sends you a letter, you can respond to it cordially, using the opportunity to tell them about your current activities and interests. If you have a question about a college or your application and you have not been able to find an answer in the college's materials, you can call the admissions office and ask to speak to a counselor. Think of the presentation process as a dialogue between you and the representatives of the colleges in which you are interested.

Reporting New Developments to Colleges As They Occur

Once you have submitted your applications—including essays, résumés, portfolios, and recommendations—your presentation and marketing efforts should continue. Keep the colleges informed about new successes: high grades, a research or creative paper that is praised by your teacher, chairmanship of a committee, the publication of your work, an award, or an athletic accomplishment. Make sure that you do not repeat what is already in your folder, and document your achievements: photocopy your report card if it is exceptional, photocopy an award, or insert a newspaper clipping. Take advantage of alumni interviews where you can, and be alert to any signals from college admissions officials that they would like to hear from you. If you receive a letter from a college in which you are interested, respond to it.

A new development should be shared with the committees. Do not hesitate to ask a teacher or coach or musical director to send a new or an updated recommendation if you are performing well for them. Most important of all, keep up your grades throughout the winter and spring terms of senior year. An improvement demonstrates true motivation to excel in your studies, while a decline shows just the opposite. Many applicants have learned the importance of this by failing to get admitted in the spring because their grades dropped after sending in their application. Others made their acceptance happen by working to improve their record right up to the end of the academic year, when they were considered for admission from the wait list.

Putting Together a Strong Résumé

Résumés—also called profiles, fact sheets, or activities lists—follow many styles, and you may choose from many models in putting yours together. You should plan to produce a résumé for the college admissions process. You may give it to teachers who will write your recommendations, guidance counselors who wish to know more about you, college alumni or on-campus interviewers who have not yet seen your application, or potential employers. You may also include the résumé with your college application, especially if it allows you to expand on a major academic or extracurricular interest. A résumé may be targeted—toward an athletic program, a musical ability, a research interest—or generalized. Remember that anything you put in a résumé that will be seen by anyone associated with a college should be something you want that college to know about you. For college admissions purposes, most résumés will include the following, as appropriate and available:

- Your name, high school, address, phone, e-mail, and social security number at the top of the page
- A list of your academic interests, honors, and Advanced Placement (AP) courses taken or registered for, standardized test scores, and other honors, awards, and recognitions
- A notation of the year in which you participated in an activity
- Explanation of activities, organizations, or awards that may not be clear or familiar to the reader

We recommend that résumés be organized by content area—sports, music, drama, academics, volunteer service, and so forth—with

SENDING SUPPLEMENTARY MATERIALS WITH YOUR APPLICATION: ADVICE FROM THREE COLLEGES

From Williams College:

Evaluation of Additional Arts Materials

If you have well-developed talent in the creative or performing arts, including samples with your application may enhance your admission prospects. Use the optional Arts Evaluation provided with the application forms. Send copies only; we are unable to return supplemental material.

Whether or not you send samples, you may include an arts résumé listing your training and experience, repertoire or roles performed, and honors received.

Music—Send a cassette labeled with your name and address, instrument (or voice), and the work's title and composer. The preferred format is in two pieces, each two minutes in length— one fast and technical, the other slow and soulful. Do not send a full orchestral, band, or choral recording unless you are a featured soloist; if so, please specify your solo. Describe with whom and for how long you have trained, any ensemble and solo experience you have, and your plans for musical involvement in college.

Visual Art—Send at least 10 (up to 20) 35mm slides of drawings, paintings, sculptures, or other works. Do not send originals. Encase slides in 9" x 11" plastic sleeves. Indicate top of work, title, date, medium, size, and your name; number each slide. The top of the work shown must be at the top of the slide when it is in the sleeve.

Theatre—Send a résumé or a videocassette of a performance of two contrasting monologues (less than five minutes total). Introduce the tape with your name and address, titles of works to be performed, and your training and experience.

Dance—Send a résumé (not a tape) listing your training and experience, repertoire, and honors received.

(continued)

Evaluation of Additional Scientific Research Materials

If you have pursued significant scientific research or mathematical projects and are considering a research or academic career, we welcome descriptions of your work. Please send a full report of your research, including an abstract and a cover sheet noting your intended field of study. Provide a résumé of related activities: independent projects, summer study or research, and recognition received.

From Bates College:

We encourage students to submit writing samples in addition to the formal essay (perhaps a copy of a term or research paper, parts of a journal, poems, or even an in-class essay) which reveal an ability to organize thoughts and defend ideas under the pressure of time.

From Princeton University:

If I have particular skills or talents which are exceptional in nature, should I send Princeton evidence of those skills or talents?

Yes. If you are exceptionally gifted in art or music, for instance, you should send a portfolio or tape directly to the Admission Office. We will then forward such things to the appropriate department or member of the faculty who, in turn, will send us an evaluation. We take such evaluations into consideration when making our admission decisions. If you are interested in the possibility of playing a varsity sport, you should write directly to the coach of that sport (see the Admission Information bulletin for the list of varsity sports offered and the names of the coaches).

individual activities organized by most recent year first. Try to keep your résumé to one or two pages, focus on your high school years, and delete any irrelevant or extraneous clutter. Your interests, strengths, and points should be clear. Most college applications ask you to list your activities, awards, and volunteer, work, and summer experiences, in prioritized order. Even if you submit a résumé, you should fill out the lists on the applications forms, presenting the colleges with your most important areas of interest. Be aware that some colleges ask you to follow a specified format if you submit an additional résumé.

GREG'S SCIENCE AND ACADEMIC RÉSUMÉ

GPA
    11th Grade: 94.5
    10th Grade: 93
    9th Grade: 93
    Overall: 93.5

Class Rank: #1

SAT I: 1510	Math: 790	Verbal: 720
SAT II: Math: 800	Writing: 790	Chemistry: 790

AP Computer Exam: 5
AP American History Exam: 4

National Merit Commended Student

HONORS

National Chemistry Exam: 99th Percentile
General Electric Computer Science Competition: Scholarship Winner
CT Chemathon Competition: 2nd in high school division; cash prize
    winner
Selected for National Honor Roll of high school students
Earned Client Server Certificate in Computer Science from Fairfield
    University
Inducted into National Cum Laude Society
High Honor Roll and Head of School List throughout high school
Varsity Letter for Baseball; Varsity Letter for Squash

STUDIES BEYOND HIGH SCHOOL

Fairfield University: Visual Basic I, GPA 4.0
                      Visual Basic II, GPA 4.0
                      Visual Basic IV, GPA 4.0
                      JAVA, GPA 4.0

Brown University: Digital Design for the Computer
Introduction to Aerodynamics
Engineering and the High Technology
     Entrepreneur

EXTRACURRICULAR ACTIVITIES

12th Grade: Technology Director/Layout Editor,
Newspaper
Technology Editor, Yearbook
Model UN
Weightlifting
Manager, Varsity Squash

11th Grade: Assistant Technology Director/Layout
     Editor, Newspaper
Technology Staff, Yearbook
Model UN: Delegate to the National
     Conference
Varsity Squash
Independent Study, Spanish
Independent Study, Computer Science
Brown University, Aerodynamics
Part-time job, Waiter

10th Grade: Assistant Layout Editor, Newspaper
Model UN
Audio Visual/Tech Crew
JV Squash
Weightlifting
Fairfield University, Visual Basic IV, JAVA
Brown University, Digital Design, Engineering

9th Grade: Layout Staff, Newspaper
Model UN
Audio Visual/Tech Crew
Varsity Baseball
JV Squash
Weightlifting
Fairfield University, Visual Basic I, II

ANDREA'S EQUESTRIAN ATHLETIC RÉSUMÉ

Background:

I have been riding for six years. I have traveled up and down the Eastern seaboard following the hunter and jumper A-circuit for the past four years. This is the most competitive level of horse show competition in the nation. It requires many hours of travel and hard work.

Significant Trophies and Awards:

1997   Eastern States Exposition Horse Show, Small Junior Hunter Champion, Grand Junior Hunter Champion, recipient of the Dillon Challenge Trophy

1997   Fairfield-Westchester Professional Horsemen's Association Horse Show, recipient of the Frank S. Grenci Perpetual Memorial Trophy

1997   Competed in the AHSA Medal and ASPCA Maclay, Devon Horse Show

1997   Class Winner Small Junior Hunter Division: Fairfield County Hunt Club Horse Show, Autumn Classic Horse Show

1996   Recipient of the Best Child Rider on a Pony award, Quentin Fall Horse Show

1996   Winner of eight AHSA Pony Medals

[A number of additional awards were also listed, helping Andrea to show her high level of competition and commitment to the sport.]

Horse Show Career Highlights:

Old Salem Farm, North Salem, NY

Upperville Colt and Horse Show, Upperville, VA

Winter Equestrian Festival, Palm Beach, FL

Vermont Summer Showcase, Wakefield, VT

Lake Placid Horse Show, Lake Placid, NY

[Andrea listed other horse shows in different states, showing the extent of her travel and time devoted to riding, as well as her exposure to different environments.]

Current Status:

Currently competing in the Small Junior Hunter Division and the Open Equitation Division (AHSA Medal, PHA Medal, USET, ASPCA Maclay, WIHS)

ALICIA'S COMMUNITY SERVICE AND ENVIRONMENTAL ACTION RÉSUMÉ

COMMUNITY SERVICE AND CLUB ACTIVITIES

Conservation Club (the student leader)—12, 11
Organized various projects, including improving the school's recycling program, running fund-raisers, eliminating Styrofoam cups from the cafeteria, and implementing a plastic drive for recycling.

Designed and created posters using computer graphics for the Conservation Club bulletin board to raise interest and awareness.

Soup Kitchen—12, 11, 10
Volunteered to cook and serve dinner at St. Luke's Shelter in Stamford.

Breakfast in the City—12, 11, 10
Served food and distributed toiletries to the homeless in New York City.

Midnight Run—12, 9
Collected donations of clothing and toiletries and prepared bag meals.

Distributed items to the homeless in New York City.

Extended Day—9
Volunteered at this after school program for lower-school children at my school.

Played games and helped them do art projects.

SUMMER EXPERIENCES

Spanish III—before 12
Completed the second semester of Spanish III because I was unable to take it during my Maine Coast Semester.

Chimpanzee and Human Communication Institute—before 11
Member of a volunteer research team (through the Earthwatch Institute) for two weeks at this Ellensburg, Washington, program.

Learned to identify the five chimpanzees, who all use American Sign Language among themselves and with their care-givers.

Collected data about their use of enrichment objects.

Contributed to the primary goal of the program, which is to improve captive primate care and animal welfare globally.

Best Friends Animal Sanctuary—before 11
Volunteered for two weeks at the nation's largest lifetime care sanctuary for previously abused and abandoned companion animals.

Attended a two-day humane education conference at the sanctuary, which is located in Kanab, Utah.

Chewonki Foundation wilderness trip—before 9
Went on a two-week whitewater kayaking trip in Maine, where we learned the Eskimo roll, whitewater kayaking, and rescue techniques.

Darien Nature Center—before 9
Volunteered as a Junior Counselor with the summer program for children.

Helped the children with art projects, went on nature walks, and participated in other activities with them.

KAREN'S MUSIC AND ACADEMIC RÉSUMÉ

MUSIC

Private flute instruction since 1992

Attended Levine School of Music for private instruction (since 1995) and music theory classes (1995–1996)

Upper School Band (1996–2000)

Interlochen Arts Camp (summers 1995, 1996, 1997)

Flute Choir at Levine School of Music (summer 1998)

School Wind Ensemble (1997, 1998)

Chamber Music Group—organized and participated (1999)

Upper School Musical Pit Orchestra (1997, 1998, 1999)

Miscellaneous flute music groups throughout high school

ACTIVITIES

Upper School Newspaper (10, 11, 12)
　Staff Writer (10)
　Assistant Editor (11)
　Copy Editor (12)

Model UN (10, 11, 12)
　Angola in Special Political and Decolonization (10)
　Algeria in Organization of African Unity (11)

Peer Listening (10, 11, 12)
　Co-advisor for group of freshmen (11)
　A leader of Eating Disorder Assembly (11)

Environmental Club (10)

SPORTS
Varsity Cross Country (10, 11, 12)
   Third Team All-WISCC (10)
   Second Team All-WISCC (11)
   Captain (12)
Crew (10)

JV Soccer (9)

Outdoor Education (9)

CHURCH
Lector since 1995
Played flute weekly in folk group at mass (9)
Annual family religious retreat (9, 10, 11)

COMMUNITY SERVICE
Soup kitchen (9, 10, 11, 12)
Community Service Day (10)
Community Christmas Party (11)

AWARDS/ACADEMIC HONORS
Headmaster's Letter (9, 10, 11)
Maryland Distinguished Scholar
National Merit Commended Scholar

SUMMER EXPERIENCES
Interlochen Arts Camp (9)
Job at Children's Bookstore (10)
Flute Choir at Levine School of Music (10)
Spanish Immersion Program (11)

ELIZA'S THEATRE RÉSUMÉ
EDUCATION
Ashley Hall High School, Charleston, SC
   Diploma anticipated: May 1998
Charlestowne Montessori School, Charleston, SC
   Completed fifth grade: May 1991
International School, Istanbul, Turkey

Second grade: February 1988
American School, Barcelona, Spain
　　First grade: May 1987
Calvert School of Home Instruction, Sailboat in Mediterranean Sea
　　First and second grade requirements
The Day School, New York, NY
　　Nursery School through Kindergarten: May 1986

TRAINING AND EXTRA ACTIVITIES

Six week summer program	American Academy of Dramatic Arts
Intro to Meisner	Midtown Theatre
One year Speech Class	Ashley Hall School
Speech and Debate Team	Ashley Hall School
Two year Apprentice program	Charleston Stage Company
Two year acting class	Martha Carter
One year private acting lessons	Donna Parker

INTERNSHIPS

MIDTOWN THEATRE: Production/Stage Management Internship. Ran box office, managed production/theatre/stage and designed lighting and sets.

CHARLESTON STAGE CO: Wings Apprenticeship Program. Trained in set construction and design, props, costume construction and design, sound, lighting design/operation, stage and theatre/production management.

AMERICORPS NATIONAL CIVILIAN COMMUNITY PROGRAM CORPS: Summer literacy program. Taught reading skills to economically impoverished 5 year olds.

EXPERIENCE

1997 *Tony and Tina's Wedding* (Nun)	Midtown Theatre Company
1996 *One Flew over the Cuckoo's Nest* (Nurse Flinn)	Midtown Theatre Company
1995 *Varney the Vampire* (Jenny)	Pluff Mud Productions
1994 *Wait until Dark* (Gloria)	Dock Street Theatre

1993 *Anne of Green Gables* (Ruby Gillis)	Dock Street Theatre
1991 *The Best Christmas Pageant Ever*	THEatre WORKS
1991 *Pinocchio* (Pinocchio)	THEatre WORKS
1990 *Brighton Beach Memoirs* (Laurie)	THEatre WORKS
1989 *How to Eat like a Child*	Bambani Artisti
1989 *Marvelous Myths* (Persephone)	Piccolo Spoleto
1989 *The Pig*	Piccolo Spoleto

TECHNICAL WORK

1996 *Biloxi Blues*	Assistant Stage Manager
1996 *Last Night of Ballyhoo*	Stage Manager
1996 *Ancient History*	Sound Technician
1996 *Tuna Christmas*	
1996 *Christmas in Rock n' Roll Heaven*	Production Manager/Set Design
1996 *A Funny Thing Happened on the Way to the Forum*	Deck Crew
1995 *Rock and Roll Heaven*	Stage Manager
1995 *The Foreigner*	Assistant Stage Manager
1995 *A Christmas Carol*	Deck Captain
1995 *The Secret Garden*	Stage Manager
1994 *The Incandescent Young Tom Edison*	Assistant Stage Manager
1994 *A Christmas Carol*	Deck Crew

AWARDS AND COMPETITION

1997 The Martha Morgan History Award	Tuition Grant
1994 First Place, Impromptu	Lowcountry Forensic Association
1994 Award for Artistic Excellence	Ashley Hall School

Interviews

Since very few colleges require interviews on campus and many colleges do not even offer them, you should consider interviews a much less important part of the presentation process than the written essays. You may be surprised by this, but remember what has replaced the on-campus interview: the application, with which you can write in depth about yourself, and the alumni interview in your home area. Additionally, some colleges may send admissions representatives to your high school to recruit and interview candidates.

Even though most colleges that still interview on campus specifically indicate that these interviews are "informational" and not "evaluative," you should avail yourself of the opportunity to interview everywhere you can, within reason. If you cannot make a trip by plane to a college across the country for an on-campus interview, then do not be too concerned. If you are able to interview at several college campuses within several hours' drive from home, then by all means do so. Interviews are interactive events where you will be able to learn more about the colleges, and they will be able to find out more about what makes you tick and how you present yourself in person. Make sure to write a brief thank-you note or e-mail to each person who interviews you, on campus or off.

After the application deadlines have passed, the alumni schools committees, which are now a part of the admissions process for all selective colleges, will interview candidates at the request of the admissions offices. If you are contacted by a college alumnus/a, take advantage of the opportunity to meet with this college representative. While an interview with a local area alum is unlikely to have either a negative or a radically positive effect, having an enthusiastic graduate in your corner is still helpful. If you have submitted an application but have not heard anything about an alumni interview, then call or e-mail the admissions office to ask if and when such interviews will be offered and to make sure that you are on the contact list.

Alumni reports usually confirm the judgments of the professional staff in the admissions office. A highly enthusiastic alumni review, however, may turn a skeptical reader of your folder into a believer. The local interviewer is aware of high school students in his or her home area who have received publicity for success in the arts, school or community leadership, or athletics. He or she can substantiate the applicant's achievements for the admissions committee. Finally, local alumni play vital roles in encouraging students to consider their alma maters. Admissions staff are frequently tipped off to a deserving prospect by an alumni schools representative.

Contacting Supporters and Writing Letters

You will be responsible for contacting those you hope will support you during the college admissions process. Before you apply, you may write to coaches, call or e-mail admissions offices to ask for materials, or write a note and give a résumé to teachers who will write you recommendations. During the application process, you may contact alumni, additional teachers, your guidance counselor, college faculty, and others who will help you make your case to the colleges, or, within the colleges, evaluate you favorably. In many cases, you will contact people by telephone or e-mail. You will also need to word-process or hand-write personal notes and letters. Consider buying a set of simple stationery with your name and address at the top. Note cards or letter-sized stationery with matching envelopes, printed on fine quality paper, are proper and professional. A good-quality computer printout can also serve your purpose.

Asking for Recommendations

You will need at least one or two teacher recommendations to accompany your applications. You will also get a recommendation from your school guidance counselor, advisor, or academic dean. Your teachers' recommendations will probably be strong, if you have chosen the right teachers and you have been a strong academic performer. Thousands of applicants get wonderful recommendations from one or two teachers. When you secure those extra one or two letters of support from teachers in major subjects, you distance yourself from the pack. Start by asking two junior-year teachers for recommendations at the end of junior spring, then continue to think about a senior-year teacher who might write you a strong recommendation during or after the fall semester. Consider also asking a music or arts teacher, a coach, a religious leader, a supervisor at a job, internship, or volunteer project, or a peer for an additional reference.

When you ask for a recommendation, it is a good idea to make an appointment with the person you are soliciting. Bring along a résumé and plan to tell the reference writer what your plans are for college. You may be more or less specific, depending on your interests and how far along you are in your college search. Generally, if someone cannot write a positive recommendation for you, he or she will decline to serve as a reference.

Letters from Others

A number of other people may write on your behalf to assist you in the college admissions process. These may include teachers and counselors writing recommendations for you, employers or other mentors writing personal references, learning evaluators writing summaries of educational evaluations, parents or peers writing letters of reference, or alumni writing to support your application. You will have more input on some of these letters than on others, but you should have an idea of what each might look like as you consider your presentation to colleges. Sometimes, you will see the letters people have written for you and you will include them with your application packet. Other times, you will give your letter writers stamped envelopes addressed to each college in which they can enclose the letter to be sent directly to the schools. Sometimes, letter writers will provide a school counselor with a copy of their letter, to be included in a packet that the school sends to the colleges. Be certain to follow the specific procedures of each college to which you apply regarding letters of recommendation.

A Recommendation from a Teacher, School Administrator, or Counselor

You will need at least one and preferably two strong teacher recommendations to support your applications. You need not select one math and one English teacher, but do try to choose teachers of different subjects. You should have at least one recommendation from a core subject area, such as English, math, history, or science. You can add one or two additional recommendations from your strongest subjects, such as language, studio art, or music. Focus on those who know you and your work well, who can comment with some perspective on your contributions to class and school, and who can talk about their confidence in your abilities as a learner who will excel in college. You may select a teacher or two from your junior year, and perhaps one from senior year. Try not to rely solely on teachers from tenth grade or earlier, since colleges will wonder why you could find no one from your more recent and important third and fourth years of high school. As your senior year progresses, if you are deferred from Early Decision/Action, or you are wait-listed, you may ask an additional teacher to write on your behalf.

Sometimes, particularly in a smaller school, a principal, dean, or head of school will offer or agree to write for you. Such a recommendation should be considered a supplemental reference, and not a substitute for a teacher recommendation. A recommendation from someone with administrative responsibility in the school can help to present your contributions to the larger school community. If you are a school or class leader, have been strongly involved in the admissions office as a tour guide or school service club, or have been a major presence at your school in other ways, then consider approaching a school administrator to ask for an additional recommendation.

As a matter of course, you should obtain a recommendation from your college guidance counselor or advisor. Ideally, this reference will gather together comments from your teachers and insights about your overall record at the school in order to tell the colleges about your contributions to the school community and many different intellectual and extracurricular areas. Sometimes, these counselor recommendations are extensive, valuable, and full of helpful information. Sometimes, they are brief, quantitative, and essentially worthless as additional commentaries on your personality and abilities. This makes the point even clearer that teacher recommendations matter most.

Writing some time ago, Thomas Hayden, the former director of college placement at Phillips Exeter Academy, offered advice for teachers and others writing student recommendations. He suggested that the content of a recommendation should include discussion of:

- The course's content and methods, including the instructor's approach, expectations, and topics and concepts covered;
- Your performance, including your ability to handle the major concepts and themes of the class, your enjoyment and enthusiasm as a learner, your success in relation to others in the class, and your individual strengths;
- Your attitude toward learning, curiosity about the material, motivation, independence, and commitment to doing extra work and spending additional time on the course;
- Your character, aspects of your relationships with the instructor and your classmates, and your exercise of leadership and good judgment;
- Your uniqueness, including stories that may show who you are as an individual and predictions and enthusiasm of the instructor about the impact you might make and role you will play at college.

Hayden recommended that reference writers take the following additional steps to build a strong recommendation. You should try to assist your recommendation writers by taking the initiative to help them pursue these steps. Meet with them, provide them with information, and stay in touch with them. Recommendation writers should:

- Get extra information from you that will help them to get to know you outside of their particular class context.
- Counsel you to help you choose the right reference writers and colleges.
- Consult your college guidance counselor to get an overview of your strengths, the colleges you are applying to, and the counselor's perspective on your applications.
- Complete the numeric rating scales on the recommendation forms in a way that is honest but helps you by rating you as

"outstanding" in as many categories as possible, since this seriously affects the colleges' rating of you as a candidate.

- Personalize his or her recommendation by writing a short note—perhaps by hand, on each photocopied recommendation—matching your strengths and interests to each college to which you are applying and possibly follow up by writing or calling a school on your behalf later in the admissions process.
- Be aware of the power of words and avoid loaded, vague, controversial, or bland language that reflects poorly on you, often unintentionally.[5]

Each recommendation is unique, and your teachers and other supporters must match their expectations with your abilities and performance in the classroom and at school. You will likely not see your recommendations, and in the event that you do, you will have little control over their content. You should choose referees carefully, talk to them personally, and provide them with helpful information, such as a résumé and cover letter detailing your interests and goals for college. You should always thank your recommendation writers for their support and let them know the final outcome of the admissions process.

A Recommendation from a Peer

Some colleges, such as Dartmouth, encourage you to submit a reference from a peer. Others will look positively on such a recommendation if it adds something new and valuable about you. Choose your peer wisely. You will want to ask someone who knows you well, who writes well, and who has the maturity and perspective to add insights and personality to your application. Sarcastic, goofy, or sloppy writing will only reflect negatively on you, since such a poor recommendation calls into question your judgment in selecting a character reference. If you do not know anyone who can write a strong peer recommendation, then choose not to submit one. In finding a peer reference, you

---

[5]Thomas C. Hayden, *Writing Effective College Recommendations: A Guide for Teachers* (Princeton, NJ: Peterson's Guides, Inc., 1984).

may consider best friends, cousins, siblings, or people with whom you have worked or studied. Most peers will be honored by your request and will share their reference with you for your reaction.

This sample recommendation was written for a student admitted on Early Decision to Dartmouth. Note how well the writer captures his friend's personality and the value he brings to the classroom, to life, and to their relationship. There is some humor and self-reflection here, but this recommendation is clearly about the candidate and not the author. That is exactly as it should be.

September 2000

Director of Admissions
Dartmouth College

Dear Director:

Writing a peer review for Jim Thomas has been more stressful than preparing my own college applications. Although I tell myself that Jim's academic record speaks for itself, and that any admissions counselor reviewing Jim's application will read this recommendation only as an afterthought, I still worry. If I fail to show you why Jim should be admitted to Dartmouth, I will have failed both a great individual and a great university.

You don't encounter a Jim Thomas very often. He is the child that parents wish their newborn will become. He is caring, responsible, compassionate, respectful, hard working and fiercely intelligent. He studies for the joy of learning, not for grades. He uses his gifts, and also shares them generously, no matter how inconvenient that may be.

When I think of Jim an image that comes to mind is the crowd of nervous students milling around shortly before last year's Physics exam. A few days before, the department had distributed a sheet of equations that students could use during the exam. The format of the equations on the sheet was new to us, however, and the equations barely resembled the ones that we had worked with all year. There were different letters and (to us at least) unorthodox mathematical notations. As the exam was about to take place in a large gymnasium filled with folding tables, students frantically studied the new equations, trying to make sure they wouldn't blank on them. Almost everyone was alone, poring over the equation sheets and flash cards. Jim did not use these last few minutes for himself, however, but bent over a student sitting at a card table and explained a problem to him. Although Jim still got an A+ in Physics, his generosity in that circumstance tells at least as much about him as the grade does.

In class, Jim doesn't just learn the material for himself. He elevates class discussion so that everyone leaves with a better understanding of the subject. In Physics and AP Chemistry, Jim doesn't listen to the lecture passively. He actively tries to understand the issues that underlie the lecture topic, often staying after class to explore a difficult, abstract concept, or to work out a derivation too advanced for the rest of the class. I sincerely believe that I have learned more physics from discussions with Jim than from reading the textbook.

As Jim's cross-country captain, I have spent a good deal of time with him in a competitive, non-academic environment. If possible, Jim demonstrates even more strength of character as a runner than as a student. Jim started to run cross-country last year, as a junior, to get in shape for skiing (at which he excels). From the first day of practice it was evident that Jim has much more natural talent as a student than as a runner. He barely made it through our first training run, finishing almost fifteen minutes behind the rest of the team. Most new runners who have that much trouble quit cross-country within a week. Jim kept trying. He pushed himself as hard as he could in every practice and every race. He quickly earned the respect and friendship of his teammates. Jim was not one of the top seven runners picked for the varsity team in the first meet, but he came anyway and cheered his teammates on. Jim steadily improved over the course of the year, and he surprised everyone (including himself, I think) by making the varsity team for the concluding meet, the New England Prep Championships.

At the end of each season the team elects one person to receive an award for leadership and dedication. Although he had run cross-country for only one year, Jim was voted the award overwhelmingly.

Jim still continues to improve as a runner. He showed commitment to the team by training over the summer while also working two jobs.

His summer workouts enabled Jim to move up the ladder and help the team as its current number three runner. Through extraordinary dedication, in just one year Jim has become an integral part of the team, valued as both a leader and a runner. Jim encourages his teammates, and inspires the team's younger runners. The remarkable impact that Jim has had in this activity, which did not come easily to him, indicates the type of positive contribution that he makes wherever he goes.

When I was trying to select a high school to attend, a friend told me that you judge an institution not by buildings or faculty, but by the exceptional individuals you will meet there. The best part of my high school education has been meeting students like Jim Thomas. Dartmouth will make itself an even better institution by accepting him.

Sincerely yours,

A Reference from an Instructor outside School

If you attend a summer academic or enrichment program, work with an outside art, drama, music or other professional instructor, or serve as an intern or an employee, strongly consider obtaining an additional reference from your mentor, supervisor, or instructor. Such a letter should speak to the requirements and contents of your class, program, or work, the length of time the instructor has known you and in what context, your contributions in the area at hand, and your future potential in that area:

Brown University
FOCUS Program
Providence, RI

Course Performance Report
Course: Engineering and the High-Tech Entrepreneur

Instructor's Evaluation
Engineering and the High-Tech Entrepreneur is a unique summer course designed to provide high school students with a "flavor" for engineering. The primary goal was to introduce students to the many fascinating

sub-disciplines of engineering, including electrical, chemical, materials, process, and mechanical, and to expose students to the many seemingly unrelated tasks that professional engineers in industry encounter on a daily basis such as marketing, patent law, ethics and economics. The students were part of an entrepreneurial team in a mock start-up company that was engaged in the high-risk, high pay-off business of portable electronic displays. The students totally organized the structure of the business and took on roles such as CEO, Vice President of Engineering, Technical Marketing, Lead Engineer, etc. The task of this exercise was to secure funding for the start-up, design, engineer, and fabricate a hand-held electronic display prototype, and to present the prototype to a panel of experts on the final day.

Greg is a very intelligent and talented young man. He made a lot of unique contributions to the company's engineering design. Greg accomplished a significant amount during the three weeks and was certainly well-liked by his coworkers. Greg is very bright and an original thinker. I enjoyed having him in my class. Greg was really devoted to the class and took it very seriously. I think he learned a lot during his three-week stay at Brown; the most important being teamwork and cooperation. Greg has a very pleasant and easygoing personality. He is well-organized, and possesses good communication and written skills, as was evident from his final presentation and written report. He really enjoyed interacting with his team. He has a strong aptitude for science and engineering, and I suspect this will be his career choice in the future. Greg certainly left with an in-depth grasp of engineering and all of its challenges, and also learned a great deal about business decisions.

Instructor and signature:

Letter from a Trustee or an Influential Alum

We are often asked, usually by parents, when, and sometimes whether, a trustee or influential graduate of a college or other VIP should get in touch with an institution on behalf of their son or daughter. Sometimes this individual will write a glowing letter about a candidate he or she has known since birth, but provide the admissions committee with no additional information that can help them decide on the candidate's qualifications. Warmth and friendship are insufficient documentation, no matter who makes the recommendation. The question, "Is this candidate better than dozens of others?" remains unanswered. You also run the risk of alienating the admissions officers, who may wonder why the applicant had to use "a heavy connection" to help his or her candidacy. Irritating overworked admissions evaluators reading thousands of folders in the dead of winter is not an especially good idea.

Our advice is never to ask anyone of importance in the particular college—trustee, donor, diligent fund raiser, or administrator—to write a recommendation without doing two essential things: give the person a copy of your application and arrange to meet with them for a meaningful period of time.

Busy people who may have known you for years do not know the details of your school career and accomplishments, though they will usually take the time to look over your application. If they do not feel that they can honestly recommend you, they will say so in most instances, and the friendship remains intact in the long run. If they do recommend you, after your meeting and review of your dossier, their recommendation may well be persuasive. No admissions committee wants to receive a letter from someone in the university community asking why a recommended applicant was rejected, while another deemed less attractive was admitted.

One further word of warning to parents: you do not want to put your son or daughter and yourself in a compromising situation by asking a friend or acquaintance to support your child's candidacy in earnest when their college may not be of major interest. Ask yourself why this person should support your child, unless there is certainty that he or she will attend if admitted? You need to be comfortable that this college is, in fact, your son's or daughter's first choice.

October, 1999

Director of Admissions
ABC College

Dear Allen:

I want to thank you for taking the time to read my letter, and for carefully evaluating the application of John Smith. I have known John intimately for ten years, and recently came to know him as a talented and motivated intern in my internet design firm. As a graduate of ABC College, I tried to be circumspect in asking John about his college intentions. I did not want to influence his choice in any way. Nevertheless, having known John for so long, and having seen him grow from a boy into a talented and personable young man, I have long felt that ABC would be an excellent choice for him. To say the least, I was thrilled when, independently, John expressed to me his strong desire to apply to ABC as an Early Decision candidate.

I have served as an alumni interviewer for ABC for many years, and was a member of the Presidential Search committee in 1995. I know the college well, and have become ever prouder of its accomplishments and potential as an institution of higher learning. I watched the construction of ABC's new technology center with particular satisfaction, as I know from my career perspective and my discussions with college-bound young men and women the importance of the technology sector in higher education and the business world today. When John mentioned his interest in ABC, I pressed him on why he had become so committed to applying early. His answers showed his knowledge of himself, the college, his academic interests, and his career possibilities.

John worked for me last summer as an intern in the graphic design department of my company. He also gained experience in customer relations and account management by shadowing various members of our team and traveling to trade and technology shows. John proved himself to be dedicated, responsible, creative, and curious. He came to us knowing advanced Calculus, statistics, several advanced computer languages, and multiple software programs. He could thus contribute immediately to the production of valuable work on many fronts. What is more, John left at the end of the summer knowing several additional programming languages and software packages. He had influenced the creative and technical direction of several major projects and become a valued participant in weekly brainstorming meetings. I knew that John had inspired confidence and trust when long-standing customers began calling him directly for advice, ideas and support after a month on the job. John always handled himself with maturity, confidence, respect, and an eagerness to learn and to please.

John has shown to me that he possesses an awareness of the programs and curriculum that ABC has to offer, and the skills and talents necessary to succeed in ABC's competitive environment. I know that he would be an active participant in the ABC community, and make a strong contribution to the college's expanding information technology, mathematics, and graphic design programs. I recommend John as an applicant strongly and without hesitation, and remain available for further comment should you wish to contact me.

With best regards,

E. J. Jones, '65

Letters from You

There are many instances when you will want to send a letter (or possibly an e-mail) to someone associated with a college to which you are applying. You might write a coach about your interest in an athletic program, a music professor about your interest in joining the school orchestra, or the dean of admissions updating him or her on your academic progress or interest in the college. You might also write to those who have interviewed you and those who will write or who have written recommendation letters for you. A major part of presenting yourself successfully to colleges is communicating clearly, consistently, and effectively with those who will make admissions decisions and those who will influence those decision makers.

WATCH YOUR E-MAIL ADDRESS

Sometimes you may unintentionally communicate negative or disconcerting information to colleges. Carefully read through your application to look for words, phrases, names, or even an e-mail address that might send the wrong signals to the admissions office. Scott Anderson, associate director of admissions at Cornell University, asks about today's highly conscientious and inquisitive applicants, "How is it that these kids, the same ones who will lose sleep over dotless i's and uncrossed t's, can present with one big collective yawn some of the most curious e-mail identities ever contrived?" Pointing to a range of e-mail monikers, from the "cute" ("xoxo, erniebert, and the like") to the grandiose ("bundy4king or jared4pres"), to the scary ("psycho_chick28 and her 27 cousins"), to the bizarre ("MrSockmonkey," "mmmmm_cheese," "clogfrog"), to the suggestive ("kinkysax," "4letterword," or worse), Anderson jokingly suggests that "Maybe admissions committees should start choosing students based on their e-mail addresses, when everything else seems equal."

All joking aside, you should take to heart this admissions officer's core point: everything you submit reflects something about you. This includes your personal choice of an e-mail identity. Unlike participating in an anonymous chatroom online, where you can create any persona you like, applying to colleges is a highly personalized process and your name and identity are clearly known. Perhaps you should select an e-mail address with the same concerns in mind as when you choose your essay topic. How about using your name?

Scott Anderson, "For College Applicants, cleverness@anycost Can Leave Admissions Officers Cold," *Chronicle of Higher Education,* April 14, 2000.

To Contact an Athletic Coach

We recommend contacting a fairly large group of coaches during the spring of junior year, if not earlier, to test the waters for college recruiting. You might write a letter to ten to fifteen coaches at colleges in which you have some interest to inform them of your skills and intentions, to alert them to some athletic camps you might be attending during the summer, and to propose meeting the coach and learning more about the athletic program at the college. You should include an athletic résumé with this letter. Some athletes may wish to provide a videotape of their performance (usually including several full events). They may do so at the outset, or once they have established that there is some interest on the part of the coach.

> Your Name
> Address
> Phone #
> Fax/E-mail

Date
Coach _____
Sports Department
College or University
Address

Dear Coach _____,
I am a junior at (school) in (location), and am very interested in your (sport) program. I am very keen on continuing my participation in (sport) at the collegiate level.

I would like to tell you a few key factors about myself. I have played (sport) for three years at the (varsity or junior varsity) level. My preferred position is ( ). My academic grade point average for the first three years of high school is ( ). I have taken all academic prep courses, (x number) being advanced, honors, or advanced placement level. My first set of test scores are (PSAT, SAT or ACT). I am confident that I can meet the academic demands of (college) while playing at the varsity level.

This summer, I am planning to attend the (special sports camp) at (location) from (dates). I will also be playing in a competitive league at (location).

Please find enclosed a personal fact sheet, together with my (sport) schedule for this upcoming season. My school coach is (name), who would be pleased to speak with you about my skills and leadership ability at your convenience. His/her telephone number is ( ) and e-mail address is ( ).

I hope to have the opportunity to meet with you or one of your assistants either at one of the camps I will be attending or on campus. I do have plans to visit (college) on (date) and welcome the chance to meet with you then. (*or,* I will contact you in advance when my plan to visit is set.) In the meantime, I would appreciate receiving information on your (sport) program.

Thank you for your interest.

Sincerely,

To Contact a Music or Arts Instructor

Following a plan similar to that of the athlete, the talented musician, studio artist, or performing artist may contact representatives of appropriate college departments to indicate your interest and find out more about the school. You may also include a résumé, a CD or tape of your music or singing, or a DVD or video of your performance. Later, during the admissions process, the studio artist might put together a more complete portfolio for evaluation.

Your Name
Address
Phone #
Fax/E-mail

Date

Professor ————
Department
College or University
Address

Dear Professor _____,

I am a junior at (school) in (location), and am very interested in your (music/studio art/drama/etc.) program. I am very keen on continuing my participation in (music/studio art/drama/etc.) at the collegiate level.

I would like to tell you a few key factors about myself. I have (played the violin, acted in drama productions, taken art classes) for seven years (name of school, instructor, program). My theater roles have included *or* I have played first violin in my school orchestra *or* my photography work has been exhibited at . . .

My academic grade point average for the first three years of high school is ( ). I have taken all academic prep courses, (x number) being advanced, honors, or advanced placement level. My first set of test scores are (PSAT, SAT or ACT). I am confident that I can meet the academic demands of (college) while continuing to pursue my passion in (music/studio art/drama/etc.).

This summer, I am planning to attend the (special arts program) at (location) from (dates). I will also be (name special courses or arts participation).

Please find enclosed a personal fact sheet, together with (a CD of some of my music, or a few slides of my art work, for example). My school instructor is (name), who would be pleased to speak with you about my talents and interests at your convenience. His/her telephone number is ( ) and e-mail address is ( ).

I hope to have the opportunity to meet with you or one of your assistants in the future on campus. I do have plans to visit (college) on (date) and welcome the chance to meet with you then. (*or,* I will contact you in advance when my plan to visit is set.) In the meantime, I would appreciate receiving information on your (music/studio art/drama/etc.) program.

Thank you for your interest.

Sincerely,

ADVICE FROM AN OLYMPIC MEDALIST AND
FORMER IVY LEAGUE COACH

We asked Betsy Mitchell, a world-class rower and Olympic Medalist in Swimming, current athletic director of the Laurel School in Ohio, and former head coach of the women's swimming team at Dartmouth College, to comment on the athletic recruiting process at selective colleges today. You can see clearly from her background that she is one of the most knowledgeable people in her field today. Here is what she had to say:

What are the most important factors in collegiate athletic recruiting?

The amount of honest, timely, and accurate information that the student can communicate to a college coach is one of the critical factors in the successful recruiting process. Many people think that recruitment is a one-way process from the college coach to the high school students. This is simply not true. Recruitment is a two-way process, one of dialogue and information exchange. Crucial to the successful outcome of both parties is to recognize that each side may have slightly different goals. When the process is most successful, a match is made that fits the goals and abilities of the student with the needs and resources of the college. In the end, the recruitment process is about developing the relationship between students and coaches. As in any relationship, first impressions are important and communication is key.

There are several ways in which a college coach will form a *first impression* of you. The coach could read a newspaper article or see you play in a game. You might send a letter or e-mail introducing yourself, or respond to a survey that they send to you. You might call the coach or send a videotape. Regardless of the method of introduction, you want to make a strong, positive, enthusiastic first impression. This means appropriate dress, strong verbal and non-verbal communication, and well-written, grammatically correct, thoughtful, thorough letters or e-mails.

(continued)

When should I initiate contact with college coaches, and how should I do so? What should I say in a letter to coaches?

If coaches of the schools you want to pursue have not contacted you by your junior year, you should reach out to them. You will want to send an *introductory letter* or e-mail. This letter should also contain your résumé. You want the coach to create a file in their system to track you through your junior and senior years. The components of a good introductory letter are as follows:

- Complete biographical information: full name, address, phone numbers, e-mail and fax addresses if you have and use them frequently, birth date, social security number.
- Summary academic information including high school name, address and phone number, guidance counselor information, coach contact information, grade point average, test scores, and graduation date.
- Sport background: sports played and specific information about your position, common performance statistics, camps or special tournaments that you have attended (leave your awards and honors for your résumé).
- Dreams and goals: create a mission statement with your reasons for playing in college, share your current personal season goals and those longer term goals that you want to pursue in college.
- Request information: ask to be put on their mailing list, request information on their team so that you can get a sense of where you might fit on their roster, request the best time to visit their campus, request a season schedule.

What should I include on my résumé?

With your introductory letter you should enclose a résumé. Make it as complete as possible. Certainly include all relevant sports material but don't have it be only a "sports résumé." This limits its usefulness in the overall admissions process. Format the résumé with sections to show all aspects of yourself:

- biographical information
- academic information and honors
- sports achievements and honors
- extracurricular activities including volunteerism
- employment history
- hobbies and interests outside sports

Please don't feel bad or hopeless if you don't have something for every category; the main point is to show off not only your athleticism but that you will be a contributing member of the campus community when you are not on the playing field. In general, limit the items included to high school (perhaps junior high). The concepts laid out in any good general résumé writing book will apply here as well. Remember to be honest and self-promoting, but accurate, as coaches and admissions officers have been known to check the validity of items on a résumé.

Should I send a videotape of my performance? When should I send one?

Your first impression may or may not include submitting videotape of your performance for the coach to review. I recommend waiting until you have established some contact with the coach to see if videotape will be helpful to each particular coach. Team sport athletes, especially those with minimal individual statistics, have more to gain from presenting a tape than do individual sport athletes. For example, swimmers' times don't lie and in tennis you have a won-loss record that speaks volumes; however, in soccer, the stopper doesn't have many statistics, but a good one is invaluable.

What should a performance videotape include?

There can be many different components of a videotape presentation of your skills and abilities. Some college coaches may ask for specific items; others are just happy to see any portion of your abilities. Your high school or club coach is a great resource

(continued)

for determining what should be on your tape. The tape doesn't have to be fancy, but it should showcase what you can do. Ascertain in advance whether or not the coach will return the tape to you after she has viewed it. This will help in planning how many copies you will need to create. My experience says don't count on the tape coming back. The tape should include at a minimum the following components:

- General competition footage edited to provide a targeted look at you rather than the entire team. Show a couple of different games and different situations, offense and defense, if applicable.
- Specific footage of drills or standard training exercises; those which show mobility, agility, speed, technique, shooting, stick work, serves, specialty strokes, tackling, blocking, saves.
- If possible, show each skill several times and from several angles.
- If you play a particular skill position, make sure to show the specific skills of that position.
- Provide a complete look at your abilities; don't hide your weaknesses by not including them.
- Make sure to label, edit, or narrate the tape appropriately so the college coach can reference footage in conversation or ask a specific question.

How do I follow up and follow through with coaches?

If you are sent a survey or questionnaire, return it. If you are asked for further information, provide it. Make it easy for the coach to obtain the information he needs in order to evaluate you and your ability to be a recruited student-athlete and go to the next step in the process. The coach will gain valuable information about you as a prospective team member by how you interact in this relationship, regardless of the length or depth of involvement. Who wants a team member that isn't thoughtful, thorough, or persistent?

How should I set up and handle personal contact with coaches and colleges?

Depending on many factors, including the rules governing the college's division of play, your importance in the overall recruiting class, the recruiting budget, time of year, and the number of coaches on staff, someone from the college may contact you. Contact can be in person or on the telephone. Contact can be in the form of personal evaluation of your academic record or athletic performance, or they may want to get to know you and your family in more depth. At this stage, it is very important for you and your family to know the applicable recruiting rules. The rules regarding personal contact and phone calls are critical to you and your eligibility. Contact the NCAA (317–917–6222; www.ncaa.org) for helpful pamphlets and all applicable rules. Regardless of whether the coach comes to see you or you go to visit the campus and team, remember that the dialogue is two-way. The coach is continually gathering data on how you would be as a student and player on his or her team. You must remember to continue to gather data to help you make an ultimate decision on where you will attend. It is critical for you to get answers to your questions. Much of the most helpful information you will collect is during the personal contact you have with the coach or team. It will help you get an intangible feel for the situation. In the end, your decision will be made in large part by which campus and team feels right. Make sure that instinct is fueled by objective information rather than by subjective assumption.

What should I expect from collegiate athletics?

Playing collegiate athletics proves to be incredibly satisfying for the large majority of those who play, regardless of the level of play. As with many things, the impression you create and how others see you will go a long way to unlocking the doors to your future. Please make sure to keep in mind that for the vast

(continued)

majority of students, sports are over either during or after the college years so that the academic component of a college match is as important as the athletic piece. While there are expanding sports-related fields that provide fantastic career opportunities for both men and women after college, it is still a fact that less than 1 percent of all collegiate athletes will ever play sports professionally. Always put your best foot forward with a smile on your face, a firm handshake, and a twinkle in your eye; you never know what it may bring you.

A Cover Letter for Your Application to Explain Something Specific

Sometimes it is necessary to attach a cover letter to your applications to list what contents are enclosed in your package, or to explain some special circumstances outside the other essays. A cover letter can be modeled on a typical business or résumé cover letter and should be brief and to the point. The center of your application is in the rest of your writing. Here is one example of such a cover note:

Your Name
Address
Phone #
Fax/E-mail

Date

Dean/Director of Admissions
College or University
Address

Dear Dean _____:

Please find enclosed my application for freshman admission to the Class of 2004. Since I am not applying directly from my American high school, I thought I would take a moment to call your attention to the fact that I am currently taking a year off prior to entering college. I am an American citizen who graduated from Lincoln High School in 1999 and chose to pursue a "gap year" to explore some of my major interests.

During the summer, I participated in an Outward Bound adventure in Alaska. I then traveled to Asia with my family for one month. From there, I kept flying west to Paris, where I entered the Académie de Paris program. I am continuing to follow my interests in French Language and Art History, as well as International Relations and European History, while absorbing the rich culture of France. I could not imagine a more fascinating and appropriate environment in which to develop my knowledge of these subjects.

I look forward to returning to the U.S. next fall to continue my studies as a double major in French and Art History at (college). In the meantime, I will have completed an additional year of post-graduate study at a high academic level as well as an extraordinary year that has changed me forever.

Please expect to receive my transcript from Lincoln High, my two U.S. high school recommendation letters, and my SAT reports under separate cover. I am including here my application forms, essays, and first mid-term grades from Paris. I expect the Académie to forward to you my first semester's grades and an additional teacher recommendation in January.

I thank you for taking the time to consider my application, and I remain available should you have any questions or concerns. I look forward to hearing from you soon.

Sincerely,

After You Have Been Deferred

It is always a disappointment to be deferred by a college or university after you have applied for an Early Action or Early Decision plan. Although it will be difficult to gain admission as part of the regular admissions pool later in the spring, you will want to stay positive, update the college on your activities and academic progress, and let the college know the level of your continuing interest in the school. If you have won an award—for example, being named a National Merit Finalist—mention that. If the college is your first choice, say so. If not, do not overstate your case. You will want to write a letter like this in January or February, after the dust has settled in December in the case of a deferral from a first-round EA or ED decision. If you have applied through an Early Decision plan with a January deadline, and have been deferred in February, you might write a letter in March. Those deferred from ED or EA may also want to consider asking a senior-year teacher for an additional recommendation letter, sending a strong graded paper to the college, and sending other supplemental materials, such as art work, which might enhance your application file. Once you have written a letter to the college that deferred you, consider adapting it to send as a general update letter to all the colleges to which you have applied.

The student who wrote this letter found the right balance between disappointment, enthusiasm, and modesty, while letting her first-choice university know her intentions:

Mr. John Smith
Dean of Admissions and Financial Aid
College of America

Dear Dean Smith,

Although I was disappointed to be deferred from early admission this year, I would like to tell you that I still consider the College of America my first choice college. I would also like to mention a few accomplishments and experiences I have had since applying last October that you may like to consider in reevaluating my application.

Last month, I was pleased to be recognized by the biology department at my high school for fine achievement during the first semester. My forensic science teacher chose me to be one of the "Biology Students of the Month," and I am especially proud of this because forensics was a course I really enjoyed. The science of forensics allowed me to combine my experience in biology and psychology, and also taught me a great deal about the largely under-appreciated work that goes into solving a criminal case and bringing justice to the families of victims. I am now looking forward to taking more courses in criminal justice and law once in college.

This year, I was also invited to apply for the Robert Byrd Scholarship, open to residents of Connecticut who have achieved a high level of academic success, and performed well on the SAT. I was honored to meet the qualifications, and while I realize that it is a highly competitive scholarship, I hope to be among the few who are chosen this spring.

Aside from these two achievements, an experience I had recently helped solidify my desire to attend the College of America. Last week, I read an article by a College psychology professor for my psychology class. Curious, I looked in the course catalog to see which classes he teaches. I was pleased to find other familiar names there, names of other professors whose work I have studied in my course. This incident reminded me that one of the benefits of a place like the College is that it brings together the greatest minds, the people who have pioneered research in different disciplines, to teach students straight from the source. I know that I would be very lucky to be part of the extraordinary environment the College provides for its students.

I understand that you and the other members of the College admissions committee have some very difficult choices to make when evaluating the applicants and deciding who will be granted admission. I want to assure you that I am still very excited about the prospect of attending the College, and I appreciate your interest in my achievements and passions. Thank you very much for taking the time to review my application. I hope that I will be receiving good news this April!

Sincerely,

Winter/Spring Update to All Your Colleges

If you are in that waiting period between January and April, you might wonder what you are supposed to be doing. First, you are supposed to be performing well academically. Second, you should update the colleges to which you have applied as to any news, or just to touch base. You might adapt a deferral letter like the one above to read as follows:

Mr. John Smith
Dean of Admissions and Financial Aid
College of America

Dear Dean Smith,

I am writing to update you on my progress and activities since I sent you my application in December. I would like to mention a few accomplishments and experiences I have had that you may like to consider in evaluating my application.

Last month, I was pleased to be recognized by the biology department at my high school for fine achievement during the first semester. My forensic science teacher chose me to be one of the "Biology Students of the Month," and I am especially proud of this because forensics was a course I really enjoyed. The science of forensics allowed me to combine my experience in biology and psychology, and also taught me a great deal about the largely under-appreciated work that goes into solving a criminal case and bringing justice to the families of victims. I am now looking forward to taking more courses in criminal justice and law once in college.

This year, I was also invited to apply for the Robert Byrd Scholarship, open to residents of Connecticut who have achieved a high level of academic success, and performed well on the SAT. I was honored to meet the qualifications, and while I realize that it is a highly competitive scholarship, I hope to be among the few who are chosen this spring.

I have continued to remain involved in acting and writing during my senior year. As editor of the school paper, I have supervised the production of our weekly issues, and submitted my own work on such issues as political expression, AIDS, and the Presidential election. I have enclosed the most recent copy of the paper with one of my articles for your review. In March, I will play the lead in our school's production of *Guys and Dolls.* I look forward to continuing my involvement in theater and journalism at the College.

I understand that you and the other members of the College admissions committee have some very difficult choices to make when evaluating the applicants and deciding who will be granted admission. I want to assure you that I am excited about the prospect of attending the College, and I appreciate your interest in my achievements and passions. Thank you very much for taking the time to review my application. I hope that I will be receiving good news this April!

Sincerely,

Assembling and Submitting Supplementary Materials

Each college differs in its approach to encouraging, receiving, and evaluating such supplementary application materials as music tapes, artwork, creative or analytical writing, research project summaries, and résumés. The University of California at Berkeley, for example, strongly discourages applicants from submitting any additional materials, even if they are applying to a program such as architecture. Some other large universities also take this stance. Most small to middle-sized private colleges and universities welcome and even encourage the submission of materials that will help those in the admissions office, often with the assistance of faculty members or coaches, to evaluate more thoroughly your talents and application. You should check the guidelines for each college and university to which you are interested in applying. Usually, an institution will post its admissions criteria and procedures on its website. Be sure to check the guidelines for individual programs or schools to which you are applying, such as the music or arts school within a university, to find out whether supplementary materials, a portfolio, or an audition is encouraged or required. If you have questions, call the admissions office and the program in which you are interested. We suggest that all applicants with special skills and interests consider submitting supplementary materials in support of their applications, even if they are applying to a broad-based liberal arts program and not a more specialized field or school, as long as the materials they send are of high quality and add positively to their overall presentation. Always work with a teacher, art or music instructor, coach, or advisor to make sure that what you intend to submit fits these criteria.

Portfolios

A portfolio is a collection of your creative or academic work. From slides of your sculptures or architectural drawings to a sampling of your photographs or songs, a portfolio helps showcase your major talent and interest to the colleges. Few liberal arts colleges, if any, require a portfolio of their applicants. Most will accept one to supplement your application. They will usually pass the portfolio, whether in the form of a music CD or tape, a set of slides or photographs, or a bundle of essays and poems, to a qualified faculty member who can professionally evaluate the work and comment on it for the admissions committee. You should only submit work of which you are proud, in which you have confidence, and which has been previously evaluated by one of your teachers or instructors. You only harm yourself by submitting a portfolio that is carelessly assembled or which reveals substandard work in an area in which you are claiming to possess special skills.

Some colleges or schools of architecture, art, design, music, visual arts, drama, and performing arts may require or strongly recommend the submission of a portfolio. Carefully look at the admissions requirements for each school within a university or individual college to which you are applying to make sure you know how a portfolio, a résumé of your work, and an audition fit into the application process. Follow the specifications and requirements for these supplementary pieces.

ADVICE FROM ONE SCHOOL OF ARCHITECTURE

Dean Karen Van Lengen of the University of Virginia's School of Architecture shared with us the following advice for students applying to Virginia's program.

What does the admissions committee look for from applicants with an interest in architecture?

> Knowledge of the field and some beginning talent which demonstrates a candidate's possibility for growth in this area. Developed design work is not a requirement, particularly at the undergraduate level.

What should these students do to help communicate their interests and talents effectively and appropriately to the admissions committee?

> Demonstrate through their activities and statement a propensity for creative thinking and development. This need not be specifically in the area of architecture but their activities should imply that their skills and interests are related or are transferable to architecture.

How important is a portfolio for a student with interests in art, architecture, and design?

> At the undergraduate level we do not require a portfolio; however, if a student has prepared one it often helps us to gauge where they are in the area of visual arts. At the graduate level it is very important to demonstrate some experience and interest in the general field of design.

A Book List (Bibliography)

If you are a voracious reader, consider submitting a list of the books you have read, in and out of school, during the past few years of high school. Denise, a top student and active rider and outdoorswoman, read widely. Here are the book list and summary of one important title which she presented in her successful application to Harvard:

Anonymous	*Go Ask Alice*
*Jane Austen	*Pride and Prejudice*
Richard Bach	*Illusions: The Adventures of a Reluctant Messiah*
Barbara Taylor Bradford	*Remember*
Maeve Binchy	*Circle of Friends*
Olive Ann Burns	*Cold Sassy Tree*
*Kate Chopin	*The Awakening* (Short Stories)
Walter Cracken	*History of Ireland Books—Trilogy (The Silent People)*
Theodore Dreiser	*Sister Carrie*
Isak Dinesen	*Seven Gothic Tales*
Patrick Leigh Fermor	*A Time of Gifts*
*F. Scott Fitzgerald	*The Great Gatsby*
Ken Follett	*Night over Water*
Dick Francis	*Slay Ride*
Nadine Gordimer	*Jump (Collected Short Stories)*
Nadine Gordimer	*My Son's Story*
Thomas Hardy	*Tess of the D'Urbervilles*
Harold T. P. Hayes	*The Dark Romance of Dian Fossey*
Ernest Hemingway	*A Farewell to Arms*
Henrik Ibsen	*Hedda Gabler; A Doll's House*
*Henry James	*Daisy Miller*
Henry James	*An International Episode*
Rudyard Kipling	*A Choice of Kipling's Prose*
Anne Labastille	*Woodswoman*
*D. H. Lawrence	*Sons and Lovers*
Gabriel García Márquez	*One Hundred Years of Solitude; Chronicle of a Death Foretold*
Peter Matthiessen	*Far Tortuga*
Peter Mayle	*A Year in Provence*
*Herman Melville	*Billy Budd*, etc. (Short Stories)
Margaret Mitchell	*Gone with the Wind*

*Grace Paley	*Later the Same Day* (Short Stories)
Ellis Peters	*A Morbid Taste for Bones*
Alexandra Ripley	*Scarlett*
*Jean Paul Sartre	*À Huis Clos*
Jean Paul Sartre	*Les Mouches*
*Jean Paul Sartre	*Les Jeux Sont Faits*
*William Shakespeare	*Hamlet*
*William Shakespeare	*Richard III*
Anne Rivers Siddons	*Outer Banks*
Anne Rivers Siddons	*Peachtree Road*
Anne Rivers Siddons	*Homeplace*
Sodi M. Demetrio	*The Mayas*
Danielle Steele	*No Greater Love*
*Jonathan Swift	*Gulliver's Travels*
Sally Swift	*Centered Riding*
*Peter Taylor	*The Old Forest*, etc. (Short Stories)
Anne Tyler	*Dinner at the Homesick Restaurant*
Richard Wagner	*The Ring of the Nibelung*
Elie Wiesel	*Night*
Tennessee Williams	*A Streetcar Named Desire*
Tennessee Williams	*Summer and Smoke*
Tom Wolfe	*The Electric Kool-Aid Acid Test*
W. B. Yeats	*Selected Poetry*

*Assigned Reading for School

PERIODICALS:
Newsweek, Practical Horseman, The New Yorker, Vanity Fair

What book or books have affected you the most and why?

As a book that I have read many times, Anne Labastille's *Woodswoman* has impressed me in many ways, especially through Anne Labastille's independence and self-sufficiency as a woman, her concern for the environment, and also her sheer writing ability.

The first time I read *Woodswoman,* I was struck by Anne Labastille's independent lifestyle which I hope to someday emulate. As a single woman, she built her own home in the Adirondacks and she has been successful in maintaining a sustainable lifestyle on her own. While my goal in life is not necessarily to live in a log cabin in the wilderness, I admire the qualities of fortitude, motivation, and self-reliance which Anne Labastille possesses as I believe they are necessary to succeed in any lifestyle. One of the things I admire most about Anne Labastille is her obvious ecological awareness, especially regarding the Adirondack Park. Having spent much of my 17 years in the Adirondacks on weekends and during the summer, I, too, realize the uncertain future of the Adirondack Park and wonder if my children will be able to hike up Mt. Marcy or canoe through clear inlets of Lake Champlain. As I read a passage describing early morning or Black Bear Lake, I am envious of Anne Labastille's poetic prose, which so articulately describes even infinitesimal details such as the "frost flowers" on the window panes of her cabin. I hope someday to be able to write as Anne Labastille does, with a graceful, original style that is entrancing yet educational, especially relating to environmental issues such as water pollution or deforestation.

Like Anne Labastille, I would like to be able to share the beauty of the Adirondacks or any area of natural beauty with people who have never experienced it, with writing being the means of relaying this priceless information. Each time I read this book, I notice one more detail that captivates my imagination and holds me spellbound as Anne Labastille weaves the complicated web of her admirable life.

In Summary

Presenting yourself successfully is an ongoing process. You are in the driver's seat and are an active participant in helping yourself stand out in the college admissions process. Some students feel they, or their parents, are being pushy by continuing to stay in touch with the admissions offices. We suggest the following plan.

First, colleges prefer to hear from students. This shows your own interest and maturity. If you have news or a question, you call. Parents, if you have something very specific and sensitive to communicate to the colleges, do so cautiously and with care. Second, as long as you are not being overly demanding, obnoxious, or overzealous, your communication with the colleges will be seen as helpful and a sign of your dedication and commitment. Calling every week is too much. Writing about every class every two weeks is too much. Having some form of contact every month or two, or sending news of a major change or accomplishment, is acceptable. You will need to find the right balance, and work with your high school counselor to stay in contact with the colleges. Avoid either being a stalker or falling off the end of the earth. In Chapter 6, we offer some concluding advice and detailed pointers on doing it right.

CHAPTER SIX

Summary Checklist and Frequently Asked Questions about Presentation

By now, you should have a good idea about what is involved in presenting yourself successfully to colleges, writing strong application essays, and marketing yourself during the admissions process. You should also have a sense of what a good essay looks like and how to get started writing about yourself in a way that works for you. In this summary chapter, we include information to help you reflect on the presentation process and answer some common questions. First, we offer a checklist covering the major presentation steps.

Presentation Checklist

1. Complete the personal strengths assessment during your junior year to begin uncovering the important qualities you will want to convey to colleges.
2. Match your strengths to colleges looking for applicants with your talents and interests.
3. Begin marketing your strengths during spring of your junior year, when you may contact coaches, art or music instructors, and others at the colleges, and alumni, teachers, employers, and others who will support your applications. Accelerate your efforts when you file your applications during senior fall and continue right up to the closing of your folder: December 1 if you are a candidate for first-round Early Decision or Action; otherwise, late March.

4. Create a marketing plan to make use of all your self-scrutiny, as well as to raise fresh awareness of what distinguishes you from other applicants. Assess your strengths, identify the colleges that need or want them, then communicate to the colleges the nature of your strengths by means of documentation.

5. Document evidence of your strengths with outstanding personal essays, creative writing, art, newspaper clippings, recent report cards, commendations, awards, speeches, tapes, and résumés of athletic, musical, volunteer, or other talent and experience.

6. Get an outside opinion of creative work or other supplementary material before sending it to admissions offices, which will ask faculty members about its quality in most cases.

7. Avoid flamboyance or gimmickry, but do not be bashful. Admissions officers admire candidates who speak from a position of strength and accomplishment.

8. If you add recommendations to your folder, give a copy of your application or your résumé to the person who is writing on your behalf. This especially important if the person is a trustee or an administrator of the college.

9. Interview whenever you can, either on campus or with alumni, while recognizing that interviews are informational events for you and the colleges and are much less important than your essay writing. Alumni/ae admissions volunteers can help you receive close attention from the admissions committees. Get an interview with an alumnus or alumna once your application has been sent in to a particular college.

10. Send thank-you notes to anyone who has interviewed you, intervened with a college on your behalf, or written a recommendation for you.

11. Keep in touch with faculty members and coaches by telephone or e-mail. Let them know about your latest achievements.

12. Your college advisor should be informed of your marketing efforts. Give him or her copies of letters and exhibits you have sent to the admissions office. An advisor can be more helpful in backing up your candidacy when armed with new information.

THE MOST COMMONLY ASKED QUESTIONS
ABOUT THE WAITING LIST PROCESS

Being put on the Waiting List (WL) is not the same thing as rejection from a college. If the admissions committee wants to reject a student because he/she is unqualified, or there is no chance of his/her being admitted in the competition, they will turn the student down outright.

An offer to remain on the WL indicates a genuine and serious interest in an applicant, because the student is considered fully qualified for admission. The problem is the combination of a limited number of available spaces and too many qualified candidates.

Each college will guess at its traditional yield factor (i.e., the percentage of applicants offered admission who will accept the offer). If a smaller percentage than usual commits to a place, then the admissions committee will turn to its WL to accept more applicants. If the yield is on target, then WL candidates will not be accepted.

Here are questions about the WL that we are commonly asked

Q. How do I know where I stand on the WL?

A. Admissions staff *do not rank the order* in which applicants appear on the WL. They will review only those students who indicated a desire to remain on the WL. Many will decide to enroll elsewhere, thus taking themselves out of the competition for a space.

Q. How do colleges decide whom to admit from the WL?

A. The admissions staff will look for signals of serious interest on the part of the student. They will offer admission only to those who are most likely to accept their invitation. They will also take into account the composition of the entering class based on those who have been accepted and add to its mix accordingly.

Q. How do I indicate my serious desire to attend and what else can I do to help my cause?

A. Write a letter to the dean of admissions *as soon as possible* indicating your commitment. Give some specific reasons for wishing to do so; e.g., particular programs of study, extracurricular activities that you excel in and will want to continue. Offer to come to campus for a personal interview to explain your interest and your qualifications directly.

Q. What else will help my cause?

A. Have your school counselor send your most recent set of grades (and teacher comments where available) to the admissions director if they reflect a strong performance. An active counselor will not hesitate to telephone the admissions officer responsible for your high school.

Also send new teacher or coach recommendations if you have excelled in that individual's course or sport since submitting your application. This is the strategic moment to ask an active alumnus or friend of the college to call or write on your behalf, if you know such a person.

Q. What do I do about the other colleges that have accepted me?

A. You must hold a place for yourself at your next favorite college prior to the *May 1 common reply date*. Failure to do so can result in a loss of that offer of admission.

Q. When will I know if I will be accepted from the WL?

A. After the May 1 common reply date, the admissions staff will know if it has met its enrollment target. If this is the case, it will notify WL candidates that the admissions process is over. If, by contrast, the staff wants to offer additional acceptances, it will notify students immediately by letter, telephone, or fax.

(continued)

All colleges abide by this reply date process and thus understand that a student may now rescind his/her earlier commitment in order to attend his/her first-choice college. The only penalty is the loss of the enrollment deposit.

It is possible for a college to maintain an active WL through the entire spring term in order to ensure meeting its enrollment targets. It is legitimate to remain on that college's WL as long as you like, if it is truly your first choice. However, make a full and enthusiastic commitment to the college that you are most likely to attend in the coming fall.

13. Write strong application essays: complete the Personal Essay Worksheet to get started. Take an inventory of your attitudes, expectations, and achievements as you search for essay topics that will allow you to reveal your personality.
14. Be sincere, be clear, be spirited, and be personal in your writing.
15. Practice, write drafts, then polish your writing.
16. Proofread your writing. Get an A in applications—no mistakes, please.
17. See your multiple essays and application forms as pieces of a puzzle fitting together on an application to present a more true and complete picture of yourself.
18. Keep copies of all your drafts, organized by college, so you can refer to them as you rewrite. Adapt essays you have written to fit the topics of different colleges.
19. Share your nearly final draft with someone who knows you well to get feedback on whether you are perceived accurately through your writing.
20. Contact the colleges a week or so after you have sent in your applications to make sure they are complete.
21. If you are deferred or waitlisted by a college, that is a time to submit supplementary materials and stay in touch with the college to let them know the level of your continued interest.

22. If you are accepted under an Early Decision plan, send a note withdrawing applications that you sent to other schools.

23. Once you have committed to a college in the spring, send notes thanking other colleges that have accepted you for their consideration, but declining their offers of admission.

24. If you have already accepted an offer of admission from one college and are then accepted from another college's wait list, write a note to a college to which you have already committed explaining your acceptance from the wait list and withdrawing your candidacy. You will lose your initial deposit there.

25. If you decide to defer admission for a semester or a year after placing a deposit at a college, write a letter in the late spring to middle of the summer (typically, before you have sent in a full tuition payment) explaining your reasons for wanting to take time out and asking for a deferral. Do not expect to apply to other colleges while this college is holding your place, or to pursue full-time college study for credit at another institution during your interim period.

Frequently Asked Questions about Presentation

Here are some of the most oft-repeated questions we hear from parents and students about the presentation process. We have organized this list in the common question-and-answer format.

Q. How do I secure an application?

A. Call or write the admissions office to request an application. Better still, if you have internet access, go to any college's website and either follow their directions for e-mailing a request for an application or download the application directly. The Common Application is normally available in your guidance office at school, or you can download it from www.commonapp.org. If you visit a college campus and become interested in applying, you can request an application from the admissions office.

Q. Does it matter if I use the Common Application instead of an individual college's own application?

A. No. All of the colleges and universities that subscribe to the Common Application do so voluntarily. They agree to treat the Common Application without any prejudice. Be certain to complete any supplemental information or essays a college may require. Also, note the place to indicate a specific college division or program within a university that you may be applying for. Remember our earlier advice that if a college's own application is significantly different from the Common Application, and offers you more opportunities to write about yourself, then you may want to use that college's individual application if it will help you to present yourself more fully.

Q. Does it matter if I send my completed application electronically?

A. Not at all. Admissions offices are happy to receive your application this way. It saves time in processing your forms. Each year, the number of electronically submitted applications rises. You may want to check by e-mail for verification that the office received your application, and you should print out a paper copy before sending the application in.

Q. What if my essays are longer than the recommended number of words?

A. The admissions committee usually provides you with a guideline, not a precise limitation. If you need to make your essay somewhat longer, they will not mind, so long as what you have to say is worth reading. Make every word count! If, however, a college has indicated a specific space requirement for essays on their application (for example, "in the space provided below . . ."), then you should make sure to follow that restriction. Keep your font, spacing, and margins readable.

Q. Is it better to type or hand-write my print application?

A. Unless a college specifically requires you to hand-write all or any portion of your application, you are best off word-processing it. This is easier for you, since you can write the application on your computer, and it is also easier for the admission officers to read. You cannot make a mistake by completing an application on screen, since you can change anything you write. It is easier to make mistakes or be illegible in handwriting. And, once you have your essays on the computer, you can spell check, adapt, and copy essays for additional applications. Be certain to make critical changes when called for—especially the name of the college you are now addressing.

Q. What if I need more space than is allotted for an essay or activity list?

A. Unless a college specifically prohibits it, you can attach additional sheets of your response to your application. There are several rules to follow: write in the designated space on the application, "Please see attached sheet," identify the question you are answering on the accompanying sheet, and put your name and social security number on the top of each page.

Q. How do I send a portfolio of my special talent materials to the admissions committee?

A. It is best to sent photos of your art, writing samples, research reports, bibliographies of your reading, athletic or performing arts résumés, or CDs or tapes of your music in a separate envelope by priority mail after you have sent your formal application. This way, there will be an official folder in your name to receive this additional information. Be certain you have identified clearly your authorship of any supplemental exhibits you send.

Q. Should I send anything to coaches or professors to indicate my interest in their programs?

A. Absolutely. Coaches are helped greatly by knowing of your interest in their athletic program, and your cover letter and résumé will inform them of your potential to contribute to their team. Professors and art directors react the same way. They hope to attract outstanding individuals to their disciplines and programs.

Q. When is the best time to send information about myself to a coach or faculty member?

A. Send any and all relevant information well before the deadline for applying. You may want to do so in the spring of your junior year or early fall of senior year in order to get feedback from the coach or professor as to any potential interest in you. If you then plan to visit the particular campus, let these people know ahead of time so that you can arrange a meeting with them.

Q. When should I forward my applications to the colleges?

A. The best advice we can offer is to send the applications well before the deadlines. You will impress the admissions committee by your organization, planning, and enthusiasm for their college if you present an excellent application well ahead of their deadline. In many instances, the committee will read applications in the order in which they are received. This is especially true for a majority of the state universities that use a rolling admissions schedule. Also note that many colleges prefer to have a "Part 1" or "Part A" of their application, which includes mostly demographic data, and an application fee sent early and in advance of the remainder of the application, which includes your essays and activities sheets.

Q. Should I try to get a personal interview at the colleges in which I am really interested?

A. This depends on the individual college's policy. Many institutions do not grant individual interviews on campus; in their place, they encourage prospective candidates to visit the campus and attend a group information session led by an admissions officer. They also encourage you to meet with a volunteer alumni interviewer once you have submitted your application. By contrast, some colleges encourage a prospective applicant to visit campus for an interview. Be sure your personal checklist of all the colleges you are considering and their requirements indicates which, if any, urge the visit and interview. Also note if any departments or schools within a university require or request a personal interview. This is often the case for performing arts or honors program candidates. Admissions committees will note in their literature if the interview plays any role in their deliberations. If not, do not push yourself on them just because you think it will help your chances for acceptance. Do take every advantage of alumni, coach, faculty, and arts director interviews where appropriate. If you are visiting a campus at a college that encourages interviews, then try to plan ahead to secure one.

Q. Is it OK to submit more recommendations than the required one or two?

A. Yes, but do not overdo it. Submitting three to five recommendations with your applications, including two or three from school teachers, is fine. Each should add something positive and new about you, adding to the college's perspective on your strengths, interests, and personality; otherwise limit yourself to the one or two requested.

A Presenter's Glossary

With a bit of humor (we hope), we present a few final words of advice for young writers, some clichés to avoid, some grammatical lessons, and some pet peeves that continue to annoy.

Clichés you should avoid:

- "I really want to attend your university because . . ." Instead of saying "your university," use the institution's official name: "I would like to attend Georgetown because . . ."

- "I know that at Georgetown I can be the best that I can be." You are not joining the Army.
- "I will never forget the time . . ." Just relate the experience. Since you are writing about it, you obviously have not forgotten it.
- "I realized that all my hard work had paid off . . ." Another statement best left unsaid, and better shown through a story.
- "When I saw the smiles on those kids' faces, that was thanks enough . . ." Is that the impact your volunteering or service had on you? What did you learn?
- "In Asia, I learned that we are all really the same, even though there are a lot of differences between us . . ." or "While in Germany, I realized that there are both similarities and differences between Germans and Americans." Narrate the experience and show what you are trying to say. The similarities/differences construct conveys little.
- "Of all the activities I participate in, the most meaningful has been . . ." Don't begin an answer by repeating the question verbatim. Jump right in with the active voice and description.
- "Soccer has taught me good goal-setting, time-management, and leadership skills . . ." Great, but how can you show this without saying it? This is much too common a statement.
- "My trip to Peru really broadened my horizons, or opened my eyes to the rest of the world, or gave me a new perspective on my life at home . . ." All obvious points. Be specific to avoid your trip sounding like a travelog or "typical community service" essay.
- "While at this stage in my life I do not have any idea what my future career/major/interests will be . . ." Take a guess, be imaginative, and talk about your strengths.
- "Allow me to introduce myself. My name is . . ." Totally unnecessary.
- "I never thought that it would happen to me, but . . ." It happened.
- "We have to value each and every day . . ." A statement like this can decrease the impact of a powerful event you have just narrated.

- "My closet/room/car/handbag is a real statement as to who I am . . ." Pick one thing and talk about its meaning or relevance to you. Be more active. This description can wear on a reader.

Childish or adolescent or slang words and phrases you should avoid:

- I was, you know, devastated.
- I mean, what can I say?
- I was really tired.
- I was, like, really tired.
- I was pretty tired.
- Been there, done that!
- He thought he was all that.
- I was buggin'. Or bugging. And, do not contract your "ing's."
- He was freaking out.
- We do not like contractions. You should not use any in your writing. You will sound smarter.
- He was way cool, awesome, hot.
- I was weirded out, grossed out, bummed out.
- Any "four-letter" or other curse words. You will likely offend.
- Ain't gonna write like this. No way!
- Your writing should convey your "voice," but it should not sound like your familiar speech.

"Big words" and other forms of overwriting that you should avoid (unless you have a very good reason):

- *plethora, melange, cornucopia*
- *plenitude, indeed, quite, query, queue*
- Despite learning all those SAT words, say what you need to as simply and directly as possible, and avoid sounding like you are trying to impress a reader by using language that just does not fit.

- If you cannot imagine saying a sentence you have written, then simplify it.
- Avoid overloading your essay with too many unnecessary, or superfluous, incidental, repetitive, redundant, complementary, synergistic, supplementary, fabulous, excellent, wonderful, impressive adjectives. Try not to write too casually, sloppily, angrily, bitterly, enthusiastically, depressingly, or negatively, or with too many adverbs.

Grammatical goofs we see all the time (and your spell check will not catch):

- Double negatives: I do not think that I will not go to college = I will go to college.
- *Its/it's:* "Its" is the possessive form, meaning "I saw the college and I liked its campus." "It's" is the contraction of "it is," meaning, "What is the campus like? It's very beautiful." You should say, "It is very beautiful. Its atmosphere is welcoming."
- *Your/you're:* Again, a contraction problem. "Your" is the possessive, meaning "your tour guide was very informative." "You're" is the contraction, meaning, "you're going to love my essay."
- *There/their/they're:* A triple problem. "There" can be used in several ways, such as "there is a lot to be thankful for," and "I would like to go there." "Their" is a plural possessive, meaning "the president and the vice-president of the class presented their opinions to the school." "They're" is another contraction for "they are." Avoid this.
- *Affect/effect:* One letter changes the meaning. "Affect" is either a verb or a noun. You can "affect" something by trying to influence it in some way: "I tried to affect my admissions chances by writing good essays." You can have a certain "affect," or demeanor: "He was very depressed. He certainly had a negative affect." This is related to the sense of the word "affection." "Effect" can also be a noun or a verb. For example, "What was the effect of your essays on the admissions readers?" That is, what was the outcome or influence itself? "Effect" can also be used in the

sense of making something happen: "I tried to effect a change in my chances, by writing good essays."

- *Complementary/complimentary:* Again, watch that one letter. "Complementary" means fitting together: "He was quiet and she was loud. They were a complementary couple. They made a perfect complement." To please someone, however, you might pay him or her a nice compliment. In that case, you might be acting in a very "complimentary fashion" toward the person.

- Pronoun agreement: Most often, this is a problem with singular/plural or his/her/their relationships. Make sure your pronouns match. For example, "An admissions office reader will offer his or her comments on your essays," not "their comments on your essays." Or, "Each of us has his or her own views." "Each" is a singular pronoun and does not agree with "their." Or, "My parents sent me a package of different kinds of chocolates, which was sitting in my mailbox." "Package" is the singular noun that agrees, correctly, with the verb "was." Watch your pronouns carefully.

- Split infinitives: These can be confusing and annoying for a reader. A split infinitive occurs when you separate the "to" from an infinitive verb and put another word or multiple words in between. Most writers agree that infinitives should stay together: "I would like to write my essays soon" is correct. "I would like to soon write my essays" is not. Sometimes, the flow of your writing is difficult to maintain without splitting an infinitive, but, again, most grammar instructors would encourage you to keep those "to's" in place: "I want to write my essays carefully" is better than "I want to carefully write my essays."

- *To/too/two:* To be or not to be is too serious a question for the two of you.

- Incomplete sentences or sentence fragments: Each sentence should stand on its own as a complete sentence. Try to avoid fragments: "A real shame."

- Run-on sentences: If you have several conjunctions (ands, buts, howevers, and so forth and so on) connecting multiple phrases and your sentence is getting too long, but you are unsure how to finish the sentence, or you think you said it best by keeping it altogether, yet you are running on and on and on, and the reader has lost track of your point and your direction, then you probably should start from the beginning and try cutting up that sentence into a few component parts and really simplifying your writing so that the reader can then make sense of it, thereby having a better idea of what you are trying to say, so you might want to use a period, just once in a while. *You just read a classic run-on sentence!*

- Passive/active: This is simple. The active voice is better in your writing than the passive voice. If you can say it in the active, then do so. "I hit the ball right out of the stadium" is better than "the ball was hit right out."

- Writing in the first person: Use the "I voice." Your essays are about you, and, wherever possible, choose to use "I" rather than "one" or "we." For example, "Such an experience made me think about my life and I knew I wanted to help people" is better than "such an experience makes you think about your life and you know you want to help people" or "such an experience makes one think about one's life and one knows one wants to help people." The first-person voice is much more personal. Writing in the third-person he/she voice is an intentional stylistic form.

Concluding Advice for Parents and Students

Students, this process is your own. Parents, you can coach and encourage your son or daughter, but this process is about them. That is the core of our message to college applicants and their families. Presenting yourself successfully is a matter of finding appropriate colleges and then making your case as enthusiastically, honestly, directly, and completely as possible. In the end, you want to convince admissions committees that there is a logical fit between you and their institution, and that you will add something interesting and exciting to their campus. You will take full advantage of what they have to offer, and they will gain much from what you have to offer. Students, be neither too aggressive nor too passive. Be assertive. When you find colleges and universities that you are interested in, you need to present yourself in a way that helps you stand out. You have nothing to lose by saying, in the best way for you, "Colleges, this is who I am, and this is why I am interested in attending. Let me show you what I've got!"

Bibliography

Cook, Claire K. *Line By Line: How to Edit Your Own Writing.* Boston: Houghton Mifflin, 1985.

Follett, Wilson. *Modern American Usage, A Guide.* Revised by Erik Wensberg. New York: Hill and Wang, 1998.

Grammatically Correct: The Writer's Essential Guide to Punctuation, Spelling, Style, Usage, and Grammar. Cincinnati, OH: Writer's Digest Books, 1997.

Hayakawa, Samuel I. *Choose the Right Word: A Contemporary Guide to Selecting the Precise Word for Every Situation.* New York: HarperCollins, 1994.

Roget's International Thesaurus, 6th ed. New York: HarperCollins, 2001.

Strunk, William Jr., and White, E. B. *The Elements of Style,* 4th ed. Upper Saddle River, NJ: Prentice Hall, 1999.

Webster's New World College Dictionary, 4th ed. New York: Hungry Minds, 1999.

White, E. B. *Essays of E. B. White.* New York: Harper and Row, 1977.

Zinsser, William K. *On Writing Well: An Informal Guide to Writing Non-Fiction,* 6th ed. New York: HarperCollins, 1998.